WOMEN AND GOVERNMENT

WOMEN AND GOVERNMENT

New Ways to Political Power

Edited by
Mim Kelber

With an Introduction by
Bella Abzug & Mim Kelber

A Women USA Fund Study

Westport, Connecticut
London

Library of Congress Cataloging-in-Publication Data

Women and government : new ways to political power / edited by Mim
    Kelber.
            p.   cm.
        "A Women USA Fund study."
        Includes bibliographical references and index.
        ISBN 0–275–94816–1 (hardcover : alk. paper). — ISBN 0–275–94817–X
    (pbk. : alk. paper)
        1. Women in politics—History.   2. Women in politics.   I. Kelber,
    Mim.
    HQ1236.W587   1994
    320′.082—dc20   94–1147

British Library Cataloguing in Publication Data is available.

Library of Congress Catalog Card Number: 94–1147
ISBN: 0–275–94816–1 (hardcover)   0–275–94817–X (paperback)

First published in 1994

Praeger Publishers, 88 Post Road West, Westport, CT 06881
An imprint of Greenwood Publishing Group, Inc.

Printed in the United States of America

The paper used in this book complies with the
Permanent Paper Standard issued by the National
Information Standards Organization (Z39.48–1984).

10 9 8 7 6 5 4 3 2 1

Contents

Acknowledgments

Bella Abzug wrote the introduction with Mim Kelber, chief writer and editor of this book. Other writers and researchers were: Nora Lapin (Norway, Sweden, Finland), Sami Fournier (Germany), Laura Kelber (Denmark), Sissel Waage, Lisa Slutskin and Rory Kennedy. Libby Bassett did the desktop publishing.

Special thanks go to Deputy Director June Zeitlin of The Ford Foundation, which commissioned the original study on Women and Government, on which this book is based.

Thanks also to Director Pierre Cornillon and Christine Pintat of the Inter-Parliamentary Union in Geneva for their pioneering work in providing analyses, voluminous data and other information on the status of women parliamentarians around the world; the UN Division on the Advancement of Women; Joann Vanek, Statistical Division, UN Department of Economic and Social Affairs; the Center for American Women in Politics at Rutgers University; M.P. Mai Britt Theorin of Sweden; Börg Manum Andersson and Berit Äs of Norway; President Vigdis Finnbogadottir, Gudrun Agnarsdottir and Aslaung Brynjolfsdottir of Iceland; Irene Natividad of the Global Forum for Women; Dr. Gisbert H. Flanz; the Nordic and German government information services; and to the many women parliamentarians, representatives of Councils on Equality for Women, scholars and women's groups who provided information and insights and who graciously reviewed this report for accuracy.

Introduction

As the twentieth century nears its end, a constant theme of the growing world-wide women's movement has been the need for empowerment of the female half of the human race. The year 2000 has been repeatedly invoked as the goal for the achievement of feminism's holy grail of social, economic, political and legal equality. Women struggle for their rights not only because they regard equality as inherently just, but because they believe that by sharing equally with men the power to shape and govern societies, they can create a better world for all people.

Great, once unimaginable positive transformations have occurred in the status and lifestyles of millions of women, and everywhere, in the developing nations as well as in the industrialized superpower nations, women are organizing to change their lives. Although women remain a majority of the poor and illiterate in all countries, many have made remarkable progress and others are on the way. But millions remain ghettoized in cultures dominated by patriarchal and fundamentalist religious values, and in the former Soviet Union and Eastern European nations, women are caught up in a misogynist backlash that threatens even the limited rights they once had taken for granted.

With a few notable exceptions, women seeking equality have been finding it most difficult to break into the male political power structures where the decisions are made about how people—men, women and children—are to live, and how they may die. As a United Nations report pointed out, whether the countries involved are rich or poor, small or large, developed or underdeveloped, women have very limited access to decision-making posts as heads of governments or members of parliaments, cabinets or in such international institutions as the UN itself.

Only a handful of women are presidents or prime ministers. The most recent survey showed an average of 11% inclusion of women in the legislatures of the world, ranging from about a third or more in a half-dozen countries to zero in some Middle Eastern countries. In Norway, which has a strong women's movement, Gro Harlem Brundtland has been a greatly admired and effective prime minister, with half of her cabinet and 35.8% of the legislature consisting of women. In the United States, which probably has the largest and most activist women's movement in the world, in 1992 the outgoing Congress had only 6.4% women members. Despite the record-breaking number elected to the new Congress in that "year of the woman," the world's leading democracy still ranks low on the inclusion of women: slightly over 11% in the House and 7% in the Senate.

In South Africa, as major political organizations were preparing for national elections in April 1994, the first ever in which blacks would be allowed to vote, both black and white women who were urging that a charter of women's rights be written into the new constitution were largely excluded by black and white males from the electoral negotiating process. After an intensive campaign, the African National Congress leadership agreed that women would comprise one-third of their candidate list It was estimated that although women would comprise at least 54% of the population of new voters, they would face special obstacles at polling places because of their sex.

In Kenya, scene of the historic UN Decade of Women Conference in 1985, there were only five women in the parliament and none in the cabinet at this writing. Dr. Wangari Maathai—the internationally acclaimed Green Belt leader and former parliamentarian—was jailed and in a later episode beaten unconscious when she led a political demonstration against the one-party dictatorship of President Daniel arap Moi. Following recent "democratic" elections, she was forced into hiding because of her opposition to the Moi government.

In Jordan, when Toujan Faisal, a popular woman TV news commentator, announced her decision to run for political office (the country had no elected women in its parliament), Muslim religious leaders told their followers that it would be permissible to assassinate her. She lost—not only a seat in parliament but her job. She did not give up. In 1993, she ran again, and won.

And in Myanmar (formerly Burma), Aung San Suu Kyi, has remained under house arrest since the National League for Democracy, which she led, scored a sweeping victory in national elections in May 1990. Results of the election, which would have made her head of the government, were ignored by the military junta in power. Instead, people were massacred and most opposition leaders were forced into exile or arrested. Ms. Suu Kyi, the daughter of modern Burma's founder, Aung Sun, was awarded the Nobel Peace Prize in 1991 "for her nonviolent commitment to democracy and human rights." In 1992, her husband revealed that she had instructed him to donate $15,200 of her prize money to the medical care and vocational training of Burmese girls and women who had been rescued from forced prostitution in brothels along the Thai-Burmese border.

Although the cultures, circumstances and status of women vary greatly among the nations of the world, in the majority of male-led governments, the environment remains either indifferent or hostile to sharing political power with women. In the following report, we describe the historical and ideological basis for the exclusion of women from leadership, the official and unofficial efforts being made to overcome this disparity, the diverse experiences of women in seeking entry to male political strongholds, and the particular problems they face in electoral or appointive government positions. Special attention is paid to the effectiveness, advantages and disadvantages of various kinds of quota systems that are employed in some countries to increase the numbers of women in government.

Also discussed are other mechanisms and programs that have been developed and advocated as ways to achieve the still elusive goal of political equality for women and men. This issue will no doubt be on the agenda of the UN's forthcoming Fourth World Women's Conference, which will be held in Beijing, China, in 1995. It will mark the 10th anniversary of the UN's July 1985 women's conference, which produced the "Nairobi Forward-Looking Strategies" proclaiming the goal of equality for women by the year 2000. It will be a time when women will be examining the progress and setbacks of the years since 1975, when the UN launched its International Decade of Women, and also will be developing new strategies to accelerate the present slow, uneven pace of women's journey toward equality.

This study's findings show that despite historical, cultural and political differences among nations and their electoral processes, the following factors, practices and recommendations are of key importance in significantly increasing women's participation in political leadership and government:

• Presence of an active, broad-based organized women's movement that reflects the economic, social and family needs of women and makes programmatic demands, including constitutional and legislative guarantees of equal rights for women, setting specific numerical goals and timetables for women's inclusion in appointive and elective office.

• Organization of women's caucuses within political parties to promote a substantive response to women's issues and to win guarantees of roughly equal numbers of women and men in party leadership posts and policy-making bodies. Women may start by seeking less than equal quotas for women in leadership and build on those gains to secure the Nordic countries' formula of no less than 40% or no more than 60% of either sex in parties and government, or the "equal division" rule observed in the U.S. Democratic Party national committee and nominating conventions. (Studies indicate that a "critical mass" of from 30-35% inclusion of women in political leadership and government is needed to affect public policies.)

• Women should not settle for an in-name-only share of leadership but should use their positions to campaign for specific party commitments to the nomination, election and appointment of equal numbers of women and men to national office, parliaments, cabinets, courts, regional and state legislatures, commissions, advisory groups, etc.

- Parties and women's organizations should seek out potential women candidates for political office and provide them with training in political and leadership skills, funding and campaign assistance.
- Creation within the government of a ministry, department or national commission on equality for women to gather data, monitor implementation of programs and legislation affecting women, initiate new programs and act as advocates in behalf of women and their needs. As this report shows, the existence of such bodies in the Nordic countries, Canada and many other countries has been a powerful force in behalf of women's economic, social and political aspirations.
- Women must demonstrate their political power at the polls. The electoral gender gap in the United States has been shown to be critical to the success of the Democratic Party and to the nomination and election of some women candidates. Although the electoral gender gap has not been tracked as closely in other countries as in the United States, a UN publication, *WOMEN 2000*, reported that women now tend increasingly to vote for the more liberal parties and candidates, and vote in increasing numbers, outstripping men in their use of the ballot box in many countries. ["Women in Public Life," No. 2, 1992.] Laws, party campaigns and the elimination of illiteracy, particularly among women in the developing nations, should be directed to facilitating women's participation in voting.
- Structural reforms in electoral processes are also needed to bring more women into government. Although the proportional representation voting systems and multimember districts used in most parliamentary forms of government can be favorable to the election of more women, these are not applicable to the U.S. government at the federal level but could be helpful in state elections. (See last chapter on the United States for more detailed discussion of possible reforms.)

Will women sharing political power equally with men change the way we live? One woman who believes so is President Mary Robinson of .Ireland. Although she holds an office that is largely ceremonial, in a speech at the 1992 Global Forum of Women she described her election in 1991 as "the psychic equivalent of the collapse of the Berlin Wall." Since taking office, she said, she has seen women changing events, and the perception of the events. "As women lead," she contended, "they are changing leadership; as they organize, they are changing organization . . . . When women lead and articulate their purposes, it seems to me that they work together not only as individuals but with a sense of community and networking in a healthy way . . . . Women have fresh and imaginative skills of dialogue and are setting a more open, flexible and compassionate style of leadership."

From President Vigdis Finnbogadottir of Iceland came this comment: "Even if women do not make the world better, at least it won't be any worse." Her smile indicated her belief that women's leadership would bring positive change, a view held by women everywhere when they gather together to share their vision of women setting new priorities for a more secure, economically just and healthy planet.

This report indicates that women can not only change the style of leadership but can make a difference in government policies. The strong presence of women in the Norwegian government, for example, has made it a leading champion of human rights as well as women's rights, a force for peace, environmental protection and sound development assistance programs sensitive to women's needs in poverty-stricken nations. In Sweden women working inside and outside of government stopped their country from entering the nuclear arms race and went on to block the continued use of nuclear power. In Iceland the election of a woman president and the formation of a feminist all-women's party resulted in sending more women to the parliament, not only from the Woman's Alliance but from the other political parties, an overall gain reflected in improved social legislation.

And in the United States, where the new Clinton-Gore Administration owed its electoral margin to women's votes, the doubling of the numbers of women in Congress, small as the total numbers were, gave early indications that the presence of 54 women was already having a transforming effect in shaping the legislative agenda, priorities and debates.

These harbingers make the issue of political equality for women even more urgent.

In this bloodiest century in human history, which dawned at Sarajevo with an incident that launched a world war followed by hundreds of other large and small wars and is ending at Sarajevo with brutal murders of children, women and men, mass rape and violence spurred by age-old ethnic rivalries, greed and macho behavior, and with mass starvation in Somalia where two male leaders violently compete for political power, is it not time to admit that the present dominance, style and conduct of male leadership has been a disaster?

Is it not time to work together for democratic political systems that recognize the coexistence of two sexes with the equal right to make decisions about our lives and the future of the world? Is it not time to recognize that women should not be classed as a "special interest" group along with youth, the elderly, the disabled, indigenous people and others but rather as half the world's population encompassing all nationalities and all "special" groups?

When that recognition comes, the principle of equal division in governance will be put in a historical and biological perspective symbolized in the "two of every kind" survival voyage of Noah's Ark.

To those who question whether women would change the nature of political power or whether political power would change the nature of women, there can be only one answer:

Let's try it. Let's find out.

Bella Abzug/Mim Kelber

WOMEN AND GOVERNMENT

1

Overview:
From Ancient to Present Times

There is an ancient tale that in the early days of Athens, the cradle of democracy, women once had the right to vote. Told originally by Herodotus, the father of history, and revised by Saint Augustine in his *City of God*, in the fifth century A.D., it describes an experience of Kekrops, the first king of what was to become the city-state of Athens:

> An olive tree sprang from the earth, and in another spot, water gushed forth. Frightened, the king sent to Delphi and inquired what this meant and what was to be done. The god replied that the olive tree meant Athene and the water Poseidon, and it was for the citizens to decide after which of the two deities they wished to name their city.
>
> Thereupon, Kekrops called an assembly of the citizens, both men and women, for in those days the women also took part in public deliberations. The men voted for Poseidon, the women for Athene, and since there was one more woman, Athene won out. Poseidon was angry at this, and the sea flooded the Athenian territory. To appease the god's wrath, the citizens imposed a threefold punishment on their women: they should lose their right of suffrage, their children should no longer take the names of their mothers, and they themselves should no longer bear the title of Athenians.

Interpreted as representing the loss of matriarchal power and the introduction of patrilineal succession, this story of the disenfranchisement of women illuminates the contradictory nature of democracy as it has been practiced, right up to the present century. Throughout the ages, male lawmakers, philosophers and political thinkers, in the process of defining and extending the democratic rights of men, specifically and deliberately excluded women from those rights and responsibilities.

By the time of the celebrated and short-lived golden age of Greek city-state democracy in the fifth century B.C., the wives, mothers and daughters of the ruling democrats had scarcely more liberty or rights than the slaves the men brought home from their wars. Aside from a constitutional provision forbidding male guardians to sell wives, daughters or sisters into slavery (except for unmarried females who were no longer virgins), the democratic reforms of Solon and later rulers did not extend to women, whether they were aristocratic, middle class or poor women and native born.

At the apex of democratic rule, under Pericles in the last half of the fifth century, the benefits of citizenship were restricted to some 45,000 males, who by definition had to be over 21, born of two free Athenian parents, and ready and able to serve the state at any time. In their famed assembly, Athenian male citizens could debate and vote on issues of defense, finance, grain distribution, foreign policy, and war and peace. Excluded from participation in the rights and civic duties of citizenship were manual workers of both sexes, all the estimated 28,500 resident farmers, and women of all classes.

It was a male world, one in which women were condemned by law, class and the patriarchal culture to devote themselves to the comfort and convenience of the male sex. From birth, women were treated as a lesser species, even those born into propertied and rich families. Aristotle, whose knowledge of anatomy was more philosophic than scientific, described the female as "a mutilated male." According to him, the embryo was created from the union of sperm and menstrual blood, the latter being called *catamenia*. These, he explained, are semen, "only not pure, for there is only one thing they have not in them, the principle of soul"—proof of female inferiority.

(From antiquity to present times, some women achieved political power as queens, consorts and mistresses, based largely on hereditary rights, marriage and the rewards of boudoir politics as well as intellectual ability, even as their entire sex was being demeaned in religious and political thought as naturally weak, subordinate and potentially subversive. In a diatribe called *The First Blast of the Trumpet Against the Monstrous Regiment of Women* [1558], which was aimed at both Queen Elizabeth I of England and Queen Mary of Scotland, John Knox, leader of the Scottish Protestant reformation, expressed the prevailing view: "To promote a woman to beare rule, superioritie, dominion or empire above any realme, nation, or citie, is repugnant to nature, contumlie to God, a thing most contrarious to his reveled will and approved ordinance, and finalie it is the subversion of good order, of all equitie and justice.")

Athens' unique but misogynistic democracy was a brief, atypical episode in history. From the fall of the Greek city-states to the rise of constitutionalism and democratic parliamentary forms of government in the West, almost two thousand years elapsed before the rights of women to share in "democratic" government became a persistent and public issue. The principle of parliamentary representation arose slowly and unevenly, taking firmest hold in England in the late seventeenth century. In those countries in which forms of parliaments existed, representation was drawn with few exceptions from the male nobility and propertied classes. The great masses of both men and women were illiterate, poor and excluded. In his treatise on eighteenth century law in England, Sir William Blackstone grouped lunatics, idiots, minors, aliens, *females,* perjurers and criminals as properly barred from voting. The advent of the printing press, improved communications, technologic advances, the demands of the Industrial Revolution and the Enlightenment's ferment of democratic ideas about individual rights and equality provided the groundwork for advocacy of broad-based suffrage, beginning in the late eighteenth and nineteenth centuries.

But would women be included in the expansion of voting rights and participation in government?

In that great liberating document, the Declaration of Independence, the founders of the new American Republic proclaimed on July 4, 1776, that to secure men's inalienable rights to life, liberty and the pursuit of happiness, "governments are instituted among Men, deriving their just powers from the consent of the governed." The 1789 U.S. Constitution itself, in defining citizenship and voting rights, spoke of "persons" rather than males, although all references to the offices of the president and vice president used the personal pronoun "he." Like the crack in the Liberty Bell, there was a deep flaw in the way the founders perceived women in the eighteenth and nineteenth centuries, and on into the present century. Almost universally, male political leaders—whether they were radicals like Thomas Jefferson or conservatives like John Adams, who preceded him in the White House—regarded women as secondary beings and natural subjects of male power.

Adams's wife, Abigail, a brilliant and forceful woman, is famous among her many accomplishments for that much-quoted letter she sent to her husband when he was a delegate to the constitutional convention in Philadelphia. "In the code of laws," she wrote, "I desire you to remember the ladies and be more generous and favorable to them than your ancestors. Do not put such unlimited power into the hands of the husbands. Remember all men would be tyrants if they could." And she followed up with a warning: "If particular care and attention is not paid to the ladies, we are determined to foment a rebellion and will not hold ourselves bound by any laws in which we have no voice or representation."

Less well known but even more prophetic was Adams's curt, negative reply: "Depend upon it, we know better than to repeal our Masculine systems." The battle lines were formed, but not yet joined. That was to take another half century.

Disenfranchising Women

In the years immediately following the American Revolution, women voted in some parts of New Jersey and Virginia. Legally, they had been able to vote in many of the early colonies, although there is scant evidence that they did so. Colonial legislatures later took away that right, but revolutionary New Jersey restored it in 1776, allowing the vote to "all inhabitants" who were over 21 and possessed an estate worth 50 pounds. According to social historian Andrew Sinclair, the women's vote in some towns was manipulated by male politicians for local partisan and venal purposes, and the state legislature finally restricted suffrage to free, white, male citizens. By the early nineteenth century, women and many free blacks had lost whatever civil rights they had inadvertently and temporarily gained.

Paradoxically, it was ratification of the Fourteenth Amendment in July 1868 granting citizenship to blacks and former slaves that for the first time provided a constitutional basis for disenfranchising women. The amendment prescribed penalties for denying voting rights to all "male" citizens over 21, except for participants in rebellion or other crimes. In the ratification campaign, some suffragists vehemently opposed approval on the grounds that it would exclude all women, white and black, from voting rights. Later, both Victoria Woodhull, and Belva Lockwood, who ran for the presidency in the nineteenth century, took the position that although women were barred from voting, they still had the right to run and be elected to government office.

In the absence of an organized women's movement, the American founding fathers were able to avoid any discussion of women's rights before or in the aftermath of their Declaration of Independence and the writing of the Constitution. But the issue was very much at the center of the turbulence that drove the French Revolution. The progression from absolute monarchy to bourgeois republic played itself out against a background of a lively intellectual tradition in which educated and upper-class women of the *ancien regime* could hold their own with the leading male thinkers of the day and develop a feminist approach to debates about the political future of their nation. From the outset, women were drawn into the politics of reform and revolution, in both the battle of ideas and the battles in the streets where working-class and market women participated in and even led demonstrations.

Indeed, scholar Joan B. Landes contends that "the bourgeois republic was constituted in and through a discourse on gender relations." As the French Constituent Assembly debated in August 1789 its Declaration of the Rights of Man (which drew much of its inspiration from the American Bill of Rights and the Declaration of Rights by the Virginia constitutional convention), it faced the dilemma of what to do about the urgent demands from women for recognition, equality and political rights. According to Landes:

> The woman question may have been even more irksome to the new proponents of reason than to their Old Regime forerunners. Either women would have to be subsumed within the universal (and effaced) or treated as different by nature but therefore outside the universal (and its privileges). . . . Feminist demands exposed the gap between principles of liberty, equality, and universal law and the

revolutionary insistence on preserving . . . and in some cases, extending prior inequalities among the sexes.

> Landes, Joan B., *Women and the Public Sphere in the Age of the French Revolution,* p. 105, Cornell University Press, 1988.

The majority of French male revolutionaries chose not to extend legal political rights to their female comrades. The liberal Marquis de Condorcet, member of the Society of 1789 and the Society of the Friends of the Negro (an antislavery group), was one of the few men among the new thinkers to speak out for women's rights. In 1787 he proposed that women be made eligible for election to governing bodies. In 1790 he published his essay, "On the Admission of Women to the Rights of Citizenship," in an effort to influence the male legislators in the National Assembly, operating under the monarchy. Denouncing the exclusion of women from political rights, he wrote:

> Now the rights of men result from the fact that they are sentient beings, capable of acquiring moral ideas and of reasoning concerning their ideas. Women, having these same qualities, must necessarily possess equal rights. Either no individual of the human species has any true rights, or all have the same. And he or she who votes against the rights of another, of whatever religion, colour, or sex, has thereby abjured his own.

> Landes, *Women and the Public Sphere . . . ,* p. 114.

He also reminded the legislators that several noble deputies were actually surrogates for certain women of property who under medieval law were allowed proxy votes. "Why," he asked, "if it be found absurd to exercise the right of citizenship by proxy, deprive women of the right, rather than leave them the liberty of exercising it in person?"

While Condorcet was a lonely male voice for women's rights, French women were speaking out boldly in their own behalf. A leading woman of this period was Olympe deGouges, a self-educated butcher's daughter, playwright, pamphleteer and monarchist. Credited with forming the first women's society during the Revolution, as early as October 1789 she presented a feminist reform agenda to the National Assembly, in which she called for legal sexual equality, admission of women to all occupations and the suppression of the dowry system through a state-provided alternative. In her parallel 1791 Declaration of the Rights of Woman, addressed to the queen, she proposed formation of a separate national assembly to represent the women of the nation and to support the constitution, good morals, and the happiness of all.

She charged that the Declaration of the Rights of Man, by excluding people from citizenship rights solely on the basis of sex and race, defied the principle of natural equality. Like men, she said, women were entitled to the full exercise of liberty, property, security, justice, political and civil freedom, including the right to free speech and assembly, And, prophetically, she declared, "Woman has the right to mount the scaffold. She must equally have the right to mount the rostrum." (Gouges herself was guillotined in November 1793 during the Reign of Terror, ostensibly because of royalist activities, but her fate was invoked by Jacobin demagogues seeking to intimidate the increasingly vocal groups of women demanding equality.)

Women as Passive Citizens

Under the then existing monarchy, the French constitution of September 1791, whose preamble was the "Declaration of the Rights of Man and Citizen," divided the populace between active and passive citizens on the basis of wealth and property, and complicated suffrage provisions were imposed. The large majority of male citizens were excluded from full political participation, as were all women, who were assigned to the category of passive citizens. This eliminated the old legal practice under which women of property could sometimes vote and act as regents. "For the first time in centuries, women were completely barred, as a group, from the voting process." [Landes, *Women and the Public Sphere . . . ,* p. 122.]

With the establishment in 1792 of the first French Republic, all men won universal suffrage, while women continued to be excluded. Although women were granted some reforms affecting their legal status as wives and mothers, their increasingly bold activities in the public sphere unleashed a counterattack from male revolutionists and the press. These ranged from ideologic polemics insisting that women must confine their roles to caretakers of husband, home and children to a flood of satiric and pornographic pamphlets ridiculing women and accusing them of wanting to "wear pants" and carry guns.

In the never-implemented constitution of 1793, provisions for educational reform, public assistance and the right to work might have improved the lives of women in the new Republic, "but their hopes were largely frustrated," says Landes. In the fast-changing political scene of 1792 and 1773 women were increasingly speaking out, demonstrating and participating in political meetings. They "were a constant presence at the places of the Convention, determining who would enter, packing the galleries at the Convention or the Jacobin club, punctuating the debates with loud advice, catcalls or abuse." [Landes, *Women and the Public Sphere . . . ,* pp. 139-40.] Some women even joined the army, disguised as men, although this was banned by the government.

The height of women's political influence came during six months of 1793 when an all-women's radical group was formed. Called the Society of Revolutionary Republican Women, it militantly sought to protect the Revolution from the schemes of aristocrats, hoarders, and speculators and also clashed with market women who had their own agenda.

As a result, acting on recommendations from its Committee of General Security, the Convention ordered a ban on all clubs and popular societies of women, denied women the right to sit in the galleries and later outlawed all political associations of women. The attack on women's rights was a turning point in the Revolution, introducing the centralization of power under Jacobin rule and the subsequent period of the Reaction. [Landes, *Women and the Public Sphere . . .*, pp. 142-43.]

"It is important to realize," historian Candice E. Proctor wrote, "that the French Revolutionaries did not fail to grant women equal rights merely because it never occurred to them to do so. They were perfectly aware of the female sex's claim to equality, and they did not simply ignore those claims: they categorically rejected them." [Proctor, Candice E., *Women, Equality, and the French Revolution*, Westport, Conn., Greenwood Press, 1990.]

SEEKING THE VOTE: TWO CENTURIES OF STRUGGLE

Although French women's confrontations with the enduring power of patriarchy, superseding class divisions, have been credited with providing the intellectual basis for the feminist movement that emerged in the nineteenth century, their social and legal status regressed during and after the Napoleonic era. In the fields of family law and property law, the Napoleonic Code enshrined male superiority and domination. It was not until 1881, for example, that women were allowed to open their own bank accounts and make withdrawals (this applied only to a small number of unmarried upper-class women) and it was only in 1907 that married women who worked were legally permitted to keep their salaries. Until 1908, married women were treated as minors.

It took until April 21, 1944, before France recognized women's right to suffrage. From his military headquarters in Algeria, General de Gaulle issued an order that a constituent assembly was to be convened within a year after liberation. It was to be elected by a single secret ballot "by all French men and French women with the exception of those judged incompetent under laws already in force." In the fall of 1944 many working women in Paris were elected municipal councillors, in 1945 they were able to vote and in 1946 the constitution granted them equal rights with men. After the war small numbers of women were elected to parliament. (As of June 1991, they accounted for only 5.7% of the French parliament.)

According to Gisbert H. Flanz, French women failed for such a long time in their efforts "to effect the necessary legal and social reforms not because of poor leadership but because of the stubborn opposition in the senate to enacting women's suffrage. Many senators were troubled by the strong pacifist orientation of French feminists. Those who wanted revenge for the French defeat in the Franco-Prussian War would not condone any pacifist agitations." French women had to prove their patriotism in World Wars I and II before they were allowed the basic rights of citizenship. [Flanz, Gisbert H., *Comparative Women's Rights and Political Participation in Europe*, pp. 22-23, Transnational Publishers, Inc., 1983.]

American women struggled for 72 years to win their constitutional right of suffrage (starting at the first women's convention in Seneca Falls, N.Y., in 1848 until adoption of the Nineteenth Amendment in 1920) and it took almost as long for the women of Great Britain. Suffrage for British women was first advocated by Mary Wollstonecraft in her seminal book, *A Vindication of the Rights of Women*, in 1792. As in France, some aristocratic women had been allowed to select parliamentary candidates, but in 1733 when a small number of women voted in the election of a sexton to one of the city churches, the Lord Chief Justice nullified the results, saying, "I'm inclined to think women have not a right of voting." The Great Reform Act of 1832 made it official, specifying that suffrage was for "male persons" only. The formal demand for suffrage was put forward in the House of Commons in 1867 when John Stuart Mill introduced a limited suffrage bill, backed by petitions with thousands of women's signatures. In both countries women encountered opposition not only from conservatives but from some male abolitionists, liberals and advocates of democracy, socialism and other reforms who wanted the women to submerge their demands to what were considered more urgent political agendas.

In both the United States and Great Britain, as well as in other countries, suffrage was won because of the work of multitudes of militant, well-organized and dedicated women, some of whom sacrificed their health and even their lives to the struggle. But it is significant that, like the French women and women in other nations who were granted the right to vote following World War II, American and British women also had to demonstrate their "loyalty" in World War I before getting male government approval of female suffrage. In both countries, it quickly became evident that victory in war could not be achieved without the labor of millions of women who flooded into munitions factories, shipyards, offices, businesses, hospitals and volunteer organizations.

(In 1915, to demonstrate their scorn for chauvinistic rivalries, American and European suffragists had joined in organizing an unprecedented women's peace congress, which met at The Hague in April 1915, with 1,500 delegates from 12 belligerent and neutral nations. Women from enemy countries embraced each other and supported one another's peace proposals. When the United States entered the war in 1917, splits developed among the American women. Carrie Chapman Catt and other prominent suffragists chose the pragmatic path of supporting a war they felt they could no longer prevent, using their cooperation as a bargaining chip to win the right to vote and to improve working conditions for women working in the war industries. Similarly in Great Britain under the leadership of Emmeline Pankhurst and other women leaders, the major suffrage groups shelved their demands for the vote for the duration of World War I and worked to aid the war effort, while a smaller number, including Sylvia Pankhurst, retained their public opposition to the carnage.)

The Touchstone of War

Throughout history we have heard the traditional view that war is what separates the men from the boys, and even more important, the men from the women. The division of sex roles around the touchstone of war has provided the rationale for the acceptance of male domination and the subordination of women in almost every culture, from primitive to modern times. This ethos prevails worldwide even though in most wars only a minority of men actually engage in combat; women, too, may be active in combat and the overwhelming majority of victims are often civilians, including women and children.

All too often, the road to political power stretches from battlefields and military posts to the highest office in the land. This does not always happen, of course, but simply by virtue of belonging to the male sex, men are automatically endowed with the right to lead nations. The U.S. Constitution provides that the president is also commander-in-chief of the armed forces and in presidential campaigns the war or nonwar records of candidates often become a major issue. During the eight-year reign of Ronald Reagan in the White House, it mattered not that he had spent World War II in Hollywood making training films. Because of the haziness of his rhetoric many people apparently believed that he had fought in the war and his implementation of the biggest military buildup in U.S. history reinforced his image as strong, tough and macho—a political Rambo who consistently won the votes of a large majority of white males.

In the absence of significant numbers of women as heads of state or governments who, in the view of most feminists, might be expected to make acceptable more peace-oriented leadership and priorities, the few women who have actually held top posts in this century may have felt it necessary to prove that they could be as tough or tougher than a man. A case in point is former British Prime Minister Margaret Thatcher, whose greatest popular success came when she led the Falkland war. She has been credited with convincing President George Bush to initiate the air and ground war against Iraq after its invasion of Kuwait in 1991, and most recently she has been advocating armed intervention in the Balkans. Doubts about the strength and capacity of women to lead nations in war continue to remain a major obstacle to the selection of more women as heads of governments, although an examination of history discloses that individual women leaders, who are surrounded by male advisers, staff and military machines, can perform as effectively or ineffectively as men leaders in wartime.

The dichotomy that assigns the battlefield to men as their domain and the womb to women as theirs tyrannizes both sexes, distorting and stereotyping their actual and potential roles, forcing men to conform to imposed standards of masculinity and women to traditional feminine roles. Although the emergence of millions of women into the workforce and most aspects of public life has transformed perceptions of women's "place," particularly in the West, women's access to the basic right of citizenship—the right to vote—has been a very slow process, spanning some two centuries, and male models of behavior remain the "correct" litmus test for elevation to political leadership.

New Zealand Leads the Way

Before World War I, only four countries granted women the right to vote: New Zealand (1893), Australia (1902), Finland (1906), and Norway (1907), and in the United States several states, beginning with Wyoming in 1890, also approved suffrage. During and immediately after the war, 15 nations finally granted women voting rights, in some instances with age restrictions or with initial restrictions to voting at municipal or local levels. In addition to the United States (1920) and Canada, these were all European states: Austria, Belgium, Denmark, Germany, Iceland, Ireland, Luxembourg, Poland, Sweden, the newly formed Soviet Union, the United Kingdom, and Czechoslovakia. In Belgium, the law of May 9, 1919, gave the right to vote in national elections only to widows or mothers of servicemen killed during the war, citizens shot or killed by the enemy and women political prisoners. All women were not granted full voting rights until 1948. Canada also favored priority rights for women associated with the war. Women who served in the military or who had a close male relation serving in the military (a father, husband or son) were granted the right to vote at the federal level in 1917. It took another year before all Canadian women were allowed to vote in federal elections.

A more diverse array of 17 nations approved women's suffrage in the period between the two wars, including Bolivia, Brazil, Chile, Cuba and Uruguay in Latin America, Spain, Portugal and Romania in Europe, Lebanon, Turkey and South Africa, and the Maldives, Mongolia, Sri Lanka, Thailand, Pakistan and the Philippines in Asia/Pacific.

Another 31 states granted women voting rights during the World War II era, mostly in the last years of the war, 1944 and 1945, and immediately afterward. Japanese women, who had been struggling for decades for suffrage, won the right to vote in 1945, courtesy of the new constitution imposed upon them by American occupation authorities. From the 1950s until the present time, 74 nations, many of them newly formed following the breakup of old colonial systems and with newly written constitutions, enfranchised women. According to the Inter-Parliamentary Union, the remaining holdout nations are Saudi Arabia, Bahrein and Kuwait, which do not have elected parliaments and impose severe social restrictions on women, and the United Arab Emirates, where it is doubted that women have the right to vote or stand for election. The UAE's constitution excludes discrimination on various grounds but not on the basis of gender. In South Africa the right to vote and to stand for election at the national level had been denied to the black population, men and women alike, before 1994.

Discouraging the Vote

In some nations, women still encounter difficulty at the polls. In Argentina, the IPU notes, men and women vote in separate polling stations. "This enables precise breakdowns to be made of men and women who abstain, but also of the preference given to the different parties by men and women—by polling stations." [Inter-Parliamentary Union, *Women and Political Power*, Document No. 19, p. 23, Geneva 1992.] In the 1992 elections in Ethiopia, Dr. Margaret Snyder, former UNIFEM director, who served as an official observer, reported seeing long lines of women late in the day waiting to cast ballots. They told her they had been waiting for hours because men were being allowed to vote first. [Interview with Mim Kelber.]

Proxy voting is a practice that also is sometimes used to give husbands power over their women's voting rights. Of the 85 countries for which information on proxy votes was available to the IPU, only 16 made such provisions in their electoral legislation. Atypically, Sweden's model language has stringent rules to guarantee that proxy votes by citizens (a husband or wife, for example) are properly exercised. In other countries, the rules are more lax. In Algeria, where husbands casting votes in behalf of their wives has been a common practice, "spouses who can prove their conjugal status at the time of voting . . . are dispensed from proxy formalities." [IPU, *Women and Political Power*, pp. 23-24.] In 1991, the Algerian proxy vote law was amended to authorize the wife to cast her husband's vote. In Central Africa, all it takes for a man to cast a proxy vote for his wife is to produce an unwitnessed letter mentioning the name of the person to whom the voting power is delegated. In a reply to the IPU survey on proxy voting, the Gabon respondent commented, "It has been observed that this possibility was exploited to a far greater extent by men than by women, for reasons not always noble." Another major obstacle to women's voting, of course, is their high illiteracy rates in the developing nations.

WOMEN IN POLITICAL OFFICE

In several countries (the Netherlands and Guyana, e.g.), women were allowed to hold a parliamentary or local political seat before they won the right to vote. In most nations, however, enfranchisement was either linked directly with or followed shortly by recognition of a woman's right to seek election to public office. But the startling fact is that although women are half the world's population and have been voting in increasingly larger numbers in those nations that allow democratic elections, the percentages of women in elective or appointive office as we near the close of the twentieth century are, with a few notable exceptions, abysmally low. Even lower are the numbers of women who have headed governments as presidents or prime ministers. It is ironic that the number of women who reigned as powerful queens in their own right or as consorts during the more than 2,000 years before the advent of democracy far exceeds the miniscule number of women government leaders in our century.

There have been only seven women presidents: Corazon Aquino, Philippines; Vigdis Finnbogadottir, Iceland; Violeta Chamorro, Nicaragua; Ertha Pascal-Trouillot, Haiti; Lidia Geiler, Bolivia; Isabela Peron, Argentina; and Mary Robinson, Ireland. Only three—Chamorro, Finnbogadottir and Robinson—were in office at this writing.

There have been 16 women prime ministers: Margaret Thatcher, United Kingdom; Maria Liberia-Peters, Netherlands Antilles; Eugenia Charles, Dominica; Gro Harlem Brundtland, Norway; Indira Gandhi, India; Siramavo Bandanaraike, Sri Lanka; Golda Meir, Israel; Milka Planinc, Yugoslavia; Maria de Lourdes Pintasilgo, Portugal; Benazir Bhutto, Pakistan; Begum Khaleda Zia, Bangladesh; Kazimiera-Danute Prunskiene, Lithuania; Edith Cresson, France; Hanna Suchocka, Poland; Kim Campbell, Canada; and Tansu Ciller, Turkey. (In Canada, Flora MacDonald served as acting prime minister from 1987 to 1988.) Of these women, only five—Bhutto, Brundtland, Charles, Ciller and Zia—were in office at this writing.

Seven of these 23 women came into political power as surrogates of deceased male relatives. Aquino, Chamorro, Peron, Bandanaraike and Zia were widows of powerful political leaders who (with the exception of Juan Peron) were assassinated. Gandhi emerged as a national leader after the death of her father, Jawaharlal Nehru, the first prime minister of independent India, and Bhutto came into prominence in her campaign to save the life of her father, ousted President Zulfikar Ali Bhutto, who was executed in 1979 after being imprisoned for two years following a military coup.

Among these top-ranking stateswomen, only a few identified with or had roots in strong women's movements—Brundtland (Norway), Finnbogadottir (Iceland), Robinson (Ireland) and Cresson (France). Initially, Aquino had overwhelming support among women in toppling the Marcos dictatorship in the Philippines but this dwindled during her presidency as she became the pawn of male military and political advisers. During her brief, turbulent first term as prime minister of Pakistan, Bhutto, a university-educated woman with advanced views on women's roles, avoided challenging restrictive laws and traditions affecting women as she sought unsuccessfully to retain power in a male-dominated political and social culture. Thatcher and Meir had no women in their cabinets, and were criticized for failing to promote women's participation in political leadership. Planinc, who joined the Communist Party after World War II, in which she fought as a Tito partisan, became a parliamentarian as a loyal party member. A Croatian, she was appointed prime minister by Tito in 1982 when he announced a new policy of rotating this post among nationals of the various provinces. She served from May 1982 until December 1983. In Poland, Suchocka, a constitutional lawyer and a Democratic Union party representative in parliament, won approval as prime minister from her colleagues after she succeeded in forming a coalition of seven parties, ending a five-week political stalemate. Unlike her own party and a majority of Polish women, she favored strict anti-abortion legislation that repealed the nation's liberal reproductive choice laws. According to a Reuter dispatch [July 8, 1992], "political commentators said this helped her to win support of right-wing parties." Within a year, her conservative coalition lost power, after national elections in which it was reported that a large turnout of women voters, angered at the abortion ban, contributed to her defeat.

Psychological Terrorism

Kazimiera-Danute Prunskiene, chosen as prime minister of Lithuania in March 1990 after it declared its independence from the USSR, said in an interview at the 1992 Global Forum of Women [Dublin, July 10, 1992] that she was an example of the "psychological terrorism" used against women seeking political office. Dr. Prunskiene described herself as a victim of power plays by men from both the left and right that led her to resign in January 1991. At the time she was the only woman in the cabinet. She said she had wanted to bring in another woman as minister of trade, but was unable to get the required 50% approval from her male colleagues. Another woman who later became a cabinet minister has since resigned. Men welcomed "being free from competition with women," she said, and were more concerned with their power struggles than in problem-solving or practical issues affecting people's lives. Dr. Prunskiene, an economist specializing in agriculture and the market economy, remains in the parliament, where women account for 8% of the members. Previously, there had been more women deputies because of a 20 to 30% quota system for women under the old government.

Women must be freed from "one-sided patriarchal views and policies" in government, she said, noting that women were suffering most from "inhumane" policies inflicted on them. Amid growing unemployment, women were the first to be fired, had less access to job training in private firms and needed "new social and political structures for individual and family survival," she said. Despite efforts to return women to traditional roles as wives and mothers, many new women's groups were forming, but most were dealing with nonpolitical issues, according to Dr. Prunskiene. She believes strongly that women must get into policy and decision-making "to bring about humane policies and free women's capacity to use power more practically. We women will never make policies against men. We want to work with men to make policies for humanity and for peace."

Edith Cresson, a Socialist handpicked by President François Mitterrand as prime minister in 1991, lasted in office only 10 months after what was called her outspoken and "combative" manner subjected her to a barrage of criticism. In her first race for parliament in 1975, she was dubbed "la battante," the fighter, because of her vigorous campaign style. Later, she held various cabinet posts, including the minister of agriculture, minister of trade and industry, and minister of Europe affairs. As prime minister, she appointed a record number of six women to her cabinet at a time when women held only 31 of the 577 seats in the National Assembly and nine of the 319 seats in the senate. Polls taken soon after she became prime minister revealed that she had the support of 86% of women and 77% of men. [*Ms.* magazine, p. 10, July-August 1991.] Within a few months, her popularity sank to unprecedented lows—not, according to one observer, because of what she had done but "what she says and how she says it." [*The New York Times,* p. A13, July 24, 1991.]

Earlier comments she had made criticizing Japanese businessmen and her assertions in an interview that 25% of English, American and German men were gay, in contrast to Frenchmen and other Latin peoples, evoked unfavorable media coverage, as did her description of male critics in the National Assembly as "machos and hyenas." Such strong language from a woman apparently violated the double standard applied to women in matters of political as well as personal conduct. President Mitterrand has been quoted as saying of Margaret Thatcher, "She has eyes like Caligula and the mouth of Marilyn Monroe," but no public outcry ensued. [Olive, David, *Political Babble*, p. 224, John Wiley & Sons, Inc. 1992.] There were criticisms in Warsaw, however, when President Lech Walesa, asked what he thought of working with the new prime minister, Hanna Suchocka, reportedly responded with a blatantly sexist remark: "I like my women under me." [Zarembka, Paul, "Poland: The Deepening Crisis . . . ," *Monthly Review*, Vol. 44, 1993, p. 26.]

In a speech at a Women in Power conference held in Athens, Greece, in November 1992, Cresson challenged what she called the masculine model of politics as regards thinking, expression and ranking priorities. "To see power in the hands of a woman is for men a theft of what belongs to them," she said. "What counts for women who reach positions of responsibility is to solve problems, to truly and tangibly fulfill projects and not merely to discuss them or use them to score points through the media . . . . A woman is more 'naturally' vulnerable to criticism by not, by definition, corresponding to the dominant model. Every aspect of her person, the way she dresses, her attitude, her voice, the subjects which arouse her energies and which affect daily life directly, her resolve to find solutions are cause for amazement. Indeed, in the French parliament she becomes the butt of disgraceful insults, jeers, and hysterical behavior from certain males. Because she will not bow to the model, it will be said that a woman does not know the rules of what, for the ruling class, is a game."

Cresson said the only way to achieve a "massive increase in the number of women in all walks of political life" is to have electoral systems that "make it possible to allocate to women a significant and compulsory percentage of political posts . . . . If we do not institute a system which makes it compulsory, not to elect, but to make it possible to elect women in large numbers, we will never make a break with a type of representation of our peoples which is artificial, ineffective and complacent, and which will provide no answers to the very complex issues affecting our societies. Women are denied positions of responsibility not by the people but by the senior party politicians and political commentators who are all men in the traditional mold."

The difficulty of being the only woman in an all-male parliament was cited by Senator Kofoworola Bucknor-Akerle of Nigeria in a recent interview. A member of the Social Democratic Party, she is a woman with impressive credentials. In Great Britain she earned degrees in law and journalism and worked for the BBC for nine years. In Nigeria, she founded an advertising firm and a food company, was president of the Federation for Advancement of Nigerian Women, and helped organize the Nigerian Conservation Foundation. Yet she still finds the deck stacked against her—by her male colleagues. "The other senators have a lot of respect for me as a lawyer, and for my intelligence," she said. "But they are biased. It's a general bias all over the world."

She recalled that at one of the initial organizing meetings of the newly elected senate, the chairman was busy writing down remarks of the members, until she got up and began speaking. The chairman stopped writing, and it took several public reminders from her before he took notes on her views. As a legislator, her goals include revising tax laws that discriminate against women, traditional laws that bar women from inheritance rights and educating women about their legal rights—including the right to oppose forced child marriages—a tough agenda for one woman parliamentarian. [*Christian Science Monitor,* p. 14, September 19, 1992.]

> Women politicians, not to mention female prime ministers, are rare. Women who try to succeed in the world of politics discover that the hurdles they face, whether based on tradition, finances, ethnicity or organization, are compounded by the hurdle that is theirs by birth—that of gender. Thus, women's increased participation in mass politics over recent years has been predominantly concentrated in the lower echelons of public administration, political parties and trade unions and has not been matched by the same presence at higher levels of policy- and decision-making.
>
> *WOMEN Challenges to the Year 2000,* United Nations, 1991.

This has the effect, the UN report says, of "'ghettoization,' prolonging women's ineligibility for traditionally male preserves." In 1991 there were only a handful of women serving as finance ministers (in Bhutan, Finland, New

Zealand, San Marino and Taiwan); Malaysia had women in the two key cabinet posts of public enterprise and trade and industry. The report also noted:

> It is not unusual for women to be appointed as ministers without being given cabinet rank. Conversely, cabinet rank may be merely symbolic—Françoise Giroud in France, who was put in charge of women's issues, made over a hundred proposals, only a few of which were actually implemented. Success requires political support from largely male colleagues. For example, in Zimbabwe when the Minister for Women's Affairs, Joyce Mujuru, and her staff were entrusted with challenging the practice of *lobola*, or bride price, they faced enormous resistance and were subsequently accused of "cultural imperialism."
>
> *WOMEN Challenges to the Year 2000,*   United Nations, 1991.

No Room at the Top

In addition to the paucity of women in top leadership, the UN report cited the following data:
• In 1990, only 3.5% of the world's cabinet ministers were women.
• Women held no ministerial positions in 93 countries.
• Women were completely absent from the four highest levels in government in 50 countries (5 in the group of Western European and other states, 8 in Latin America and the Caribbean, 21 in Africa and 16 in Asia and the Pacific).
• Women similarly occupied less than 5% of the top positions in international organizations, including the United Nations and the European Community.
  Another UN report, *World's Women, Trends and Statistics 1970-1990*, points out: "Most women in government leadership are in such ministries as education, culture, social welfare and women's affairs. In some regions they are also making inroads in justice and legal affairs. But even in the 'social' fields, women average only 12 to 14% of the positions in developed regions, excluding eastern Europe and the USSR, 9% in sub-Saharan Africa and 6% or less in the rest of the world. Overall, women are least represented in executive, economic, political and legal ministries in Africa and in Asia and the Pacific. Men maintain a stronghold on such key areas as defense, economic policy and political affairs in all regions."
  Women's lack of direct participation in top-level policy-making in most nations of the world is a reflection of their lower economic and social status and at the same time reinforces the barriers against achieving substantial progress for women, who are now slightly less than half the world's population. Although women live longer than men, on average, and until recently were described as a majority of the world's population, the UN's statistical study reveals that of the world's 5.3 billion people in 1990, fewer than half (2.63 billion) were women. In most regions, women do outnumber men, but in the Asia-Pacific area there are

only 95 women for every 100 men—"enough to offset the world balance for men," according to the UN study. It attributes this to social and cultural factors in many areas that "deny girls and women the same nutrition, health care and other support that males receive. In a few countries widow burning and dowry deaths persist, and female infanticide is still suspected in some rural areas . . . .

"A new phenomenon—abortion on the basis of male preference—is also now known to occur. In these circumstances, women have higher death rates than men, especially at early childbearing ages and sometimes throughout their childbearing years." The study noted that of 8,000 abortions in Bombay after parents learned the sex of the fetus through amniocentesis, only one was male.

Global Status of Women

Other key UN statistical findings on the current status of women worldwide included the following:

ILLITERACY: Between 1970 and 1985 the number of illiterate women rose by 54 million, to almost half a billion, while the number of illiterate men rose by only 4 million.

FAMILY STATUS: Women now head more than a third of all households in the developed regions, Africa, Latin America and the Caribbean. Most often, households headed by women are poorer than those headed by men. In some rural areas of Latin America and Africa, the number of female-headed households reaches 50%, and in areas where civil or military conflicts are in progress, the figure is closer to 80%.

WORK AND PAY: Women everywhere work as much as men or more, up to 13 hours more each week in Asia and Africa, not counting unpaid, undervalued housework and other under-recorded or unvalued work. Although women in the industrialized nations spend less time on housework, because of time-saving appliances, smaller households, more help from men and other factors, the UN report notes, "First, women everywhere have nearly total responsibility for housework. Second, men in developing regions generally do even fewer household chores than men in the developed regions . . . . Even when women do the same work as men, they typically receive less pay—30 to 40% less throughout the world." The International Labor Organization has estimated that if the unpaid "invisible" work done by women in the home were to be quantified, it would contribute up to 40% of the gross national product of industrialized nations. [See also, *WOMEN, Challenges to The Year 2000*, UN, 1991.]

It is self-evident that if the economic and social status of women is to be raised and prevailing inequities overcome, women's access to and inclusion in the policy- and decision-making bodies and institutions that shape our societies must be broadened and strengthened. This was the consensus at an unprecedented IPU Symposium on the Participation of Women in the Political and

Parliamentary Decision-Making Process, held in Geneva, Switzerland, in November 1989, and attended by some 150 women and men MPs from all political horizons and regions, and some 60 experts. A synthesis statement based on the presentations and discussions at the four-day conference asserted:

> The political space belongs to all citizens; politics belongs to all citizens; politics is everyone's business and affects the lives of each of us . . . . There is no doubt that the more women are associated, in numbers corresponding to their percentage of the population, in the political decision-making parties, in elected bodies in Governments and in international bodies, the more they can be associated with this process as protagonists and the more they can change the modalities and outcomes of politics. Only then will the concept of democracy find concrete and tangible expression. Indeed, it has been underscored that democracy and the participation of women go hand in hand and promote each other mutually.

The statement also noted "that in countries where they (women) already represent a rather high and stable percentage of members of decision-making bodies, some problems facing society are no longer viewed as secondary or 'soft' issues; on the contrary, they have been included in Governments' priorities."

A Terribly Slow Pace

At the 1989 symposium, the IPU, which made its first survey of the numbers and percentages of women in the parliaments of 73 countries in 1975, reported on the progress made as of 1988. It found that the gender division in single or lower chambers averaged 87.5% men and 12.5% women in 1975, and over a 13-year period had changed to 85.5% men and 14.5% women, a 2% gain for women overall. A breakdown showed that in 15 countries the percentages of women in their parliaments had actually decreased, in three countries there had been no change, and increases ranged from 1% to 5% in the remaining countries. It was also estimated that as of 1988, in those nations that had bicameral legislatures, about 10.5% of the seats in the upper chamber were occupied by women.

A more recent IPU survey, reporting on the parliaments of 143 nations, showed that as of June 30, 1991, the world average was down to 11% women's inclusion in the single or lower chambers, with the data on 16 nations not available. On a regional basis, the percentages were: Africa, 9.2%; Americas, 12.0%; Arab states, 3.7%; Asia, 12.5%; Europe, 12.5%; and Pacific, 5.6%. In the upper chambers, women's inclusion ranged from 0% to a high of 29.9%. [IPU document No. 18, Geneva, 1991.]

"With a few exceptions, women are gaining ground in politics," the IPU said. "This is obvious, but . . . at a terribly slow pace and sometimes with severe set-

backs, as can be seen from the results of the latest elections held in various
Central and Eastern European countries or other parts of the world which have
opted for a change in their political and institutional systems." This was a reference to the collapse of the former governments of the Soviet Union and Eastern
Europe whose largely powerless, rubber-stamp legislatures had above-average
percentages of women members, elected or assigned under quota systems. In the
fast-changing post-revolution political scene in the Eastern bloc, women's inclusion in legislative and executive political positions has declined precipitously,
nor does the issue of women's participation appear to be on the male agendas of
the emerging political groups in that region, whether they profess to be democratic, autocratic, new-line, old-line, nationalistic, ethnic, or religious.

Quotas in the Eastern Bloc

A derisory view of the way quotas had been applied in the former Soviet
Union appeared in a *Moscow News* article by Natalia Kraminova reprinted in the
first issue [March 1992] of *Woman and Earth,* a magazine published in the
United States and Australia by Russian writer Tatyana Mamonova, who was ex-
pelled from her homeland in the pre-glasnost era for circulating a feminist newspaper. "The last few years of the Supreme Soviet's work have shown that after
seventy-plus years, the process of sexual leveling has triumphed: these women
who have become deputies through Committee for Soviet Women (CSW) quotas
(75 people, exactly half of the corps of women deputies) are completely equal to
the male majority in their total lack of originality, sparkle and distinctiveness,"
Kraminova wrote, adding that "we're getting tired of only seeing male faces at
presidiums and roundtable discussions on television. We're concerned about the
way new social organizations are turning into male strongholds. And it's really
sad to see that they didn't find space for a single woman in the Presidential
Soviet."

She noted that in the most recent parliamentary elections in the republics,
women accounted for only 5% to 8% of the deputies. She disagreed with
Alevtina Fedulova, first deputy chairperson of the Soviet Women's Committee,
who called for restoring the quota system to assure protective legislation for
women—"those same quotas," Kraminova commented, "which Galina
Starovoitova, a people's deputy of the USSR, has rightly dismissed as
'loopholes' for women. I'm just thinking that quotas are only arithmetic, and
what we'd like to see from politicians of both sexes is some higher mathemat-
ics."

Kraminova argued that "the woman question is not a question of minor socioeconomic discrepancies, but part of the general question of human rights in
this country . . . . And it's about progress in the woman question being impossible until the word 'equality' is returned from post-revolution decrees into real

life. And the CSW should be seeking leaders for a political movement, which would at last pose the question of the second-rate status of women in our country, and occupy itself with the specifics of consciousness-raising in this area."

With their decreased representation in national and local legislative bodies, both as the result of the elimination of quotas and fewer women candidates, women in Russia and other former republics are being subjected to a concerted effort to drive them out of the labor market by eliminating social welfare programs. Journalist Katrina vanden Heuvel, who specializes in Russian politics and society, reported recently in *The New York Times* [September 12, 1992] that as the Soviet welfare system was collapsing, "the feminization of poverty may become the new Russia's largest and cruelest problem." In Moscow, she said, 70% of the newly unemployed are women between the ages of 45 and 55 and legislation, backed by a coalition of new democrats and old-style conservatives, was expected to be adopted that would prevent women from participating equally in the emerging market economy.

"Mothers of children under the age of 14 would be allowed to work only a limited number of hours a week, thereby disqualifying them from the best jobs," she wrote. In addition, the parliament and some city governments were dismantling the once elaborate Soviet system of child care, with the Moscow city council proposing to shut down a third of the city's day care centers in the next two years. Russian women were organizing activist and self-help groups, she said, adding that they were "unlikely to find allies among the overwhelmingly male political class."

The Soviet experience was duplicated in other Eastern bloc elections. In July 1990, the IPU reported that the number of women in European parliaments had "dropped dramatically," down to 13.6% as compared with 19.1% in January 1988. It attributed this to new elections held in the former Communist Eastern European nations. Percentages of women dropped in the Romanian parliament from 34.3% to 3.5%; Czechoslovakia, from 29.5% to 6%; Hungary, from 20.9% to 7%; Bulgaria, from 21% to 8.5%; and the German Democratic Republic, from 32.2% to 20.5%.

Women in the Former Yugoslavia

Following the breakup of Yugoslavia and before the tragic civil war among some of the constituent republics killed thousands of men, women and children and created huge numbers of refugees, the deteriorating position of women was described at a Regional Seminar on the Impact of Economic and Political Reform on the Status of Women in Eastern Europe and the USSR, held in Vienna April 8-12, 1991, by the UN Division for the Advancement of Women. Svetlana Arsenic, a counselor for the Yugoslav Federal Secretariat for Labor, reported that instead of the 30% quotas for women that had prevailed in the national parliament, there had been a "dramatic decrease in the number of women in the newly formed representative bodies and organs of authority, which is considerably at variance with the percentage of women in the total population and their actual presence in the spheres of production, science, culture, art." Also, she said, the past practice of appointing women to certain posts had been abandoned.

The most recent elections, she said, showed that Slovenia was down to 13% of women in its parliament, Croatia 4.56%, Montenegro 4%, Macedonia, 3.33%, Bosnia and Herzegovina 2.9%, and Serbia 1.6%, adding that women feared that the new parliaments would "not even put on the agenda, let alone solve, problems which are of special interest and significance for women." Restructuring processes were leading to massive layoffs of workers, forcing women to return to the household in large numbers. "Women have not failed to react to this situation," she said. "Within the framework of the general pluralization of political life, women's parties and women's liberation groups are being set up as associations of a democratic orientation which counter in an organized fashion the pressures of nationalism, clericalism and other forms of conservatism. Associated women's parties and groups in Serbia had demanded that the National Assembly of Serbia set up a Ministry for Women, but that proposal was not accepted, and on their part, in protest to the virtual absence of women in the assembly, they also established a parallel women's parliament."

Both the governments of Serbia and Croatia have rejected women's demands and in the other newly independent republics, women's concerns are being ignored, according to Vesna Pesic, a sociologist at the Institute of Social Sciences in Belgrade, "Up to date," she reported, "both left- and right-wing authorities have shown the greatest interest only in the reproductive role of women, threatening thus the individual constitutional right of the free decision of giving birth and, potentially, other women's rights."

Internationally known journalist Slavenka Drakulic, an outspoken feminist and critic of the former Communist government, agreed that there was a concerted drive on "to put women 'where they belong,' back into the house, with children, recognizing them only in their maternal function" and observed that this "is a phenomenon in almost all countries where the Communist regimes have lost power. These governments see them only in the role of mothers, giving birth to the little Croats, Slovenians, Hungarians, Poles, Czechs, Slovaks . . . in fact, to the Nation. One of the first issues on the agenda of the (new) parties in power was the restriction on abortion." She noted that abortion restrictions or prohibitions were also being pushed in Poland, Hungary, and the Czech and Slovak Republics.

Democracy with a Male Face

"Once again in history," she said, "women have been led to believe that democracy is more important than their rights—rather than that democracy is all about their citizens, human and women's rights . . . . they themselves haven't learned yet that their rights are a litmus test for democratic changes. Once this kind of 'democracy' with a male face establishes itself here, together with the capitalist economy, I am afraid that women will find themselves stripped of their basic rights (such as reproductive rights), without social privileges granted by the previous system, and without the possibility to influence the political decisions and to bring about changes. As if 45 years of the emancipation of women under socialism had never happened."

She noted that "emancipation" grew out of the leading role the Yugoslav Communist Party played in organizing resistance to the Nazi invaders during World War II and mobilizing women into the Antifascist Women's Front (AWF), a broad patriotic front that included some two million women. One hundred thousand women fought in the Partisan forces, 25,000 of whom died and 40,000 of whom were seriously wounded. "The fact is that many women did indeed find liberation in the war because they were treated as equals rather than as sex objects or household property, for the first time in their lives," she explained. "In the immediate postwar period, the CP built into legislation the emancipatory policy and the 'woman question' no longer existed." Later, she said, the AWF was transformed into a bureaucratic women's organization that served to assure CP power over women. "Self-organizing didn't exist, any kind of spontaneous grassroots organization (peace, ecological, feminist, workers, etc.) was suspicious, therefore forbidden—because if an organization is not institutionalized, it cannot be efficiently controlled."

Referring to the 30% quota for the representation of women in politics that existed under Communist rule, she said, "The problem, of course, was that these women were tokens, without power to influence politics or decide for themselves." But, according to Vesna Pesic, various women's organizations in the post-Communist era were returning to the idea of quotas as the only way to restore women to potentially influential political positions. One reason women fared so poorly in the Croatian, Serbian and other republics' most recent elections was that few women were allowed to be nominated and those that were, she said, found themselves at the bottom of the candidate lists offered under proportional representation voting. Party steering committees formed after the elections also bypassed women, she reported, pointing out that in Slovenia only two of 27 appointed ministers were women, only one out of 20 in Serbia, and none in the other republics.

Furthermore, she said, women have not only been excluded from "top politics" but from local governments where they had been most active. Centralization in the republics had abolished local political bodies, she said, and "in this way, practically all institutional avenues for women's public activity have been closed." In an effort to preserve women's rights that had been guaranteed under the former Yugoslav government and to promote constitutional, economic, social and political changes to raise the status of women, she said, some independent women's organizations and some political parties were demanding quotas for women in party leadership positions. They were also calling for including women's issues in party programs, establishment of separate female lists for future elections, preservation of local governments and participation of women in decision-making, and safeguarding of the right to and availability of contraceptives.

Rape as a War Tactic

Since these reports were presented at the April 1991 seminar in Vienna, the situation in former Yugoslavia has disintegrated into civil war, "ethnic cleansing," and increased violence against women. There followed reports of mass rapes of young women by soldiers, with women in one small town in Bosnia, who had been held hostage for days and raped repeatedly, asserting they had been told by their Serbian attackers that they were under government orders to rape Muslim women "as a principal tactic of the war."

This brutal way of demonstrating the subjection of women was described by some of the young victims in interviews with a New York *Newsday* reporter, Roy Gutman. His report included a charge by Dr. Melika Kreitmayer, leader of the gynecological team that examined 25 of the 40 victims from the town of Brezovo Polje, that "the object of the rapes was to humiliate Muslim women, to insult them, to destroy their persons and to cause shock." [*Newsday*, p. 7, August 23, 1992.] According to a representative of the German-based International Women's Peace Archives, at an international women's conference held in Zagreb, Croatia, October 24, 1992, some participants estimated that 30,000 women and girls aged 10 to 70 years had been raped, with hundreds left pregnant and denied abortions. A later European Community investigation put the number of estimated rape victims at about 20,000, and indicated that forced impregnation was a deliberate government policy to produce more "Serb babies." Historically, from ancient to contemporary times, rape and forced prostitution have been a weapon of all sides in military conflicts.

THE IPU FINDINGS ON QUOTA SYSTEMS

At the IPU symposium in Geneva in November 1989, when the upheavals in the Soviet Union and Eastern Europe were just getting under way, the discussion focused on how quota systems and other mechanisms to increase women's participation could provide more than tokenism in multiparty democratic nations or at least give them a foot in the door in authoritarian societies. Participants suggested that a minimum of 30% women members, or about a third, is needed to provide the "critical mass" of gender balance in a legislature that can lead to fundamental policy changes and female political leadership reflecting the views, needs and concerns of women. In several democratic European countries (as will be discussed later), a formula of no less than 40% or no more than 60% of either sex to be included in the legislative and executive branches of government has been instituted.

In the IPU's June 1991 survey, only six parliaments in the world had achieved the goal of including more than 30% women. These were: Finland, 38.5%; Sweden, 38.1%; Guyana, 36.9%; Norway, 35.8%; Cuba, 33.9%; and Denmark, 33%. The Nordic countries are generally regarded as the most democratic and advanced in the world on women's rights issues and also have the highest number of women in top executive government positions.

Cuba is a one-party state with a government-controlled women's organization that has developed extensive social, economic and legal "guarantees" and programs to raise the status of women, provide education, employment, child care, etc. A constitutional provision that men must share household duties equally with women is often cited, with little evidence that it is honored in practice.

In Guyana, where women won the right to sit in the Legislative Council in 1945, eight years before they won the right to vote, the relatively high percentage of women was explained this way in a report to the IPU: "Politically, women's image has undergone a revolutionary change. Women politicians generally see themselves not as mere appendages to the party hierarchy but as being equal with their menfolk. Generally, political parties accept this new-found concept women have of themselves, and recognize that women do have an important part to play." [IPU, *Women and Political Power,* p. 168.] In an interview with the author, Jocelyn Dow, a leading Guyanan feminist, said that women in the small island republic (population 765,000) have a tradition of being independent and outspoken. She also credited former Prime Minister Cheddi Jagan, a Marxist, and his U.S.-born wife with having encouraged women's participation in political life, without applying specific quotas. (Jagan was reelected prime minister in October 1992.)

Thirteen nations that responded to the IPU survey had no women in their parliaments. These included four Arab states: Jordan, Lebanon, Morocco, and United Arab Emirates (no information on Libya); two African states, Comoros and Djibouti (no information on Equatorial Guinea, Gabon, Guinea-Bissau, Sierra Leone and Swaziland); Americas: Belize and Santa Lucia (no information on Antigua/Barbuda, Colombia, Dominican Republic, Grenada, Guatemala, Haiti, St. Vincent and Suriname); Asia: Bhutan; and the Pacific: Kiribati, Papua New Guinea; Solomon Islands, and Tonga (no information on Western Samoa). Saudi Arabia has no legislature, nor did Kuwait until it held its first elections on

October 5, 1992. Voting for the 50-member parliament was confined to men over 21 whose families had lived in the emirate since before 1921—a select group of 81,400 men out of Kuwait's 606,000 nationals. No women were allowed to vote. Some staged protests at the polling booths.

As of 1991, the United States, self-proclaimed leader of the free, democratic world, was among the bottom 71 countries that had legislative bodies with fewer than 10% women members (it had 6.4%), and within this group it ranked 21st. (See chapter on the United States.) Also in this below-10% group were such leading democracies as Australia (6.7%), Belgium (8.5%), France (5.7%), Israel (6.7%) and the United Kingdom (6.3%). In June 1992 elections, Israeli women picked up three more seats in the Knesset, raising their number to 11 among the 120-member parliament.

Next in rank to the top six were Iceland, 23.8%; Austria 21.8%; The Netherlands and China, each 21.3%; Germany, 20.4%; and Democratic Republic of Korea (North), 20.1%, four of which are multiparty democracies. Among the 10 nations with percentages of women legislators above 15% and below 20% were two that are now defunct: the USSR, 15.3%; and Yugoslavia, 17.7%. In the former USSR, according to a December 1988 law on elections to the USSR Congress of People's Deputies, women's councils, coordinated by the Soviet Women's Committee, as noted above, had the right to appoint 75 women as deputies on behalf of those national public organizations, regardless of electoral constituencies. This system of reserved seats for women was in effect a quota system; however, it did not exclude direct election of additional women. Also in this group of 10 nations with above-15 percentages were Vietnam, 17.7%; New Zealand, 16.7%; Nicaragua, 16.3%; and various small developing nations.

Among the 23 nations in the 10%-15% range of inclusion were several Western nations: Canada, 13.2%; Italy, 12.8%; Luxembourg, 13.3%; Poland, 13.5%; Spain, 14.6%; and Switzerland, 14.0%; and the remainder were Middle Eastern (Iraq, 10.8%) and developing nations.

With the exception of Japan, 2.3%; Liechtenstein, 4.0%; South Korea, 2.0%; and Turkey, 1.3%, all the countries that had lower percentages of women in their legislatures than the United States, France and the United Kingdom were poor developing countries. Iran, 1.5%; Kenya, 1.1%; and Pakistan, 0.9% ranked lowest.

In the Middle East, as previously noted, Muslim-led nations have the lowest percentages of women in their parliaments and usually none at all. Just how formidable the odds are against women asserting their rights can be seen from the episode noted in the introduction. The woman seeking election to Jordan's parliament was Toujan Faisal, a 41-year-old TV commentator and university graduate, married to a gynecologist. In 1988, she had become the hostess of "Women's Issues," a TV series that each week considered a different problem of special interest to women. It immediately became the most controversial series in the history of Jordanian television, particularly when she exposed the physical abuse and violence suffered by women in every stratum of society. The Muslim fundamentalists sought to have the program banned, and after almost a year of denunciations and threats from religious fanatics, the Ministry of Information cancelled the program.

It was then that Faisal decided to file as a candidate to run for a seat in the parliament. A central part of her campaign was a proposal to amend Jordanian family law to give women greater rights. Under existing laws, she pointed out, the Muslim woman is kept powerless by the husband's control over her property and income. He can keep three or four wives, divorce and remarry at will, deprive a divorced wife of her home, children and income. She particularly angered the fundamentalists by pointing out that such behavior toward women was not authorized in the Koran, but was a tradition established by men in the interests of men.

After she announced her candidacy, Muslim fundamentalists brought charges of apostasy against her in a religious court, with the penalties for conviction including dissolution of her marriage and loss of her children. Her accusers also called for the lifting of punishment from any Muslim who might choose to assassinate her. She was subjected to a series of pretrial hearings, which finally ended when the court disclaimed jurisdiction. She had to conduct her campaign under the protection of bodyguards, and her husband had to close his clinic. She came in third among six candidates for the seat she was contesting and charged that she had lost because of electoral fraud. She was unable to find work after this episode, and her husband had to go abroad to find employment. In an interview with journalist Milton Viorst, she predicted that the abuse she had suffered would discourage women for a long time from running for office. [Viorst, Milton, "A Reporter at Large (Jordan)," *The New Yorker*, January 7, 1991.]

Nevertheless, Faisal herself was not discouraged. Two years later, she and two other women were elected to the lower house of the legislature.

THE ISSUE OF TOKENISM

The mere presence of women in a legislative body does not necessarily mean that they got there via a democratic process or that they can act independently to influence policy, but sometimes even as tokens they can symbolize potentially expanded political roles for women. Thus, at the 1989 IPU symposium in Geneva, participants from countries in which women had the lowest level of parliamentary representation were the most supportive of the system of reserving a certain number of seats for women, filled by means of a separate election or co-optation, or through appointment. According to the IPU, this is an uncommon mechanism, found only in Bangladesh, Nepal, Pakistan and Tanzania at present and formerly in Egypt. In the last-named country, the late President Anwar el Sadat decided in 1979 to reserve 30 seats for women in the People's Assembly, and he also decided to include women in municipal councils. This policy was later contested on the grounds that it was contrary to a constitutional provision prescribing equality between men and women in the field of rights and responsibilities and that women had reached a state of political maturity that qualified them to assume the same political and parliamentary responsibilities as men. The Egyptian parliament, as of June 1991, had 2.2% women. Although there are no longer reserved seats for women, some women are still appointed.

In Nepal, a constitution adopted in 1990 provides that at least 5% of candidates of political parties and organizations for the house of representatives must be women; in addition, three of the 35 members of the National Council who are co-opted by the house of representatives must likewise be women, which, in effect, means reserving three seats for women on the council.

In a report to the IPU, a spokesperson for the government of Pakistan, which had less than 1% women in its parliament, said Pakistani women "have been encouraged to participate in politics, but in view of our cultural and social conservatism, special seats were also reserved for women in the Assemblies. Their participation at the grassroots level in politics has also been ensured by reserving a minimum of two seats in the Union Council, elected through either direct or indirect election. Women local councillors are actively playing their role in the local government institutions and in spite of the fact that men and women have equal opportunities to participate in politics and to stand for general elections, there have also been special reserved seats for women in both the National and Provincial Assemblies (20 seats in the National Assembly, and 5% of the membership of each Provincial Assembly)." In 1990, however, the system of reserving special seats for women expired and in the last general elections for the National Assembly, only three women ran for election, and two won. In a reference to former Prime Minister Benazir Bhutto, who was defeated for reelection after a political scandal involving charges of corruption against her husband, the Pakistani report asserted that she had given no priority or consideration to extending the term of seats reserved for women. It said the present government was drafting new legislation "to restore the reserved seats for women in the parliament and the provincial assemblies, in order to have adequate representation of women." There was no self-consciousness in this statement about the validity of stating that half a country's population could be adequately represented by 20 women. (Bhutto was returned to office in a later election.)

A reply from a government spokesperson in Morocco to the IPU survey said it would be preferable to reserve seats for women "during a transitional period," leading the IPU to comment: "This remark is particularly relevant in view of the fact that the Moroccan parliament, to which women have had the right to be elected since 1963, has not yet had one woman member of parliament." [IPU, *Women and Political Power*, p. 99.]

In India, where women are 14.1% of the parliament's House of the People, there has been a shift to decentralized politics that encourages women's participation, according to Dr. Devaki Jain. An Oxford-educated economist who has spent the past 30 years studying the situation of poor women in her country, she told the 1992 Global Forum of Women that India's constitution was being amended to reserve 30% of legislative seats at the grassroots level for women. Already, she said, 12,000 women have been elected to local councils in several states. Women are emerging in large numbers at the grassroots level and "moving from individual to collective leadership," she said.

The system of appointing members of parliaments may apply to men as well as to women but, according to the IPU, "in many countries it is the only way of getting women into parliament and..., in relation to changing mores, it is sometimes applied as a veritable 'positive action measure.'" It listed 44 countries in which a specific number of seats in parliament are filled through appointment, and said this procedure remains for women one possible means of access to parliament. [IPU, *Women and Political Power,* p. 99.] It added that in the few countries where the entire second or upper house is appointed, a number of women can (or in any case would be able to) enter parliament by appointment instead of being elected to the lower house. (Aside from Canada and Germany, these are mostly developing nations.) At present, appointed women sit in the upper houses of Barbados (six, or 28.6%); Belize (two, or 22.2%), Jamaica (four, or 19.0%), Jordan (one, or 2.5%), Saint Lucia (two, or 18.2%), and Trinidad and Tobago (four, or 12.9%). In the United Arab Emirates, where all the members of the national parliament are appointed, there has never been a woman member.

THE CONCEPT OF POSITIVE DISCRIMINATION

The word "quotas" has become political anathema in the United States as part of the conservative backlash against affirmative action programs of the civil rights and women's movements that seek to end discrimination and employment inequities affecting minorities and women. But the concept of setting specific goals, timetables and numbers to assure genuine equality between men and women is widely accepted in international bodies such as the United Nations, in international law, and by some governments and political parties, both in theory and words. (How the concept is applied practically will be discussed in more detail below.)

Called "positive discrimination," rather than affirmative action or quotas, the concept, says the IPU, "is based on the assumption that, temporarily and pending achievement of a proper balance, women should be given an institutional or other 'helping hand' to compensate for the de facto discrimination they suffer." [IPU, *Women and Political Power,* p. 95.] This approach is enshrined in Article 4(l) of the UN Convention on the Elimination of All Forms of Discrimination against Women, adopted by the UN General Assembly in December 1979 and effective in September 1981. It says:

Adoption by States Parties of temporary special measures aimed at accelerating de facto equality between men and women shall not be considered discrimination as defined in the present Convention, but shall in no way entail as a consequence the maintenance of unequal or separate standards; these measures shall be discontinued when the objectives of equality of opportunity and treatment have been achieved.

Article 7 says:

States Parties shall take all appropriate measures to eliminate discrimination against women in the political and public life of the country and, in particular, shall ensure, on equal terms with men, the right:

(a) To vote in all elections and public referenda and to be eligible for election to all publicly elected bodies;

(b) To participate in the formulation of government policy and the implementation thereof and to hold public office and perform all public functions at all levels of government;

(c) To participate in non-governmental organizations and associations concerned with the public and political life of the country.

Article 8 says further:

States Parties shall take all appropriate measures to ensure to women of equal terms with men and, without any discrimination, the opportunity to represent their Governments at the international level and to participate in the work of international organizations.

The general principle of equality was laid out in the United Nations Charter (1945) and the Universal Declaration of Human Rights (1948). In 1952, the UN General Assembly approved the Convention on the Political Rights of Women, which became effective two years later. The UN-sponsored World Decade for Women, 1976-1985, gave tremendous impetus to women's rights activities and consciousness in all areas of the world, from the developing regions to the industrialized nations. It also provided the pressure that led to adoption of the Convention to End Discrimination against Women and the Forward-Looking Strategies statement, adopted by the UN International Women's Conference in Nairobi, Kenya, in 1985 and later approved by the General Assembly.[1]

According to a report presented by Professor Eliane Vogel-Polsky of the Free University of Brussels to the Council of Europe's symposium on "Equality between Women and Men" [Strasbourg, 1989], Article 4 of CEDAW provides the legal mandate for remedial action by all signatory governments to end discrimination against women. (The United States has not yet ratified the Convention.) She said:

This is the first-ever clear statement in an international and universally applicable legal instrument to the effect that positive action neither constitutes discrimination nor derogates from the principle of equality (provided the measures are temporary and aim to correct inequality where it is actually experienced.) [The Convention] recognizes that such action encompasses all aspects of sexual discrimination.

Describing the legal implications of this article, Professor Vogel-Polsky noted: "It does not simply proclaim acknowledgment of a fundamental right or freedom, nor is it a special provision relevant to one aspect of women's rights. It is an internationally accepted interpretation of a general principle of law, the principle of equality between men and women." Once a state has ratified the UN Convention without making reservations in respect of Article 4, paragraph 1, it should recognize that "three guarantees of crucial significance become entrenched in its domestic legislation. These are:

1. that where positive discrimination or preferential treatment is granted to a person or group of persons of one sex, it will never be construed as an illegal derogation from the general principle of equality between the sexes provided that any such special measures are temporary and serve to bring about equality more rapidly;
2. that such measures will be adopted and continued until the objectives of equality of opportunity and treatment have been achieved;
3. that special positive action measures will be adopted by states in their relations with citizens, groups and institutions, whenever they appear to constitute the most appropriate means of achieving one of the rights enshrined in the UN Convention, a right incorporated in their domestic legislation by their own procedures which will depend upon the provision made for the purpose in their constitutions.

She added, however, that the purpose of Article 4, paragraph 1, is not a standard establishing a right that must be enforced by national legal procedures. Rather, she said, "It is a principle of interpretation that has entered directly into the domestic legal order of every state ratifying the Convention; for a principle of interpretation is by definition one that does not require special measures for its transposition. Once the principle has entered into a state's domestic legal order, it applies to all the laws, collective agreements or statutory provisions in which equality of opportunity and treatment is guaranteed to women and men."

Professor Vogel-Polsky said it seemed doubtful that many of the governments ratifying the Convention were aware of the legal implications of accepting Article 4, paragraph 1, without reservations. She said the principle of interpretation described above "is not static; in essence it is dynamic since it enters into every field where the issue of sexual equality arises (civil, political, social, economic and cultural) and lends a new dimension to legal standards adopted in the country's constitution, its general or specific legislation, or the clauses of any collective agreement. Positive action measures must be adopted whenever and wherever they are seen to be necessary for the achievement of equality in this sense."

Against this background and with legal commitments to women's equal participation in political life and decision-making, the 1970s and 1980s produced a growing number of official actions and statements reinforcing this commitment and in some cases providing for quotas, particularly in Europe.[2] At a seminar on "The democratic principle of equal representation—forty years of Council of Europe activity," held in Strasbourg November 6-7, 1989, Marit Halvorsen, assistant professor, Norwegian State College of Public Administration and Social Work, Oslo, reported:

> The 1970s was the era of legislation on equal rights and equal opportunities, in Norway as well as in other European countries. The number of measures adopted is breathtaking. International organizations also promulgated an astonishing number of documents on the subject. The Council of Europe alone published 90 documents relevant to the equal rights question between 1950 and 1988, of which five are Declarations, 36 Recommendations and 25 Resolutions. Given the sometimes slow progress, it seems fair to question the effectiveness of this kind of paperwork.

Quota Experiments Advocated

At a Council-sponsored European Ministerial Conference on Equality between Women and Men at Strasbourg [March 4, 1986], the meeting approved the following typical declaration on quotas: It recommended "use of positive action and special measures to accelerate the achievement of equality in participation in political life and the nomination, the appointment and the election of women to positions of responsibility in all areas of the decision-making process, for instance, experiments with various forms of quota systems."

Among the Council's most recent statements was a Declaration on Equality of Women and Men, adopted at a meeting of its Committee of Ministers (from 21 member European states) November 16, 1988. Reaffirming its commitment to equality of the sexes, it included among its action proposals: "VI. Declare that the strategies to be applied for this purpose must enable women and men to receive equal treatment under the law and equal opportunities to exercise their rights and develop their individual gifts and talents. These strategies should provide for suitable measures—including temporary special measures aimed at accelerating de facto equality between women and men—relating to the following in particular: a. protection of individual rights; b. participation in political, economic, social and cultural life;" and it enumerated eight other rights.

At the 1989 Council seminar in Strasbourg, the boldest intellectual challenge to the enormous discrepancy between the constant reaffirmation of principles of equality and the "realities which need to be changed by action, struggle and mobilization of all our energies and all our talents" came from Professor Elisabeth G. Sledziewski, University Robert Schuman of Strasbourg.

Calling for a reexamination of principles which have shown themselves to be incomplete, she asked: "Does not the fact that women's social and political emancipation is making so little headway in a Europe in which openness to democratic ideas is a matter of consensus suggest that it is in this consensus, this openness and these very ideas that a misunderstanding is concealed?"

She traced the root of the problem to the "resolutely universalist" modern ideal of European democracy, in which "the rights of the individual are set out in a universal, abstract form: equal rights for a featureless individual, whether he be of noble or humble origin, rich or poor, good or bad, intelligent or stupid. The modern doctrine accentuates the universal and abstract nature of rights, because, furthermore, it attributes them to man and woman indifferently, unlike French revolutionary democracy, which imposed the lasting model of the civil incapacity of the female sex. It is also worthy of note that it has been regimes based on liberal democracy which have, up to most recent times, maintained women's civil incapacity, thereby contradicting the universalist ideal while playing on its abstract formulations.

"For the abstract formulation of rights is indeed the paradox of democratic universalism, and therefore the point at which it is in danger of turning into its opposite. By omitting to specify that the citizen's civil and civic capacity is also that of the citizeness, modern democracy confirms its universalist choice and at the same time the humanist dimension of a definition of the social agent as a rational subject, man made mind by abstraction from his biosexual identity. Conversely, however, this refusal to sexualize the definition of the citizen also confirms the latent power of a sexist scheme of things, which automatically masculinizes all social and political responsibilities. When European languages speak of the rights of the citizen, or even, the rights of man, they generally give the subject of these rights the masculine gender. Universalism as an approach to rights is therefore the most dangerous gift humanism can make to democracy.

"To refuse to acknowledge that there are human beings who are men and human beings who are women," Professor Sledziewski continued, "is one way of refusing to acknowledge that there may have been discriminations. . . . The disavowal of the sexual condition of human beings is not content merely to cast an angelic veil over reality. It authorizes the negation of all the infringements of human rights which may take place in a particular sphere, that of the difference between the sexes . . . . The universalism of asexual human rights quickly becomes an opportunity to enhance the rights of the male, by claiming that they are those of all mankind."

But, she continued, "the definition of the human subject cannot omit the difference between the sexes inasmuch as it is as a man or as a woman that this subject lives out his or her humanity . . . . The idea that there can be no human substance without sexual identity implies that we cannot legitimately define human rights, which are attributes of this substance, otherwise than as the rights of man and of woman . . . . The democracy which does not acknowledge as its own the task of safeguarding the rights of man and woman is, logically, just as suspect as a self-styled democracy which does not specify that the rights and freedoms of the people can be exercised by individuals."

Contending that no real democracy is possible if the question of equality between men and women is not posed as a political precondition, she stated the case for quotas: "Only the introduction of participation quotas imposing equal representation of the sexes in all decision-making authorities can make women's active participation in the *polis* effective and irreversible. If democracy is to acknowledge the difference of the sexes, it has no other response to suggest than this: the human race is twofold, debates and decisions must be the acts of men and women, otherwise they cannot be the acts of the human race as it is.

"This is absolutely not a demand for a corporatist arrangement, since a sex is not a corporation, but a physical datum of human existence. Nor is it a question of bending the principle of equality whereby all citizens are eligible, regardless of their social origin: for preventing discrimination constructed by society (class, case, religion, etc.) does not in any way imply the negation of physical differences; on the contrary, it implies their recognition in order to prevent them from the outset from working in favor of inequality. This is precisely what quotas, infelicitously referred to by some as positive discrimination, seek to achieve, as their purpose is to disarm all forms of discrimination."

Quotas, by which she means equal numbers of men and women, must be regarded as a political, not a technical process, she said. "Measures put forward to foster the involvement of women in political life must not be presented, as they too often are, as conjunctural arrangements for the achievement of results on an ad hoc basis and devoid of any doctrinal justification. This approach could not fail to confirm the unfair suspicions voiced in connection with quotas and suggest that the involvement of women in politics can only be enforced by unlawful means. On the contrary, it is necessary to affirm that these provisions are envisaged in the very name of the principle of equality . . . .

"The advent of democracy based on equal representation," she concluded, "will mean not only a turning point in relations between men and women and consequently in the social being of the human race, but also a turning point in the democratic construction process. Equal participation by female citizens in the affairs of the *polis* will henceforth be considered a *sine qua non* of the completion of democracy. A democracy without women will no longer be seen as an imperfect democracy, but as no democracy at all."

QUOTA SYSTEMS IN OPERATION

The IPU study focused on two types of electoral quotas: (a) The quota applied to the election and therefore concerning the percentage of women candidates in relation to the total number of persons seeking election. (b) The quota applied to the result of the election and hence concerning the number of seats that must be occupied by women after the vote.

"In many cases," the IPU reported, "replies to the survey did not show whether the quota mentioned referred to the proportion of women candidates (probably the most common case) or, on the contrary, to the proportion of those elected. There nevertheless do not appear to be any examples of dual quotas: one for candidates and one for the results of the election." In regard to parliamentary seats, a further distinction must be drawn between a quota embodied in the constitution or electoral law, and a quota introduced by a political party, and included in its statutes or an internal directive. After a bitter debate lasting several months, Argentina's parliament voted in November 1991 to include in its electoral law a compulsory 30% quota for female candidates for all elective posts, an unusual action. The several other countries in which quotas ranging from minimal to substantial have been specified in national legislation include Angola (which reserved 15% of seats for women in the People's Assembly elected by indirect ballot in December 1986); the Philippines (whose 1987 constitution included women among a number of under-represented groups to share 10% of Chamber of Representatives seats chosen or elected on the basis of a list); the former Soviet Union (discussed earlier); and Sweden.

Although comparatively few political parties around the world have established a quota system, the IPU survey showed that some 56 political parties in 34 countries have adopted quotas of varying percentages either for legislative elections (22) or for elections to posts in the executive structures of the party (51). The quota may be compulsory or indicative, with about the same number of parties choosing each quota system.

Among those countries in which some or all of their political parties have adopted fixed percentage quotas for inclusion of women in party governing bodies and/or electoral candidate lists are the following, based on country responses and comments to the IPU survey and other sources. (CQ indicates a compulsory quota):

AUSTRIA: Socialist Party, 25%-38%; Greens, 50%; In the October 1990 national assembly elections, Socialist Party women held 26.3% of the party seats and Green Party women had 50% of their party's seats. [Snyder, Paula, *The European Women's Almanac*, p. 38, Scarlet Press, London.]

BELGIUM: Three parties have quotas for party governing boards and two of these have quotas for legislative electoral candidates. The quota (CQ) for party leadership posts was 20% (as of 1990). In a report to the IPU, the Socialist Party said women members were calling for a 30% quota, noting that the quota has had "a positive effect: more women elected at all levels of the party." It added, however, that the quota has also had "a perverse effect; the quota of 20% has not always been taken as a minimum target but is often considered as a contract to be executed. Thus, women are elected via the quota system whereas they sometimes have enough potential votes to be elected without the quota." In October

1990, women held 7.5% of SP seats in the house of representatives. The Christian People's Party, in which women held 14% of its house seats, reported that "the quota introduced by the CVP has proved to be effective and militant women members are calling for it to be increased."

CANADA: While the Liberal and Progressive Conservative parties have inclusion of more women in their governing bodies as an objective, only the New Democratic Party has specific goals. Its constitution provides for a mandatory "gender parity" policy under which at least 50% of all federal executives and members of committees at the federal level must be female, and since 1985 it has established an objective of having women comprise 50% of its candidates in federal elections. In a speech at a Socialist International Women's meeting in Paris in December 1988, held to discuss the role of women in Socialist parties, Tessa Hebb, a member of the federal executive of Canada's New Democratic Party, described how it decided to move toward a quota system:

> We pledged ourselves to voluntary affirmative action to have women participating in the various levels of our party, and this pledge was very solemnly made by all those present. But voluntary affirmative action did not work. There was no dramatic increase in the numbers of women participating.
>
> And so, in 1983, we established a quota system. And my party took the very radical approach of immediately going to 50/50, equal representation, and insisting, in fact, that 50% be women. The fact is that in the six years that have followed, we have moved on the executive board of our party to 60% representation of women, so we have already exceeded that goal. The fact that women now hold the positions of both president and treasurer in our party ensures for women the kind of power and the kind of access that means many more women can join in the political process in Canada.

(In 1992 the quota issue arose when the Canadian government conducted closed negotiations at Charlottetown for a new constitution designed to forestall secessionist threats from the Quebec French-speaking provincial government by assigning more political power to all the provinces and providing for an elected senate, the upper house. The National Action Committee on the Status of Women, the largest feminist group in Canada and partially funded by the government, successfully convinced the leaders of four provinces—Ontario, Nova Scotia, Saskatchewan and British Columbia—to set aside 50% of their senate seats for women. But the NACSW later decided to oppose the new constitution in a national referendum on the grounds that its decentralization of policy-making and funding would undermine equality protections for women in its Charter of Rights.

The NACSW decision, controversial within the women's movement and among the public at large, was based on the belief that funding for long-sought women's programs would be scuttled by provincial government male leaders and that the rights of the disabled and the large population of aboriginal Indian women would be nullified. They were particularly concerned that aboriginal women would not be guaranteed the right to vote or to run for office in native self-governments dominated by men nor would their equality rights be covered by the Charter. The Charter was rejected in an October 1992 national referendum.)

CHINA: Although China does not have a formal quota system, Chinese women delegates to the 1989 IPU symposium reported that as a result of official state encouragement and the 1945 constitution granting women equal rights with men, there were 634 women deputies in the National People's Congress, accounting for 21.3% of the members. Within 41 ministries and ministerial commissions under the State Council, 15 women had been appointed as ministers, deputy ministers and the like. Nationwide, they reported, there were 8.7 million women officials, 70,000 of them leaders above the county level. (Of the 175 members of the ruling Communist Party's Central Committee, where effective power lies, there were only 10 women, or 6% of the total.)

Despite legal and constitutional guarantees of women's rights, popularized in the slogan, "Women hold up half the sky," the Chinese statement conceded that considerable obstacles remained against full political participation by women, including "thousands of years of feudal history, where feudal ideas, practice and traditions, such as 'respectful gentlemen, humble women,' still exist today." With women making up 70% of China's illiterates and women, particularly in rural areas, bearing the double burden of agricultural labor and household work, there is little time for them to participate in politics, the IPU delegates said.

In a speech to the Global Forum of Women [July 1992, Dublin], a 24-year-old woman university student, Jinquing Cai, who fled China after the massacre in Tiananmen Square, said the Communist Party had done a lot to promote the emancipation of women by educating them and pushing them into the professions and into political posts. But, she said, people were constrained by the whole political system and government corruption. "A few senior people decided everything and would not listen to anybody," she said. "Anyone criticizing the government can be accused of sabotage." Nevertheless, she said, in the wake of the student demonstrations, "a new image of women as leaders has emerged."

DENMARK: The Social Democratic and Socialist People's parties have 40% minimum quotas for inclusion of women in party leadership and candidate slates. (See CLOSE-UP: DENMARK)

GERMANY: The Social Democratic Party has a 40% quota for inclusion of women in party leadership and election slates and the Green Party has a compulsory 50% quota. (See CLOSE-UP: GERMANY)

GREECE: The New Democracy Party has an unspecified "proportion" of women for inclusion in its governing body, the Greens have a 50% quota and the Coalition of the Left specifies a 40% quota for women in its governing body. As of April 1990, women held 5.3% of the New Democracy Party's 152 seats in the parliament, 7.1% of the Coalition of the Left's 14 seats, and 100% of the Green's single seat. [Snyder, Paula, *The European Women's Almanac*, p. 160.]

ICELAND: In both the Social Democratic Party and the People's Alliance, according to party rules, both sexes are to have at least 40% of the total membership in all elective party governing bodies, provided there are enough candidates of each sex. In the parliament, the five parties have an average of 23.8% women members, including 100% (5 seats) from the all-women Women's Alliance. [Snyder, Paula, *The European Women's Almanac*, p. 184.] (See CLOSE-UP: ICELAND)

IRELAND: The Labour Party is the only one of the major parties that had a quota (10%) for women in its governing body, as of July 1991. Women held only 8.7% of the seats in the parliament, but in a stunning victory Mary Robinson was elected the country's first woman president in November 1990. Her winning margin was provided by second-choice votes transferred to her from another party candidate. On the first count, Robinson, the candidate of a Labour Party coalition, received 39% of the vote compared with 44.1% for Brian Lenihan, leader of the major party, Fianna Fail, and 19% for Austin Currie, the unpopular candidate of the largest opposition party, the conservative Fine Gael. Almost 77% of Currie's supporters listed Robinson as their second choice and only 14% chose Lenihan, enough of a swing vote to give Robinson a comfortable victory.

A feminist, former senator and highly respected constitutional lawyer, Robinson held views on women's rights, abortion and divorce that were at odds with those of a majority of Irish voters, as recorded in national polls and referenda. Traveling the length and breadth of the Emerald Isle, she attracted and apparently inspired crowds of women wherever she went during her vigorous seven-month campaign. Running for what was regarded as an essentially powerless post in which she could not even take positions on pending legislation or controversial policy issues, Robinson, without renouncing her personal beliefs, was able to make a successful above-party appeal to voters. In her acceptance speech after she was declared elected, she said: "I was elected by men and women of all parties and none, by many with great moral courage who stepped out from the faded flags of the Civil War and voted for a new Ireland. And above all by the women of Ireland . . . who instead of rocking the cradle rocked the system, and who came out massively to make their mark on the ballot paper, and on a new Ireland." [See Finlay, Fergus, *Mary Robinson, A President with a Purpose*, The O'Brien Press, 1990, Dublin; and O'Reilly, Emily, *Candidate, The Truth Behind the Presidential Campaign*, Attic Press, 1991, Dublin.]

In this instance, the transfer voting system gave Robinson an unprecedented opportunity for political leadership. She has gone on to become enormously popular and influential among the Irish electorate and in international affairs, helping to provide a climate that resulted in the election of more women to parliament in 1992 and moving Ireland toward a more open society.

ISRAEL: The IPU did not have data on political quotas in this country. According to Na'Amat, the women's division of Histadrut (General Federation of Labour), the Labour Party and Mapam Party have quotas (percentages unspecified) for women candidates for seats in the Knesset and other political bodies. Because citizens vote for a party list of Knesset candidates on a nationwide basis rather than from geographical constituencies, top placement of candidates on the list can be crucial to success. The most seats ever won by women in the 120-member parliament were 11 in the years 1949, 1951, and 1955 and that number was not attained again until the 1992 elections. Until this most recent election, only four women had served as ministers in the 12 governments since the establishment of the state in 1948: Golda Meir, Shoshana Arbeli-Almozlino, Shulamit Aloni, and Sara Doron.

In the new coalition government put together by Prime Minister Yitzhak Rabin of the Labour Party, two women were named ministers: Ora Namair (Labour) as minister of environment and Aloni, founder of the Meretz Party, as minister of education and culture. The Meretz Party, noted for its strong stand on women's rights and peace issues, also elected two other women, Naomi Chazan and Anat Maor. Both Na'Amat and the Israeli Women's Network, a coalition group dedicated to improving the status of Israeli women, support quota systems to increase women's participation in government.

In 1989, Na'Amat conducted a public referendum in which 400,000 people, two-thirds of them women and one-third men, were asked, among other things, whether they favored "affirmative action programs for women in the apportioning of senior political and administrative positions." Sixty-six percent said "yes." Na'Amat then proposed that affirmative action be carried out over a period of several years until men and women were treated equally in the economy, the Knesset, the government and in local municipal governments. Its initial demand was for 25% of all positions in the public and private sectors to be held by women.

In 1991, IWN announced an "Empowering Israeli Women" campaign for electoral reforms to benefit women. It called for continuation of proportional representation but with candidates selected on a regional constituency basis (no more than 12 from the whole of Israel). It also proposed a significant change in the mode of voting:

> While parties would continue to present voters with a list of candidates, these would have to be local candidates, resident in the constituency, and would have to include at least 40% women candidates. Each voter would then be able to rank the candidates nominated by the party for which he/she is voting. Thus, it would be possible to promote a low-ranked woman candidate and demote a highly ranked male.

ITALY: The Greens have a 50% quota for party leadership and electoral candidates, and the Communist Party has a 30% quota. Based on more than 12 parties, the average percentage of seats held by women in the Chamber of Deputies, as of June 1987, was 12.7%, and 6.5% in the senate. [Snyder, Paula, *The European Women's Almanac*, p. 215.] Figures were not available for the most recent elections, but apparently the Socialist and Social Democratic parties have adopted some forms of quotas. In an impassioned speech to the Socialist International Women's Paris meeting, Margherita Boniver, international secretary of the Italian Socialist Party, a senator and member of the European Parliament, said:

> Let me say very bluntly that I don't like quota. It smacks of Indian reservations; it smacks of ghettos. But having said that I absolutely feel that the quota is totally necessary. If the quota had not been introduced, I really wonder where we would be standing today. The only logical explanation we could give is that this is how it was in the past. Because women did not have access to positions of power, obviously women were somehow to be considered inferior. Of course we know the opposite is true. And that is why so many Socialist and Social Democratic parties, including my own, have introduced the quota to guarantee a minimum participation of women in the structures of political power and decision-making.
>
> What is quota about? Quota is about equality of opportunity. Quota is about giving women a sporting chance to compete in the very complex and very male-dominated world of politics. Quota is, very simply, setting right what was wrong from the very beginning.
>
> Socialist International Women, *The Long March of Women Towards Equality,* p. 16, May 1989, London.

(Immediately following the Socialist International Women's Paris meeting, the Council of the SI, headed by President Willy Brandt, adopted a resolution declaring its full support for the goals of the Socialist Decade for Women, announced by the SIW at a meeting in Lima, Peru, in 1986, "namely an increase in the number of women in all positions of power in SI member parties and as candidates for elections.

"To this end," it said, "affirmative action is necessary, be it quota or other regulations in party statutes, with the right of women's organizations to have a say in the selection process." Expressing dissatisfaction with the slow pace of progress in the affiliated parties' inclusion of women in their governing structures "and the resistance from our own parties to the implementation of positive action programs such as quota regulations," the SI concluded its statement by calling on its member organizations "to give political power for women the highest possible priority, including and encouraging its members to take leadership positions." [SIW, *The Long March of Women Towards Equality,* p. 23.]

LUXEMBOURG: The G.A.P. has a quota of 40% women on its governing bodies. The P.O.S.L. (Socialist Party) plans to introduce a minimum number of three women on its 28-member managing committee, one of whom would be a vice-chairperson. Socialist women won a demand that at least one woman be included in the four electoral district commissions that propose national candidates for party lists in national elections. As a result, more women's names were placed on the lists and the party had its first successful women candidates in

1989, three in the parliament and one in the executive branch. In addition, the Christian Party elected four women, and the Democratic Party one: overall, 13.3% of the 60-member Chamber of Deputies are women.

NETHERLANDS: Three parties have quotas for women on electoral slates: The Labour Party, 33% (CQ); Green Left Party, 40% (CQ) and the Christian Democratic Alliance, 26%. In the September 1989 elections, women won 32.7% of the Labour seats, 50% of the Greens' and 18.5% of the Christian Democrats. Two smaller parties' successful candidates were 36.4% and 33.3% women, and four conservative parties had no women winners. Overall, the average for women-held seats was 27.3%. Three of the 14 cabinet ministers are women. [Snyder, Paula, *The European Women's Almanac*, p. 253.]

At the SIW meeting in Paris earlier in the year, Marjanne Sint, president of the Netherlands' Labour Party, commented: "There is currently more understanding and attention than ten years ago for the demands of women. However, there is no reason yet for us to lean back satisfied. The position of women is on the political agenda, but in daily practice, there is still much work to be done . . . . Our culture has retained a pronounced masculine bias. Women active in the sciences, in the arts, in politics and society are only gradually winning acceptance. The media is male-dominated. Advertising passes on outdated role stereotypes. Women are poorly represented in political positions, and that applies also to the Socialist International . . . . We are seeking a society in which one half of the people is not brought up to dominate the other, and that other half conditioned to submit."

A Netherlands Women's Party, founded in March 1989, did not have enough time to organize support for its parliamentary candidates and was focusing on fielding more women candidates in the municipal elections scheduled for early 1994. Party Secretary Christine Soenario, who belonged for 11 years to the Red Women, a group within the Labour Party, said that despite Labour's 33% quota for women candidates, men still treat women's concerns as unimportant. "They don't say so," she said in an interview with *The New York Times*. "It's more subtle. The issues are postponed, put aside. You can't get through." Lottie Schenk, a founder of the new Women's Party, said: "We are not against men and we have a lot in common with women of other parties. But we want to follow a different strategy." Although women have long formed a "subculture" in the main parties, she said, "these are still male clubs where men set the agenda and define the debate." She and other Women's Party supporters said the need for a different approach was made urgent by economic concerns, such as cuts in welfare benefits, with women—single mothers, part-time workers, divorced women and widows—making up the fastest growing segment of the poor. At the other end of the scale, it was pointed out, Dutch women hold only 2% of managerial posts, the lowest rate in the European Community, along with that of Italy. [*The New York Times*, p. A4, September 18, 1992.]

NEW ZEALAND: The New Labour Party and Green Party have 50% compulsory quotas for inclusion of women in their party governing boards. In the

October 1990 elections for the house of representatives, 21.4% of the candidates were women and 10.4% won.

At the IPU November 1989 symposium in Geneva, a critical view of quotas was presented by Margaret Shields, then a member of parliament and also minister of women's affairs, minister of statistics, minister of consumer affairs and associate minister of education in the Labour Party government. (After the Labour Party defeat, she became director of the United Nations agency for women's training programs, INSTRAW.)

Ms. Shields contended that while some parties that use quota systems have impressive records of getting women into decision-making posts, particularly in the Scandinavian countries, quotas can be "an artificial construction" that may not be sustainable over time. "We need to expose who are the gatekeepers and therefore which women will make up that quota," she said. "If women are chosen by the existing patriarchal power holders then they may be beholden to that patronage and unable to challenge the system for other women."

Preferable to "top-down" strategies such as quotas, she said, are "bottom-up" strategies such as those used by New Zealand women in their organizations and in the Labour Party, which at the time was headed by a woman, to encourage more women to run and to promote their candidacies. A women's group called the Women's Electoral Lobby and the Women's Council of the New Zealand Labour Party run skills training programs for women prior to local and national elections, raise funds, seek out potential candidates and conduct research to demonstrate that women are electable and that female candidates draw more support from women voters. Ms. Shields said her party attracted more support from women in its 1984 election campaign "because we promised to establish both a Ministry of Women's Affairs and a full cabinet position for a minister of women's affairs. Women should argue that parties should not only develop platforms that target women, but that those platforms will be more convincing if they are articulated by female candidates."

A significant factor in her comments was that New Zealand, like the United States, United Kingdom and France, did not then use proportional representation in its electoral system. The proportional representation system, in which voters do not necessarily vote for individual candidates but rather for a preselected party slate of candidates, has been shown usually to help women achieve a greater share of political positions. (See CLOSE-UP sections on particular countries.)

NIGER: Although this nation's constitution states that women represent more than 50% of the population and play a key role in production, the MNSD Party-State (National Movement for the Society in Development) currently in power has set aside only five seats (CQ) for women in the parliament. Five women also sit on the national executive bureau of the Party-State.

NORWAY: The Labour Party and Socialist Left Party have a minimum 40% quota for women's inclusion in their governing bodies and most of the other parties list the same percentage as an objective. All the parties state that from

40% to 60% is their objective for women's inclusion in legislative elections. (See CLOSE-UP: NORWAY)

PORTUGAL: The Socialist Party has a 25% quota for women in its governing body. Socialist Maria de Lourdes Pintasilgo served as prime minister in 1979. Women won full rights to vote only in 1976 when a new constitution was adopted guaranteeing equality in law to all citizens and allowing temporary measures under law to remove existing inequalities. It specifically allows positive action with regard to employment. As of June 1991, 7.6% of parliamentary members were women. [Snyder, Paula, *The European Women's Almanac*, p. 298.]

SENEGAL: The Socialist Party has a 25% quota (CQ) for women in its governing body. In 1988, 25% of the parliamentary candidates were women, and half of them won seats (15).

SPAIN: The leading party, the Socialist Workers Party (PSOE), and the Communist Party are the only ones that have quotas (25% CQ) for women in their governing bodies. In the 1989 elections, women held 13.4% of the seats in the Congress of Deputies, with 18.3% of PSOE seats held by women, the highest for any party. In the senate, women averaged 11.2% of seats, with the PSOE women holding the highest percentage, 15.6%. [Snyder, Paula, *The European Women's Almanac*, p. 322.) Even though the PSOE does not prescribe quotas for women candidates, the inclusion of more women in its leadership provides an atmosphere that encourages more female candidacies.

SWEDEN: Three parties—the Social Democratic, Left and Green—have 50% quotas (in effect, gender balance of women and men) in their governing bodies and the Liberal Party has an objective of a 40% maximum for women in its governing body. The Conservative Party told the IPU that it is opposed in principle to quota systems, but said that one-half of the first five to 10 names on its lists for parliamentary elections are women, in almost every voting district. In the 1988 elections, women held 38% of parliamentary seats, ranging from a high of 45% of Green Party winners to a low of 27% for the Conservatives. Women are 42% of county councillors and 34% of municipal councillors. [Snyder, Paula, *The European Women's Almanac*, p. 338.] (See CLOSE-UP: SWEDEN)

SWITZERLAND: The Christian Democrats have a 35% quota for women in their governing body and electoral slates and the Greens have a 50% quota for their governing body. After the October 1991 elections, with more than a dozen parties represented in the National Council, women held an average of 17.5% seats, ranging from the Greens' 57.1% women among its successful candidates to 31% for the Socialists to zero for five parties. Women were 8.7% of the members of the Council of States. In 1989, 33 out of 100 elected deputies to the Geneva canton parliament were women, after the Association of Women's Rights launched a "Vote for Women" campaign. Swiss women did not win the right to vote in parliamentary elections until 1971. [Snyder, Paula, *The European Women's Almanac*, p. 352.]

TURKEY: The Social Democratic Popular Party has a 25% quota (CQ) for women in its governing body, the only party to do so. As of 1987, women held six of the 450 seats in the unicameral legislature, or 1.3%.

UNITED KINGDOM: The Conservative Party, which has held power since 1979, has no quotas for women either in party leadership or candidate lists. Since 1989, the Labour Party has required that its shadow cabinet must include at least three women, including a spokesperson for women's rights. Five seats have been reserved for women on the national executive committee since 1918 when the Women's Labour League was incorporated into the party. Since 1988 there must be at least one woman on every shortlist (preferred) selected for parliamentary elections. The Liberal Democrats require that one-third of the members of its federal executive committee be women. A minor party, Plaid Cymru, reserves for a woman one of the 25 seats on its executive committee.

In the April 1992 elections, the percentage of women elected to the 651-member House of Commons increased from 6.3% to 9.2%: 59 women won, including 19 newcomers. Conservatives elected 20 women, five for the first time; Labour elected 37, including actress Glenda Jackson and 13 other newcomers, and the Liberal Democrats elected two. In addition, Margaret Ewing was elected as parliamentary leader of the Scottish Nationalist Party. For the first time, a woman, Labour Party M.P. Betty Boothroyd, was elected Speaker of the House, with the approval of the Conservatives in a vote that reflected the nonpartisan nature of the presiding officer's duties. (One of the speaker's first acts was to announce that she would not wear the traditional white wig used for the office.)

The 300 Group, a nonpartisan group of women, campaigns for equal numbers of women in the House of Commons and monitors party list nominations for inclusion of women, as well as election results. In addition to holding training programs for women interested in political careers, each year it conducts a one-day "shadow cabinet" meeting of women M.P.s to demonstrate how they would deal with national issues and problems.

UNITED STATES: After the Nineteenth Amendment granted women suffrage in 1920, the Democratic Party national committee directed that each state delegation include at least one committeewoman. Under the present Democratic Party charter (adopted in 1974) Article 3, Section 2 requires national committee membership "for the chairperson and the highest ranking officer of the opposite sex of each recognized state Democratic Party." It also states that "the members of the national committee from each state shall be divided as equally as practicable between committeemen and committeewomen." The president of the National Federation of Democratic Women (or her designee) and two additional members selected by the federation are also accorded membership on the committee. Article 3, Section 2 also provides that the national committee leadership be composed of "a chairperson (and) three vice chairpersons, two of whom shall be of the opposite sex of the chairperson." Since 1980, the charter also has specified a 50-50 division of male and female delegates to the national convention, held every four years, and approximately equal numbers have been present at succeeding conventions. Despite these mandates, the charter states in Article 10, Section 4 that the approved level of representation of women and minorities in Democratic Party organizations and activities "shall not be accomplished either directly or indirectly by the national or state Democratic parties, [by] imposition of mandatory quotas at any level."

Beginning in 1924, Republican Party rules required that "each state, territory and territorial possession shall nominate, through its chairman, one man and one woman to the national committee." Presently, Rule 19 provides that committee membership is comprised of "one national committeeman and one national committeewoman and the chairman" of each state party, who may be either a man or a woman. The rules also mandate that the membership of the national committee, excluding officers, be composed of at least 33% women. In addition, Rule 23 provides for representation of women in the national committee leadership including a chair and co-chair of the opposite sex and "eight vice chairmen, one man and one woman" from each of the party's four regional groupings. No percentages are indicated for women delegates to the national convention. In 1988, women constituted 35% of the convention delegates; in 1992, following the Democratic Party convention at which at least half of the delegates were women, some Republican congressmen and other male delegates turned their seats over to women to increase their visible numbers. In the absence of party commitments to quotas or other mechanisms for assuring approximately equal numbers of male and female candidates in elected or appointive government positions, as of 1992, only 6.4% of members of the House of Representatives and 2% of the U.S. Senate were women. President Bush had two women in his cabinet. (See the United States chapter for updated information.)

UNITED NATIONS: The IPU study was confined to national governments. Studies of international institutions have shown wide gaps between their commitments to inclusion of more women and their performance. The United Nations, which has played an indispensable and noteworthy role in reporting on the status of women, held innumerable meetings and conferences on women's roles and rights, and committed itself to quota systems to increase the numbers of women in professional posts within the UN Secretariat, has come under sharp criticism from women within the Secretariat.

According to Ciceil Gross, former president of the Group on Equal Rights for Women at the UN, "The lack of improvement in the status of women in the UN system is the best-documented history of failure in the annals of the UN. We've had special committees, study groups, advisory groups, statements, goals, promises. What we haven't had is action. There is always some excuse—restructuring, financial crises, etc.—and when these occur, it is the less powerful who suffer first, and women in the UN fall into that category."

Ms. Gross disputed the claim by UN personnel officers that a goal of 30% of professional posts to be held by women was reached in May 1992 (two years late), or that a subsequent goal of 35% by 1995 would be met, and she was equally skeptical that a goal of 25% in middle management posts would be achieved. In fact, she contended, the situation for women within the UN was deteriorating. In 1986, she noted, there were four women assistant secretary-generals, but by 1992 there was only one, assigned to overseeing conference services, a position that can hardly be described as dealing with urgent policy-making. Despite a budget crunch, she said, recruiting still was going on in high-level policy jobs regarded as outside the regular budget. She estimated that about a third of UN positions are not subject to official requirements and these go overwhelmingly to men. Ms. Gross and others in the Women's Rights Group believe that gender balance will not be achieved within the UN system until "preference is given to women and they fire or retire male incompetents." [Personal interview, August 1992.]

Reflecting the overwhelming male character of the 178 UN member governments, in September 1992 only seven UN delegations were led by women ambassadors. In an interview with *Ms.* magazine [September-October 1992 issue], a veteran UN staff member, Isel Rivero, commented: "We (women) are not sitting in the Security Council. The political commissions, like disarmament and the Fifth (budgetary) Committee, have few women. They're all boys' clubs." Of the 15 nations represented on the powerful Security Council, only five had women in their delegations, and no delegation was headed by a woman. Similarly, at the UN Earth Summit held in Rio de Janeiro, Brazil, in June 1992, only three women government heads addressed the gathering of world leaders, summoned to act on the global environment/development crisis. (See discussion of women's roles in the UN Conference on Environment and Development below.)

Women Under-Represented in UN Missions

An October 1989 report by the UN Secretary-General stated that while most high-level UN posts are filled by promotions within its existing civil service system, a number are filled by outside recruitment, which "has frequently been considered unfavorable to women. Outside recruitment of women depends on the submission of candidates by member states and many countries still do not submit any female candidates at all for positions in the United Nations, while most countries continue to submit mainly male candidates. This is particularly noticeable for the higher positions."

A contributory factor to the lack of women in top positions, it said, "is the general under-representation of women in delegations to the UN, one of the traditional sources of outside lateral recruitment. In 1989, there were only 337 women in the diplomatic staffs of the permanent missions to the UN in New York, out of a total of 1,695 (20%). Sixty missions had no women among their diplomatic staffs. Only eight women held the rank of ambassador." The report also pointed out that at a June 1989 meeting of a preparatory committee working on International Development Strategy for the Fourth UN Development Decade (in which women's roles and needs are central to any proposed solutions), there were only 20 women delegates out of a total of 210 (9.5%) and in 65 delegations out of 89 there were no women at all.

By 1993, however, some slight improvements in nongeographical appointments were noted under the leadership of Secretary-General Boutros Boutros-Ghali, who repeatedly voiced his commitment to an overall 50-50 gender balance within the Secretariat by 1995, the 50th anniversary of the founding of the United Nations. Goals of 25% for senior-level posts and 35% for posts subject to geographical distribution were projected. He reported that as of December 1993 the percentage of women in higher-level posts was 13.6% and 32% in posts subject to geographic distribution. Among the 43 under secretary-general positions, seven were held by women, compared with none in 1992. The number of women ambassadors, however, had dropped to seven, with U.S. mission head Madeleine Albright being the only ambassador from a major power and the only woman on the Security Council. (The others were from Kazakhstan, Trinidad and Tobago, Canada, Jamaica, the Philippines and Leichtenstein.) And, despite an international women's campaign for a gender-balanced War Crimes Tribunal established by the UN General Assembly in 1993 to try accused criminals in connection with civil war atrocities in the former Yugoslavia, the assembly elected only two women to the 11-member court.

Responding to the slow progress in elevating women to high policy posts within the Secretariat, Boutros-Ghali took the extraordinary step of approving a preferential hiring formula for qualified women. In an Administrative Instruction to staff members of the Director of Personnel on March 3, 1993, it was stated that women UN employees "who have served at least one year within the previous three years, under any type of appointment, may be included in a special pool for priority consideration."

In accordance with an October 20, 1992 directive from the secretary-general, it was said, "in departments and offices with less than 35% women overall and in those with less than 25% women at levels P-5 and above, vacancies overall and in the latter group, respectively shall be filled when there are one or more female candidates whose qualifications match all the requirements for a vacant post, by one of those candidates."

Furthermore, the Instruction said, "vacancies that occur in departments and offices that do not meet the required percentages of women both overall and at the higher levels will not be available for the appointment of male candidates until serious efforts have been made in good faith to identify and secure a qualified woman. Where male and female candidates have equivalent merit and suitability, preference shall be given to a woman candidate. The post will become available for male recruitment only after it has been vacant for 12 months and despite the best efforts of all concerned, as certified by the Office of Human Resources Management, it has not been possible to identify or secure a qualified woman during this period. It is therefore in the interests of both the department and the Organization as a whole to start the search for women candidates well before the vacancy is likely to occur."

While some veteran female employees of the Secretariat remained skeptical that genuine progress would occur, citing ingrained discriminatory attitudes among senior male officials as well as recurrent instances of sexual harassment, in some UN specialized agencies, however, significant progress was being made on affirmative action for women. Dr. Nafis Sadik, executive director of the UN Population Fund (one of the two women who headed UN agencies or commissions in 1992), reported that her agency has a 43% female professional staff and is aiming for 50% by the year 2000. UNICEF, the UN Children's Fund, reported increasing its female professional status staff members from 24.6% in 1985 to 35% in 1991, with a goal of 40% by 1994 and parity by the year 2000. Sadako Ogata, head of the UN High Commission for Refugees (UNHCR), said that because 75% of refugees worldwide are women and children, there was a definite need for more female professional staff to work overseas. But, she noted, relocation overseas poses difficulties for married women whose husbands may object to moving with them. Another obstacle to women's assignments to overseas posts is resistance, overt or subtle, from host countries.

A different view was held by William F. Lee, New York representative of the UN Relief and Works Agency (UNRWA), which works in Palestinian refugee camps and in Egypt, Jordan, Lebanon and Syria. Pointing out that 37% of UNRWA's field positions are held by women, he said: "People say that women won't make it because of the attitudes in the Middle East. They've been proven absolutely wrong . . . . We have managed to break down a lot of perceived barriers for women, which is a key element to the overall success of our agency's work there." [*Ms.* magazine, pp. 18-19, September-October 1992.]

* * *

The above analysis of existing quota systems shows that this mechanism for increasing women's participation in government and access to political power displays a chameleon quality, with its varying degrees of effectiveness in particular countries reflecting indigenous cultural, social and religious traditions, caste systems, the democratic, authoritarian or flexible nature of the electoral process, the strength of women's organizations and movements, and the level of women's consciousness and action in challenging the patriarchal attitudes prevalent in all societies.

Quotas range from token percentages that segregate women into marginal positions to larger percentages that have genuinely expanded women's access to political power to the "no less than 40% or more than 60%" formula for either sex which comes closest to the ideal democratic concept of equality posited by Professor Elisabeth G. Siedziewiski. But even in the Nordic nations in which women have attained the greatest political presence in government, the view is sometimes heard that this has been made possible because real power has been shifting elsewhere, to multinational corporations and male-controlled international institutions, for example. Or, as Irish theologian Mary Condren said at the Global Forum for Women in Dublin (July 9-12, 1992), "The powerful only give up the degree of power which will enable them to retain power."

Nevertheless, in its summation of the discussion of quotas by participants in its 1989 symposium, the IPU reported that many supported quotas "as a temporary measure," on the grounds that "(a) Quotas are a means of rapidly increasing the number of women candidates; (b) quotas have resulted in increased numbers of women politicians who can act as role models for other women; (c) quotas and reserved seats ensured some women MPs in situations where there would otherwise be none, or so few that they could not be politically effective. Some felt that quotas would probably work best where there was a proportional representation list."

Reservations expressed by a significant number of participants ranged from the unconstitutionality of quota systems in their countries to the belief that the system might be manipulated by men to promote women who would not "rock the boat." Some stressed the need for mechanisms to ensure that women themselves, through their organizations, could propose women candidates.

"The importance of specialized bodies, such as Ministries of Women's Affairs, was emphasized by many," the IPU report said. "They could actively support and assist the process of gaining equality for all women—even though it was also stated that unless they were strongly supported they could become a 'ghetto' for women's issues and powerful but troublesome women.... The need for 'gate-keepers' at all levels of political parties was mentioned, and the importance of mobilizing both women and men to support women's political participation was emphasized."

There were also repeated references to the need for women's organizations to "avoid the risk of relieving governments of their responsibility for education, health, welfare, child care, and so forth. These must be mainstream issues, central concerns for all governments." [IPU Symposium, *Reports and Conclusions*, No. 16, Geneva, 1989.]

Women Lack Confidence

Most of the participants agreed that a major barrier to women's equal participation in political life was the lack of self-confidence among women, as well as such objective factors as their lack of time to get involved because of the double burden of family and child care responsibilities and outside employment, the practice of holding political meetings and legislative sessions at night when women could not easily get away from home and children, lack of education and professional skills as well as financial resources, and discouragement from entrenched male leaders.

While many women parliamentarians have professional backgrounds and university degrees, it was also noted that the entry point for women can be grass-roots and local community political activism, as in India and other countries. In her report to the IPU symposium, feminist Jacqueline Pitanguy of Brazil, a sociologist, writer and teacher, said that although Latin American women were traditionally excluded from party politics, "women participating in various social movements and organizations have made their presence felt in the political arena, especially since the 1970s when, in many Latin American countries, the exercise of party politics was curbed by government authorities . . . .

"During the 1970s and early 1980s," she said, "authoritarian regimes restricted parliaments' scope of action to a considerable extent . . . . The Women's Movement for Amnesty in Brazil, the Mothers of the Plaza de Mayo in Argentina, Women for Life in Chile, the Women's Group in Uruguay are all examples of women's organizations that played an important role in strengthening political parties struggling to reestablish democracy. A number of other rural or urban organizations worked specifically to defend women's rights, for example, feminist groups, study and research cells, communes and women's centers, peasants' organizations, women's sections within trade unions, and professional associations, mothers' clubs, etc."

In the 1980s, with the reestablishment of democracy in a number of Latin American nations, women's movements started to develop closer relations with legislators. In 1985, Dr. Pitanguy said, the Brazilian National Congress adopted a law creating the National Council for Women's Rights, which, in turn, developed a women's list of demands, 80% of which were incorporated into the new constitution. She reported that Brazil has 37 councils at the state and municipal levels together with 70 all-women special committees that deal solely with violence and sexual abuse against women. Special police offices staffed by women officers have been set up at which women can lodge complaints against abusive husbands, relatives and other males, with comparative safety.

Women's institutions have also been set up in Uruguay and Argentina, Dr. Pitanguy said, while Venezuela and other Latin American nations have Ministries for Women's Affairs or similar bodies. It is also important, she said, to establish women's committees within parliaments to submit laws, lobby for them and monitor their implementation. (The IPU reported that 24 responding countries have a Ministry for the Status of Women, while "57 countries boast some other governmental body in charge of such matters. Thus, 81 countries out of 96, or a big 84.4% majority, have a governmental body specially responsible for questions relating to the status of women. Without prejudging the efficacy of government action, that cannot be assessed from the survey results, this points to a substantial effort by Governments to promote the status of women.")

Despite these advances, Dr. Pitanguy conceded that political parties remain male-oriented. "Women's participation is very limited," she said. "There are fewer women candidates and in general they have very restricted financial resources and less logistic support for their campaigns. Women's participation in decision-making is minimal. The outlook is sombre and, because of its own internal dynamics, the situation is self-perpetuating as few women seek participation in political life, excluding themselves from an area that excludes them. Such a picture can only be changed if there is the political will to power."

Margaret Shields of New Zealand stressed the need for women parliamentarians to serve as role models and "never to forget where you came from and who supported you." She told the IPU symposium: "Women moving into male-dominated and often alien environments need to be part of a wider network of women from where they can draw advice and support. That is essential if the goal is to change a historically patriarchal environment into one that is accessible to everyone regardless of their agenda."

The positive symbiosis of women working together inside and outside of government was pointed out by Barbara McDougall of Canada. "Increasingly," she told the IPU, "efforts being made by women outside the government to effect change and reform are being complemented by women who are inside the government—members of parliament, cabinet ministers, parliamentary secretaries and opposition critics, and women who hold senior positions within government bureaucracies.

"The further broadening and widening of women's participation in the labor force, in the professions, in academia, in government bureaucracies—and especially as women gain more leadership and key decision-making positions in these spheres—will certainly augment women's influence in the political process from within and without," she continued. "Issues traditionally championed by women and their organizations, such as child care, the integration of work and family responsibilities, equality in employment, human rights, and health and well-being, are now in the mainstream of government attention and activity throughout the world."

Israeli Women Seen as More Dovish

In Israel, once led by Golda Meir, who had no women in her cabinet, feminists believe that a united front, the raising of many female voices to change the system will be more effective than the lone woman in power. According to Professor Galia Golan, head of the political science department at Hebrew University, "Politics in the pre-state Yishuv and in Israel was always a man's world." She added: "We've had the experience of queen bees in politics in this country, of women who make it and feel no responsibility to help other women. Golda was a perfect example. She made it much more difficult." A lack of ambition, based partly on the traditional religious image of women's subordinate role in society, was cited by parliamentarian Sara Doron as the reason more women were not pushing their way into politics. "Women have the brains and the heart, but no elbows," she said. [*Na'Amat Woman,* September-October 1988.]

Professor Naomi Chazan, a political scientist at Hebrew University, believes that because Israel has been in a situation of continuing warfare and military alert, the image of society is transformed into a very male-dominant image and society develops values that underestimate the role of women as well as their needs. Since military experience is often considered a prerequisite for holding public office, women are blocked from significant political power. In an article on "Women, War and Peace" by Amy Avgar [*Na'Amat Woman,* March-April 1990], the author cited data showing consistent differences between men and women on policy issues. In the November 1988 elections, she reported, more women than men voted for left-wing and center parties and fewer women than men supported rightwing parties. She also cited a longitudinal survey by political analysts Asher Arian and Raphael Ventura on Israeli-Palestinian differences that found a hardening of positions among Israeli men and an increasingly dovish attitude among women. Over a 10-month period, from December 1987 to October 1988, women became more moderate in their position on negotiating with the PLO, and more prepared to trade territories for peace.

Professors Golan and Chazan, both central figures in the Israeli peace movement, have conducted an extensive study of differences in the way men and women conceptualize war, conflict and peace, and styles of political activism. According to Dr. Chazan, there is a logical link between feminism and political action in the context of the Israeli-Palestinian conflict. "If equality is a principle, then it is universal and must extend to self-determination for all," she said. "If we oppose the oppression of women, how can we fail to oppose the suppression of another people?" Although they found feminists who were nonactivists and activists who were not feminists, overall the number of "superhawks" was found to be lower among women than among men, and at the other end of the spectrum there were more women doves than male doves.

For a significant number of women, Professors Golan and Chazan concluded, feminism and pacifism are inextricably bound together "and, in the world view of such women, the quest for peace, equality and human rights extends to all individuals." [Avgar, Amy, "Women, War and Peace," *Na'Amat Woman,* March-April 1990.]

In the early months of the Rabin government, which launched a peace initiative on the Palestinian issue, his minister of education, Shulamit Aloni, was already coming under strong attack from orthodox religious leaders for her outspoken secular views. A multiparty democracy that includes nonreligious as well as religious Jews, and a minority population of Muslims and Christians, the state since its inception has ceded all issues related to marriage and divorce to the respective religious leaders. As education minister, Aloni also quickly challenged arrangements under which the majority of state funding went to religious Hebrew schools, leaving secular schools underfunded and operating on half-day schedules. While religious leaders were demanding Aloni's ouster from the cabinet, Israeli feminists were citing the attacks on her as what happens to a forceful woman political leader who breaks out of imposed, restrictive traditional roles.

Differences among Women Class-Linked

In contrast, the ideological differences between educated, middle- and upper-class women who attain political careers and organizations of poor, uneducated women with urgent life survival problems were seen as a major problem by a Filipina analyst, Socorro L. Reyes, writing in the *Asia Pacific Women's Studies Journal* [No. l, 1992, Institute of Women's Studies, Manila, the Philippines]. In an article titled, "Strengthening the Linkage Between Women's Groups and Women in Government," written when Corazon Aquino was still president, Ms. Reyes said:

> In the political empowerment of women, the Philippines can be considered the most advanced and progressive among Southeast Asian countries. Female partici-pation in the policy-making arena covers both the executive and legislative branches. Aside from the presidency, women also hold positions as secretaries, undersecretaries and assistant secretary. In Congress, there are two women in the (24-member) Senate and 19 (of 200) in the House of Representatives.

Most of the women in the executive branch previously had positions in academe or government service, she reported, while the majority of the women legislators came from the business, trade and banking sectors. Fourteen of the 16 women legislators interviewed by Ms. Reyes "believe their blood relationship with a male politician helped them win their electoral seat. The male relative can be from any or all of the following generations: grandfather, granduncle, father, uncle, brother, husband, and son." One congresswoman was the sister of the slain husband of Corazon Aquino and of another parliamentarian, Senator Agapito Aquino, all members of the wealthy, land-owning Aquino family.

"For the majority," Ms. Reyes said, "their entry into electoral politics was largely motivated by their desire to continue a 'family tradition.' At least two women ran for office because their husbands were unavailable for drafting, while another joined politics because her father suffered a stroke." Only three re-spondents argued that their candidacy was triggered not by any family-related cause but by their desire to work for reforms in the system and by the "genuine intention to serve the public." But most of the female legislators "recognized the strength of the women's vote as one of the factors that helped them win."

In the executive branch, women are circumscribed in effective policy-making if they hold ranks below cabinet department secretary. In congress, Ms. Reyes said, "female legislators have a more direct hand in the formulation of public policy because of their active participation in the various stages of the legislative process, particularly in the introduction of bills, committee work, and organizing majority support for their passage. This participation appears less evident, however, in other aspects such as floor deliberations (few make speeches), conflict resolution in the conference committee and liaising with the Executive." She noted that most bills introduced by women legislators were mostly of local application, with hardly any on women's issues.

Within the executive branch, she said, individual women officials have a working agenda and vision about upgrading the status of women in society to achieve political and socioeconomic equality with men. But the congresswomen "do not have any specific legislative agenda for women. In fact, most of the pending bills and resolutions on women's issues and concerns in the lower house were sponsored by their male counterparts, such as the legislative proposals on mail-order brides, overseas Filipina workers and the dissolution and annulment of marriages." While praising the legislative proposals of the congressmen, which "truly seek the protection and promotion of the interests of women," she noted that they lack "feminist substance."

"But feminism means more than just a reform of structures in society and modification of existing laws which discriminate against women," she argued. "It means that it is for women to say what women are like, what women want, what women enjoy, and what women can do." She cited the failure of either the senate or house to support freedom of reproductive choice for women, including access to all forms of contraception or family planning.

Describing the numerous women's organizations that exist in the Philippines, ranging from traditional to reformist to radical feminist groups, she concluded: "The top women officials of government are limited to the middle- and upper-class women's groups they are affiliated with and whose agenda usually calls for equal pay and the elimination of all forms of gender-based discrimination in the workplace. For most women in the Philippines, however, the basic problem is getting a job that will provide them a gainful source of income. This explains the high influx of women migrating to different parts of the world to work as domestic helpers, entertainers and even as mail-order brides. Within the country itself, women sell themselves as hospitality girls catering to the sexual needs of tourists from Japan, Australia, the Middle East, Europe and the United States. The problem in the Philippines is thus not based on gender alone but on more fundamental structural problems affecting the economic and social base of society.

"It is thus important for any feminist agenda to reflect the prevailing condition of women in the other strata and respond to their needs and demands within their own material context. Otherwise, career feminism will not only liberate merely a tiny sector of the female population but also continue to perpetuate the socioeconomic order that oppresses and exploits the majority of women."

The challenge to women's groups, Ms. Reyes said, "is to sensitize the females in Congress to gender issues and concerns and to raise their feminist consciousness. This can be done through seminar-workshops, informal dialogues, lectures and workshops." Although many organizations have written off the congress as ineffective, she concluded: "The fact remains, however, that this institution is in place and receives a huge amount of annual appropriations from the national budget. It will thus be worth the taxpayer's money if women's groups can harness them to work not only for gender concerns but for national purposes as well. They have to be carefully monitored, however, and a system of political accountability has to be firmly established and implemented." [Reyes, Socorro, *Asia Pacific Women's Studies Journal,* pp. 66-87.]

OTHER MECHANISMS FOR CHANGE

The importance of a close working relationship between female legislators and women's groups was also stressed in a comprehensive report prepared by The Division for the Advancement of Women, United Nations Office at Vienna, based on an Expert Group Meeting on Equality in Political Participation and Decision-Making, held September 18-22, 1989.

The report cited as continuing obstacles to equality the lack of adequate recruitment and promotion mechanisms, preventing women from entering the civil service in significant numbers, and "insufficient applicability of quotas and other affirmative measures, aimed at ensuring the adequate participation of women at all levels of political parties, parliaments, trade unions, including their governing bodies and executives."

It noted approvingly that women seeking increased political participation "have also started developing their own networks, building connections among grass-root organizations, women's issue associations, women's movements, female researchers, politicians, social workers and career women representing various professions.

"The experience shows," it continued, "that in the countries with such developed networks, advanced studies and training courses (in political science, law and management) accessible and attended by women as well as developed social support services, women's mass participation in politics is high and participation in decision-making higher than average region-wide and worldwide."

As long as the external obstacles "are not compensated by strong support of women's groups and special temporary measures, like for example quotas," the report said, "women's equal access to political decision-making will be extremely difficult to achieve."

The specific conclusions and recommendations of the UN expert group were included in a report to the UN Commission on the Status of Women from the UN Secretary-General [E/CN.6/1990/2] on October 27, 1989. The recommendations, including renewed support for quotas, outlined proposed changes in the policies of national governments, political parties and other organizations, civil service and international bodies, including the UN.

Although there has been a plethora of meetings in Europe and within the UN on the need for increased participation of women in political life, the goal of 50-50 or roughly equal inclusion of women and men in government leadership had not been a prime focus of international women's meetings until recently. That began to change in 1990 when the Women's Environment & Development Organization (WEDO), founded by Bella Abzug and Mim Kelber, organized an international network of women concerned with what would happen in the decision-making process leading up to and including the UN Conference on Environment and Development—the Earth Summit—in Rio de Janeiro, Brazil, in June 1992.

Women's Action Agenda 21

Under the rallying cry, "Women must have an equal say in 'fate-of-the-Earth' decisions," WEDO held a World Women's Congress for a Healthy Planet in Miami, Florida November 8-12, 1991, attended by 1,500 women from 83 nations in every region of the world. Together, they worked out a multi-issue Women's Action Agenda 21 that was presented to UNCED and included an unqualified demand for equality:

> We come together to pledge our commitment to the empowerment of women, the central and powerful force in the search for equity between and among the peoples of the Earth and for a balance between them and the life-support systems that sustain us all.
>
> Women are a powerful force for change. In the past two decades, thousands of new women's groups have been organized in every region of the world, ranging from community-based groups to international networks. Everywhere, women are catalysts and initiators of environmental activism. Yet policy-makers continue to ignore the centrality of women's roles and needs as they make Fate-of-the-Earth decisions.
>
> We demand our right, as half the world's population, to bring our perspectives, values, skills and experiences into policy-making, on an equal basis with men, not only at the United Conference on Environment and Development (UNCED) in June 1992 but on into the 21st century.

Specifically, the women's agenda demanded "full and equal participation for women and men in public policy analyses, at senior levels in government and non-government organizations, in decision-making, implementation, administration, and funding at international, national, and community levels.

"We recommend that the democracy-strengthening principle observed in some nations—that no more than 60% or no less than 40% of either sex be included in government bodies—should be applied universally to all public policy-making groups. The guide to women's empowerment is achieving a critical mass of representation in decision-making, not mere tokenism. Gender balance must be observed in the national delegations to the UN Conference on Environment and Development (UNCED); in the permanent missions of UN member states; in the UN Secretariat's professional staff; in the World Court, World Bank, International Monetary Fund, and UN specialized agencies and programs."

The agenda served as a launching pad for an effective and still ongoing international campaign to increase women's participation in the UNCED process and that succeeded in getting many of the women's demands on environment and development issues included in the official Agenda 21 approved at the Earth Summit. A WEDO-organized women's caucus operated throughout the process, lobbying and negotiating with UNCED delegates to strengthen programmatic language. No count was made of women members of government delegations but it appeared that about 10% were women, with many delegations again being all-male. Nevertheless, some female delegates served as intermediaries in negotiations and were a valuable resource for inside information.

During the two-year preparatory process, the active involvement of thousands of women from the nongovernmental organization (NGO) sector served to sensitize UN delegates and bureaucrats as well as parallel NGO caucuses to women's concerns. In response to pressure from women, the UNCED Secretariat included Filomena Steady, a female specialist on women's issues, who was invaluable in helping to transform the official Agenda 21, Bella Abzug was appointed as a special adviser to UNCED Secretary-General Maurice Strong, and the International Facilitating Committee, representing the NGOs, became gender-balanced. During the Earth Summit itself, Ms. Abzug and Wangari Maathai of Kenya, also from WEDO, were invited to address a plenary session of the world leaders, a recognition of how far women had come.

But still not far enough. As noted earlier, only three women headed delegations to Rio and while women could lobby, most could not vote. It was a particularly bitter experience for women to realize during prolonged negotiations on reproductive rights and family planning language, which ended in compromise wording, that on this issue which most profoundly and intimately affects the female half of the world's population, representatives from the Holy See and from male-led governments could vote but they were disenfranchised.

Political Equality on the Agenda

Still, women who participated in the World Women's Congress and the UNCED process returned to their homelands with a heightened sense of self-confidence and empowerment. Both nationally and as part of a growing international network, they can be expected to push harder for political equality. A few weeks after the Earth Summit, more than 400 women leaders from some 50 countries gathered at the 1992 Global Forum of Women in Dublin to review the status of women and discuss "new visions of leadership."

After hearing reports by Bella Abzug, Irene Natividad, Betty Friedan and parliamentarians, the participants agreed on a Call to Action that included these recommendations to the 1995 UN International Women's Conference in China: Women should hold at least 40% of the seats in national and international public policy groups by the year 2000. Political parties should develop ways to get women involved in politics and should raise money to allow women to develop campaign skills and strategies. Women should demand equal numbers of women and men in policy-making groups such as the UN and the World Bank.

The campaign for political gender balance received even stronger impetus from a "Women in Power" conference of women political leaders, held in Athens, Greece, November 2-3, 1992. It was sponsored by the European Expert Network "Women in Decision-Making," established in the spring of 1992 to support the activities of the Commission of the European Communities. The commission also assigned the European Women's Lobby to organize the first European Women's Summit, a gathering of present and former women government officials, held in conjunction with the conference. The summit was initiated by Vasso Papandreou, member of the European Commission responsible for social affairs.

From both the conference and the summit came a number of recommendations on how to expand equal opportunities for women in decision-making bodies and especially how to involve more women in the decision-making process at all levels. One roundtable, whose participants discussed specific strategies for increasing the numbers of women in political positions, reported: "Planning mechanisms such as quotas or reserved seats must be considered as a strategy to hasten the natural, but slow, evolution of women into power, which could take till the year 2500 to become a reality. It is critical to remember that the central struggle is over power, which is never easily yielded to outside contestants.

"This realization underlies the concept of gender quotas at selection conventions, which proposes that 40% of candidates must be women. In this way, 40% of a party's elected representatives would be women under some electoral systems. Cross-cultural caution is urged, for electoral systems differ. Nevertheless, perhaps a different architecture could be plotted to ensure that quotas could be shaped to suit other electoral systems."

The report also stressed the necessity for having relevant data concerning selection procedures to facilitate planning for gender equality: "Learn the system first, if you want to beat it."

The summit, attended by 14 former and present women cabinet members, prime ministers, parliamentarians and leaders of the European Parliament, issued a Declaration[3] that noted a "profound inequality in all public and political decision-making authorities and bodies at every level—local, regional, national and European" and cited a significant decrease of women in decision-making in some European countries, a reference to the Eastern bloc and the former Soviet Union republics.

Proclaiming the need to achieve a balanced distribution of public and political power between women and men to "produce different ideas, values and styles of behaviour suited to a fairer and more balanced world for all, both men and women," the Declaration called upon all political leadership at the European and national levels "to accept the full consequences of the democratic idea on which their parties are built, in particular by ensuring balanced participation between women and men in positions of power, particularly political and administrative positions, through measures to raise awareness and through mechanisms."

The 400 women attending the conference also signed the Declaration, and messages of support were received from President Mary Robinson of Ireland, President Vigdis Finnbogadottir of Iceland as well as from other women politicians, including cabinet ministers and parliamentarians. Commissioner Papandreou also addressed a letter to all women in European parliaments— European, national and regional—asking them to join in signing the Declaration. The statement was distributed to all governments in Europe and to the 48 member organizations of the European Women's Lobby, which have an estimated overall membership of more than 100 million women in the 12 member states of the European Community.

Spokeswoman Irmeli Karhio said the summit Declaration and the conference documents were providing the basis for a Europe-wide campaign in preparation for the European elections in 1994 and "marked a turning point in the discussion on women's access to positions of political responsibilities . . . . In this way," she said, "the Athens conference was an important step to bring about the equality of the sexes, which is an essential attribute to a truly democratic society."

As the Athens Declaration made clear, the enormous gap between words and performance on gender balance evident in male-dominated governments and institutions demonstrates that women cannot expect men voluntarily to step aside to make room for the "other" sex. It will take continuing pressure, organization, skills training and strong, popular women's movements in the countries of the world to reach the natural quota of 50-50 leadership in governments around the world.

In the following chapters, political strategies and accomplishments of women's movements in Sweden, Norway, Denmark, Finland, Germany and Iceland are described. The final chapter discusses new mechanisms for achieving political equality for women in the United States.

NOTES

[1] Paragraph 86 of *The Nairobi Forward-Looking Strategies for the Advancement of Women* says: "Governments and political parties should intensify efforts to stimulate and ensure equality of participation by women in all national and local legislative bodies and to achieve equity in the appointment, election and promotion of women to high posts in executive, legislative and judiciary branches in these bodies. At the local level, strategies to ensure equality of women in political participation should be pragmatic, should bear a close relationship to issues of concern to women in the locality and should take into account the suitability of the proposed measures to local needs and values." Paragraph 88 says: "Governments should effectively secure participation of women in the decision-making processes at a national, state and local level through legislative and administrative measures. It is desirable that governmental departments establish a special office in each of them, headed preferably by a woman, to monitor periodically and accelerate the process of equitable representation of women. Special activities should be undertaken to increase the recruitment, nomination and promotion of women, especially to decision-making and policy-making positions, by publicizing posts more widely, increasing upward mobility and so on, until equitable representation of women is achieved. Reports should be compiled periodically on the numbers of women in public service and on their levels of responsibility in their areas of work."

[2] The European Parliament approved a policy statement by its Committee on Women's Rights calling on political parties "when deciding on their candidates or lists of candidates, to operate a clear-cut and monitorable quota system aimed at increasing numerical equality between men and women in all representative political bodies within the foreseeable future." The 12-member-state European Parliament, as of 1992, included 107 women, or 20.7% of its 518 members. This percentage was higher than the average numbers of women in the individual member-state parliaments. It has been said that it is easier for women to get elected to the European Parliament because it lacks the power to initiate legislation, though it can amend and vote on legislation submitted by the European Commission. However, the Committee on Women's Rights, chaired by Christine Crawley (Labour Party, U.K.), plays an effective leadership role in advancing policies raising the economic, social and political status of European women. A breakdown of women's representation in the European Parliament follows: Belgium 29.2% (7 of 24 members); Denmark 37.5% (6/16); Germany 37% (30/81); Greece 0% (0/24); Spain 15% (9/60); France 22.2% (18/81); Ireland 6.7% (1/15); Italy 13.6%; Luxembourg 50% (3/6); Netherlands 28% (7/25); Portugal 12.5% (3/24) and United Kingdom 14.8% (12/81).

[3] Among those signing the Declaration were Vasso Papandreou; former President Simone Veil of the European Parliament and still a member; former French Prime Minister Edith Cresson; Rita Süssmuth, president of the German parliament; Erna Hennicot-Schoepges, president of the Luxembourg parliament; Miet Smet, minister of labour and equality, Belgium; Lone Dybkjaer, M.P. and former minister of environment, Denmark; Melina Mercouri, former minister of culture, Greece; Matilde Fernandez Sanz, minister of social affairs, Spain; Mary O'Rourke, minister for trade and marketing,

Ireland; Tina Anselmi, former minister of labour and health, Italy; Hedy d'Ancona, minister of health, welfare and culture, The Netherlands; Leonor Beleza, vice-president of the parliament, Portugal; Lady Trumpington, whip of the House of Lords and former minister of agriculture, U.K.; Pirjo Rusanen, minister of housing, Finland; Inger Davidson, minister of public administration, Sweden; Judith Stamm, M.P. and president, Committee on Women's Affairs; Anna Roschova, member of the presidency, Czech National Council; Kriszlina Dobos, deputy under secretary of state of the ministry of culture and education, Hungary; and Chafika Meslem, director of the UN Division of the Advancement of Women.

2

Close-Up: Norway

When Nora Helmer in Henrik Ibsen's 1879 play, *The Doll's House,* walked out on her authoritarian husband, the sound of the door closing behind that independent Norwegian heroine resonated for women throughout the Western world. A century later in 1979, Norway was again at the forefront of feminism when it implemented the innovative Equal Status Act to provide women with an equitable role in both government and society as a whole. By 1992, the country was led by a woman prime minister who had recently been returned to office for a third term, eight women members of a 19-member cabinet, and a quota system that seeks to guarantee women between 40 and 60% of representation on all levels of government. In fact, according to a recent report by the United Nations, Norway is one of only a very few countries in which women are at least 30% of the participants in government and thus constitute a "critical mass" that can make "a visible difference on political decisions and agendas, as well as on attitudes, behaviors and styles." [Report of the Secretary General, E/CN, .6/199, p. 5.]

Why does this small, relatively rich Nordic country with a homogeneous population of about 4.2 million people lead the world's nations with regard to political representation for women? There are several contributing factors, including a deep appreciation of equity and democracy and a women's movement that has been well-organized, active, and outspoken for a long time.

Additionally, Norway fits many of the indicators that, according to an international study presented by Professor Wilma Rule at the UN International Women's Conference in Nairobi in 1985, predispose countries to have a relatively large proportion of elected women officials. According to Dr. Rule, the significant factors include the Lutheran religion (as contrasted to Catholic), women who belong to left-wing or socialist parties, a high percentage of women in the workforce, election rules that build on proportional representation, and ballots with many candidates on them. Norway ranks high in all these categories. [Äs, Berit, *Which Positive Actions—At This Time in History*, p. 13.]

DEMOCRACY, EQUITY & WOMEN WHO DEMANDED THEIR RIGHTS

Some feminists trace the country's tradition of equity all the way back to ancient Viking laws that provided equal rights to women. As Bitten Modal, a Norwegian feminist, has pointed out, Viking women needed legal rights because they were in charge of homes and farms all along the Norwegian coastline while the men were away, as fishermen, sailors, and Viking warriors. ["The Price We Pay," *Ms.* magazine, January-February 1991, p. 12.]

In reality, there were actually several factors in Norway's history that led to solidarity among women and the tendency among men to support women's right to equity that were important prerequisites to women's recent rise to political power. Unlike other Nordic countries, Norway has experienced long periods of occupation by or forced submission to other nations—first Denmark for 400 years, then Sweden, and finally Germany from 1940 until 1945. This national history of domination—which meant, among other things, that Norway did not have its own constitution until 1814 —is generally acknowledged to have imbued Norwegians with a strong respect for democracy and equity, as well as a tendency to identify with the oppressed and underprivileged.

The fact that Norway never had a land-owning aristocracy (although it does have a royal family) may also have contributed to the country's egalitarian attitudes. As Gisbert H. Flanz pointed out in his 1983 book on *Comparative Women's Rights and Political Participation in Europe*, "The roots of democracy in Norway are deep and strong. A comparative study of Norwegian social history shows that unlike all the other countries of Scandinavia, Norway did not attach much importance to social stratification. A remarkably equalitarian outlook was in evidence long before the French Revolution." Additionally, a Norwegian observer, Beatrice Halsaa of Oppland Regional College, noted in a paper on *Policies and Strategies for Women in Norway*, "The power elite . . . has been pliable, showing a remarkable capacity to grant access to new groups and their arguments and to meet political pressure without the use of violence." [p. 3.]

Another factor paving the way for the unique political progress of Norwegian women is the national predisposition to organization, which helped women to come together to work collectively for increased rights and participation in the political process, regardless of what political party they belonged to. Norway currently has about 1,300 organizations for virtually every purpose from religion, languages, leisure activities and humanitarian work to occupational and industrial groups and these groups have a total membership about three times the size of the country's population, with 81% of all Norwegian women, and 87% of

Norwegian men belonging to at least one organization. [*Women's Status in Norway*, p. 5.] Traditionally, women have been most active in grassroots movements concerned with such issues as social welfare, education, and peace. However, not surprisingly, the numbers, proportion, and power of women members are traditionally less significant in national organizations with more status and power.

Special organizations for women and organizations whose members are mostly women have been active in Norway since the second half of the nineteenth century. Thus, the Norwegian Association for the Rights of Women (NARW), which has played an invaluable role over the past hundred or so years in advocating women's rights, was established in 1884 by well-known and influential women from the middle and upper classes, along with a few male supporters, to work for equal rights and responsibilities for women in education and economic life and to improve the rights of married women. A few years later, in 1889, the more radical members of the NARW broke away to form the National Association for Women's Suffrage (NAWS) which, as its name implies, had the specific goal of achieving universal suffrage for women on equal terms with men, a right that was finally obtained in 1913. [*Policies and Strategies for Women in Norway*, p. 14.]

While the NARW and NAWS had an overtly political purpose from the very start, most of the other early women's organizations had religious, social, or humanitarian goals. For example, the Norwegian Women's Public Health Organization, which today is the largest women's organization in the country with 240,000 members and runs 600 hospitals, nurses' training schools, kindergartens, maternity homes, and other institutions, was founded in 1886, when women were afraid that war would break out between Norway and Sweden and wanted to provide a medical corps for the army. Similarly, the Norwegian Housewives Association, which is now the second largest women's organization with over 40,000 members and runs kindergartens and other programs for children and families, was established in 1915. The National Council of Women in Norway, created in 1904 to be an umbrella organization for other women's organizations and which eventually had over 20 member organizations, played an important role both nationally and internationally until it was dissolved in 1990.

Working women began to organize to protect their interests as wage earners around 1890 and about 20 women's unions were started during the following decade. Although women primarily organized to protect their jobs against men who wanted to shut them out of the labor force, other more enlightened men supported the women's organizing efforts. Working women have traditionally belonged to the women's groups of the labor unions, as well as to the women's groups of the Labour Party. Today, women constitute about 30% of the 750,000 individuals who belong to the Norwegian Federation of Trade Unions. [*Policies and Strategies for Women in Norway*, p. 14.]

In 1912, after the women's labor movement was fairly well established, women nurses and teachers, who had not been organized by unions, also formed vocational organizations. They were followed in 1925 by women in agriculture who formed a Women's Committee which was closely associated with an existing organization of male farmers. It still exists in the form of the Norwegian Country Women's Organization, which now has about 30,000 members. There are currently about 60 women's organizations in Norway. [*Women's Status in Norway*, pp. 6-7.]

Women's political associations have traditionally been closely linked to the male-dominated political parties. An association of socialist women was started in 1895 in Oslo and the Norwegian Labour Party's Women's Association was formed in 1901. It was then abolished as a separate organization in 1923 when a Women's Secretariat connected to the party's central board was established. [*Policies and Strategies for Women in Norway*, p. 15.]

From the very beginning of the women's movements, socialist and nonsocialist women had different priorities and strategies. While socialist women often emphasized the common struggle of working-class men and women for better living conditions and a more just society, nonsocialist women usually stressed their special grievances as women. One issue over which these two wings of the movement were deeply divided was special protection for women workers. While working-class socialist women worried about the dangers of night work for women and thus favored special protection, middle-class, nonsocialist women opposed special protection for women workers because they thought it would hamper women's ability to be competitive in the labor market.

Similarly, when Katti Anker Moller, an upper-class feminist, successfully campaigned for a parliamentary act that in 1915 made Norway the first country to give children born out of wedlock the right to carry the names of their fathers and to inherit from them, the Housewives Association opposed the new reform as an attack on the integrity of the family. Then, when Anker, who was also the first to discuss contraception and the need to liberalize abortion legislation, led a movement to establish health centers that offered advice on contraception, some traditional women's association, and religious and conservative groups again objected strongly. [*Policies and Strategies for Women in Norway*, p. 17.]

Later, during the great international depression of the 1930s, women of the Labour Party split over whether or not to support legislation to keep married women out of the workforce so that they would not take jobs away from men who presumably needed them more. After World War II, the Labour Party's Women's Secretariat organized about 40 women's organizations into a Cooperation Committee but the committee fell apart in 1950 because of a dispute over the position that the committee should take on abortion.

THE SEEDS OF THE WOMEN'S MOVEMENT

Despite such positive factors as the Norwegians' long-standing respect for democracy and the country's active women's movement, women still had a long and sometimes hard struggle before they achieved their significant victories of the 1970s and 1980s, including the Equal Status Act and a woman prime minister. As long ago as 1885, the year after NARW was formed, Norwegian women began to demand the right to vote in both municipal and national elections. By 1898, all Norwegian men had the right to vote regardless of their income and three years later, in 1901, women with incomes over a certain level were allowed to vote in municipal elections and to be elected to municipal office. A few courageous women actually ran for and were elected to local offices that year, subsequently comprising .8% of all representatives on Norway's municipal councils.

The rising expectations which arose from these small but meaningful victories led Norwegian women to demand more representation and power and in 1909, Fernanda Nissen, a women's rights activist, wrote, "Women must enter politics if they are to have an influence on their own lives." [Nissen, *Women in Norwegian Politics*, p. 7.] Soon afterwards, in 1913, Norwegian women became eligible to vote, joining the ranks of women voters in New Zealand, Australia, and Finland, the only other countries that had already instituted women's suffrage. Norwegian women led the way for women in the other Nordic countries who won the right to vote before women in most other Western nations; they became eligible in 1915 in Denmark and Iceland, and in 1919-21 in Sweden.

After these early advances, however, women's participation in Norway's political life generally stagnated for several decades. The first woman was elected to Norway's parliament (called the Storting) in 1921. In 1937, women's representation in Norway's municipal councils had only inched up to 2.4% from .8 in 1901. In 1945, Norway had its first woman minister, Kirsten Hansteen, but she lacked her own ministry and had the relatively unimpressive title of "consultant minister." [*Women in Norwegian Politics*, pp. 7-9.] As recently as the end of the 1960s and beginning of the 1970s, women composed only 9.5% of the membership of local councils, 5.4% of the membership of county councils, 8% of the membership of parliament and 7% of the cabinet. [Torild Skard, "Women in the political life of the Nordic countries," *International Social Science Journal*, p. 639.]

EARLY SUCCESSES OF THE WOMEN'S MOVEMENT

Perhaps the contemporary women's movement in Norway really began the year *before* the progressive, tumultuous decade of the 1960s which ushered in so much change not only in Norway but throughout the Western world. In fact,

1959 was the year of an event that was an important first step in the recent advances towards equity for Norwegian women—the creation of the Equal Pay Council. This followed Norway's ratification of the International Labour Organization Convention No. 1000 endorsing equal pay for work of equal value. Considering that the principle of pay equity has made only slow progress in the United States more than 30 years later, the establishment of a Equal Pay Council can be seen as a significant indication of the Norwegian predisposition to equal rights. The council, which in 1972 was renamed the Equal Status Council and was subsequently responsible for drafting Norway's landmark Equal Status Act, had a number of responsibilities related to advancing the concept of equal pay. They included providing information about the issue, studying existing labor market conditions, and advocating measures to facilitate women's participation in the labor force. One result of the council's work was the Framework Agreement on Equal Pay of 1961 between the Norwegian Employers' Confederation and the Norwegian Federation of Trade Unions which affected most of the private sector and was implemented gradually between 1961 and 1967, unfortunately without completely solving the tenacious problem of wage inequities between men and women. [*Equal Status Between Men and Women*, p. 2.]

But it was not until the second half of the 1960s that women in Norway had acquired enough energy, coordination, and momentum to bring their movement for equal rights into the political arena. This initiative, which ultimately had a dramatic impact, was sparked by a 1965 Labour government initiative to follow up on a United Nations recommendation that all countries should develop their own plans of action to solve the problems facing women. Labour responded to the UN mandate with a major effort to increase the number of women members elected to local councils in the 1967 nationwide elections which attracted women of all political stripes, as well as a number of men in the country's political leadership. Thus, although the campaign was actually organized by the well-established Norwegian Association for the Rights of Women and women were the driving force behind it, the campaign committee was led by two men, the prime minister who belonged to the Agrarian Party and the former prime minister who belonged to the Labour Party. All of the country's political parties were represented on the committee, as were the country's leading women's organizations. Working primarily through the mass media and the public schools, the committee launched a broad educational campaign that stressed the valuable contribution of women to politics, urged the various political parties to nominate women as candidates, and encouraged the electorate to support them.

This well-organized, broad-based, and sustained effort ultimately paid off in substantial gains in the number of elected women officials in the 1967 election, when the overall representation of women in public office increased from 6.3% to 9.5% and the number of municipal councils without a single woman representative fell from 179 to 79. [*Policies and Strategies for Women in Norway*, p. 36.]

PUTTING WOMEN FIRST

Perhaps the most innovative and ultimately significant aspect of the 1967 campaign was the strategy developed by a group of 17 enterprising women to maximize the impact of the women's vote in their local election. First, however, it is necessary to understand a unique aspect of the Norwegian electoral system that allows voters not only to vote for a political party but also to influence who will represent the party on local councils. Norwegian elections are based on proportional representation, with the number of representatives a party receives determined by the number of votes it obtains. Consequently, the parties present their slates of candidates in order of priority. If the voters wish, they can change this order to put the candidates they like best at the top of the list, and traditionally voters have done so to favor male candidates. This time, however, this small group of women utilized this system in their own favor. They systematically crossed out the names of male candidates, thus moving to the top of the slate the names of the women candidates who had been listed last. They also transferred women candidates from the slates of other parties to their own party's slate. Thus, by using their legal rights to the full, these women managed to have 24 women elected out of a total of 43 representatives to the local council.

Not surprisingly, this clever and successful strategy attracted both negative and positive attention. Some men considered it to be unfair even though men had traditionally reordered slates of candidates to favor men over women. On the positive side, some members of the new, more radical women's movement who had previously been uninvolved in the electoral process were sufficiently impressed by the creativity and militancy of the technique to join with more traditional women's organizations in a unified effort to elect more women to political office.

When it was time to organize a campaign to elect more women in the 1971 national election, the activists were more experienced than they had been a few years earlier. This time, the campaign was spearheaded by Norway's largest women's organization, the National Council of Women, which launched a major voter education drive about the international commitment to the goal of equality, the obligation of Norway's political parties to respect the rights of women, and the ability of voters to have an impact on the election. At the same time, women members of the various political parties urged their parties to nominate greater numbers of women. Additionally, women voters all over the country borrowed the technique which had been so successful in the 1967 campaign of crossing out men's names and transferring women candidates from one party's list to another as a means of electing more women. The cumulative effect of these diverse efforts was what leading politicians called the "women's coup"—female representation on 428 of the country's 450 municipal councils and a female majority on the municipal councils of three of Norway's largest cities, including the capital of Oslo, Trondheim, and Asker.

These election results created a national uproar with newspaper headlines that read, "Female Knock-out in the Elections," and "Political Amazons Take City Hall by Storm." Again, as in 1967, some men objected to the rearranging of names on the party slates to put women at the top as an "undemocratic procedure"—even though the strategy of reordering candidates was completely legal in Norway and had often been used by men. In reality, however, the so-called coup hardly brought Norwegian women to political parity with men. After the election, women still comprised only 15% of the country's elected officials, up from 9.5%. [*Women in Norwegian Politics*, p. 6.]

Nevertheless, the 1971 election represented real gains for women and had many consequences, the most important being an increased interest in politics and greater political activity and ambition among Norwegian women. Many men also began to understand that women were serious about their demands for political and social equity and intended to use their votes to accomplish those goals. They also realized that women could be effective politicians and that their ascendance to power did not lead to revolution or catastrophe. [Skard, *International Social Science Journal*, pp. 639-42.]

Not long after the 1971 elections, the electoral laws were changed to minimize the voters' ability to influence the parties' choice of candidates and thereafter women were less able to increase their political representation by putting women's names at the top of their parties' slates. In fact, however, the change in the electoral laws also benefited women by mandating direct elections for county councils. Until 1975 when those elections were introduced, women constituted only about 5% of the members on county councils. The reason for this particularly low representation was that the members of county councils were chosen by and from the members of municipal councils which were still largely male-dominated. As soon as the law changed so that members were directly elected by the voters, the percentage of women members climbed to nearly 25%.

Despite their undebatable progress in increasing their representation in government, Norwegian women faced considerable hurdles both to being elected in significant numbers to their country's national parliament called the Storting and to achieving decision-making powers in such areas as economics and foreign policy, which were traditionally considered to be the province of men.

As Torild Skard, a former member of the Storting and a delegate to the United Nations, noted at the beginning of the 1980s, "As the number of women in political bodies has increased, a pattern of sex segregation has become evident. Basically the pattern has two dimensions: a vertical dimension by which men get more important positions than women and a horizontal dimension which displays a division of labor in keeping with the traditional sex roles . . . . As for horizontal segregation, men are mainly occupied with questions relating to production and women with questions relating to reproduction." [Skard, *International Social Science Journal*, p. 650.]

Skard also pointed to a study of the Norwegian parliament in 1973-77 showing that women generally wanted to serve on the same committees as men did but that their requests for committee assignments were not complied with to the same extent as were the men's. The women thought the men were more likely to be assigned to committees of their choice because of direct sex discrimination and because men often seemed more qualified for the posts due to seniority, previous political experience, business connections and other factors that tended to work in their favor. [Skard, *International Social Science Journal,* p. 651.]

But despite the limits imposed on their areas of influence, the growing number of women who became elected officials during the 1970s unquestionably helped to put some important issues on the political agenda and even, in some instances, to bring about important reforms. Thus, a study indicated that between 1973 and 1977, 20% of issues that women members raised concerned women's rights and benefits as compared with only 4% of the issues raised by male members. Similarly, in the municipal councils of Oslo, Trondheim, and Asker, where women had obtained a majority in 1971, demands such as the need for more child care, widows' and widowers' pensions, equal pay for equal work, and assistance to enable single parents and married women to join the workforce finally received long overdue attention. In fact, the feminist majority on the Oslo, Trondheim, and Asker councils actually brought about some concrete reforms, including pay increases for the lowest paid women workers, part-time jobs and flexible working hours for working parents, and compensation for parents for the cost of child care during council meetings. [Skard, *International Social Science Journal,* p. 652.]

INEQUITIES IN THE STATUS OF MEN AND WOMEN

During the 1970s, Norwegian women were not simply gaining strength and a more commanding voice in the country's legislative chambers, they were also making their presence and concerns known in various governmental bodies. Thus, in 1972, when the Equal Status Council was established to assume the responsibilities of the Equal Pay Council, it expanded its scope of responsibility beyond the single issues of pay equity to also advocate equity in the areas of business, education, and community and family life. As one of its first acts, the council issued a publication entitled *Facts about Equal Status,* which aired some stark facts about the discrepancy between men's and women's status in Norway at the beginning of the 1970s. Among the findings included were:

• The extent and nature of women's participation in the workforce varied greatly depending on their age and the size of their families while men's economic activity was not influenced by their family status.

• Women's level of employment was linked to their level of education to a greater degree than was men's.

• A large percentage of married women were only able to work a limited number of hours because they bore most of the responsibility for their families.

- Women worked in low-pay occupations and sectors and were generally paid 10 to 15% less than were men when they did the same jobs.
- Although equal numbers of boys and girls took the final examination at upper-secondary school, the girls usually chose to study for traditionally female, often service-oriented occupations while men chose technical and economic subjects that would qualify them for well-paying jobs in traditionally male occupations, thus perpetuating the division between the male and female labor markets for some time to come. [*Equal Status Between Men and Women*, Norwegian Information publication, 1990, p. 2.]

Slowly but surely, however, some of these deeply rooted inequities were beginning to be overcome through changes in Norway's legal system that made the country's laws almost entirely gender-neutral and, at least theoretically, made women more nearly equal with men. Thus, in 1974, the Allodial Act, which governed the inheritance of land, was changed to overrule the ancient right of men to inherit their families' land and to give women the same privilege. Not surprisingly, this age-old tradition has not died easily. Reactions to the new, gender-neutral legislation were strong, especially in the countryside where the question of which child inherited the family farm had enormous economic ramifications. Some families even tried to circumvent the intent of the new legislation by pressuring female children to relinquish their right to inheritance in favor of their brothers. And as recently as 1988, 14 years after the Allodial Act was changed, two Norwegian professors wrote, "No other law is today discussed with such engagement, even passion as this one." [Tove Stang Dahl and Helga Maria Hernes, "After Equality," *Scandinavian Review,* 1988, p. 1.]

Another blow to tradition that also increased women's legal rights was the 1979 Law of Names which removed a man's right and privilege to give his name to his wife and family. Since it was enacted, women have been free to choose whether or not to take their husbands' name and, if no other arrangements are specified, children automatically receive their mothers' surname. Perhaps the last area regarding inheritance in which tradition finally gave way to equity for women was the ancient provision in the Norwegian constitution that succession to the Norwegian throne was still reserved for princes. This provision somehow managed to remain intact until 1990, when the paragraph of the constitution concerning succession to the throne was amended so that beginning with the next generation of the royal family, a woman can become the head of state.

Of course, the victories of Norwegian women in the political and legal arenas during the 1960s and 1970s did not occur in a vacuum. In large part, they resulted from and then reinforced and interacted with a general awakening of women's consciousness and activism that spread throughout Norway—and the Western world—like bubbling yeast which gradually causes bread to rise. In fact, Norwegian feminists attribute much of their own vitality to international trends and to International Women's Year in 1975. In Norway, however, the women's movement seems to have had a uniquely political orientation. As Professor Berit Äs has pointed out, "During the 1970s when consciousness-raising groups were formed everywhere . . . while sexual liberation may have been a stronger theme in Denmark at that time and the peace movement drew women in Sweden into action, in Norway women's politics were discussed all the time." [*Which Positive Actions—At This Time in History?*, p. 9.]

In fact, the new women's movement was really the second wave of a women's movement that had emerged around the turn of the century, the time at which the old-line Norwegian women's organizations had been founded and women received the vote. This wave, however, led both to a revitalization of the traditional women's groups and the rise of new, more radical ones. Women now began to demand reforms to enable them to fulfill their growing role as wage earners at the same time that they remained the primary caretakers for their families. Thus they called for six-hour working days, equal pay for work of equal value, one-year maternity leave, and free kindergarten for all children. [*Women's Status in Norway*, p. 7.] Additionally, formerly taboo subjects, including women's sexuality, domestic violence, incest, sexual harassment, and abortion rights, were also put on the agenda. In fact, abortion was a controversial issue in Norway during the 1970s when the existing law favored women of wealth who could afford to go abroad to have abortions while working-class women had to deal with demeaning red tape before they could obtain abortions in their own country. The right to free abortion on demand up to 12 weeks and up to the second trimester on medical, eugenic or rape grounds, was finally won by the smallest possible majority in parliament in 1978. [*Policies and Strategies for Women in Norway*, p. 21.]

In contrast to the older women's organizations which emphasized equal rights, professionalism, and the need for government reforms, the new women's movement did not devote most of its efforts and energies to working within the system, but instead tried to raise the consciousness of women throughout Norway with a feminist counterculture. During the 1970s, the new feminism developed its own literature, theater, music, and films, informal networks, innovative political action, festivals, and innumerable conferences. It also created alternative institutions to respond to women's special needs, including crisis centers, women's centers, and self-protection classes. [*Policies and Strategies for Women in Norway*, pp. 18-19.]

During the 1970s, an active lesbian movement also emerged in Norway and attitudes towards sexual preferences became more tolerant. Additionally, a campaign against pornography was organized in the late 1970s, with support from women across the political spectrum, from the traditional Norwegian Housewives Association to the radical Women's Front. Norway's first crisis center was established in Oslo in 1978, signalling a national movement for crisis centers and crisis telephones for battered women and children. During that decade, women in the universities also began to protest the disproportionate number of male professors and the male-dominated curricula, a movement that led to the development of women's studies and feminist research, which, with the support of the women's organizations and women in parliament and other branches of government, has gained funding and credibility over the years. [*Policies and Strategies for Women in Norway*, p. 20.]

For a few years during the 1970s, there was considerable tension and ideological debate between adherents of the older, reform-minded women's organizations and believers in the new liberation, grassroots and women-oriented feminism. Gradually, however, the various groups realized that their common goals were more important than their strategic differences and overcame their differences to work together for legislative reform that would benefit all Norwegian women.

Probably the ultimate proof that women were finally being taken seriously in Norway was the passage in 1978 of the landmark Equal Status Act, which had been advocated by the Labour Party's Women's Association since the early 1970s. The act is unparalleled around the world in that it not only regulates the workplace but also all other sectors of society, including education, advertising, and even family and personal life. Thus, advertising is prohibited if it denigrates either sex or portrays either men or women in a degrading fashion and a family cannot discriminate against a man or a women when renting a room in their house. Only internal conditions in religious communities are exempted on the grounds that freedom of faith is guaranteed by the Norwegian constitution.

DIFFERENTIAL TREATMENT TO PROMOTE EQUALITY

The first paragraph of the act clearly articulates its sweeping purpose: "This Act shall promote equal status between the sexes and aims particularly at improving the position of women. The public authorities shall facilitate equality of status between the sexes in all sectors of society. Women and men shall be given equal opportunities for education, employment and cultural and professional advancement. The Act applies to all areas of society and states that differential treatment of men and women is prohibited. Differential treatment to promote equality between the sexes, however, is not prohibited." [*Equal Status Between Men and Women*, Norwegian Ministry of Foreign Affairs, April 1990, p. 2.]

The act also established an apparatus to enforce its provisions, which includes an Equal Status Ombud and a seven-member Equal Status Appeals Board with representatives of labor and business and other members appointed by the king. The Ombud position continues the Scandinavian tradition of appointing or electing an "Ombudsman" to address allegations of injustice from individuals and groups but because the term ombudsman might be considered sexist, the Equal Status Act instead created a more neutral Ombud. The Ombud has the job of making sure that the act's provisions are followed. He/she can respond to complaints of violations by individuals or groups and also intervene on his/her own initiative. In the case of a complaint, the Ombud first tries to reach a voluntary settlement but if mediation fails, he/she will bring the case to the Appeals Board, which has the power to prohibit actions that violate the act.

Additionally, the Equal Status Council, which, as mentioned earlier, was created in 1972 to assume the functions of the Equal Pay Council along with other responsibilities, plays a fundamental role in implementing the intent of the Equal Status Act. The council operates as an independent advisory body to the Norwegian government and also coordinates information and activities related to equal rights among the government, women's organizations, and the public. [*Policies and Strategies for Women in Norway*, p. 33.] Both sexes and all parts of the country are required to be represented in the council and some of its members must have experience with women's issues and organizations and equal status work. The Council changes its focus as time goes on to deal with issues it considers to be of the highest priority. Thus, in recent years, the Council has focused on the labor market and particularly emphasized the need for pay equity, more manageable working hours for women and local equality committees to advocate for equal rights on the grassroots level. To publicize its concerns, the council holds conferences and issues publications. It also serves as an advisory body for the equal status committees in counties and municipalities which are charged with encouraging sex equity in local communities. [*Women's Status in Norway*, p. 13.] Moreover, a Department for Family Affairs and Equal Status was established in the Ministry of Consumer Affairs and Government Administration, which has since changed its name to the Ministry of Family and Consumer Affairs to coordinate government policies concerning equal status.

The act was intended both to ensure equal treatment in all possible areas and to encourage more equitable attitudes towards sex roles. It bluntly states that, "Discrimination between women and men is not permitted," and defines discrimination as treatment differentiating between women and men because they are of different sexes and places one sex "at an unreasonable disadvantage as compared with the other." The Ombud who enforces the act has interpreted discriminatory treatment to include unequal access to pension plans and restaurants. Also, if the girls at a boarding school had to clean their own rooms while the boys' rooms where cleaned for them by hired staff, this differential treatment would be considered discriminatory. [p. 3.]

While affirmative action may still be controversial in the United States, it has become an established fact of Norwegian life ever since the passage of the Equal Status Act. Thus, although the act prohibits discrimination that puts women at a disadvantage, it is also explicit in noting that "different treatment which . . . promotes equal status between the sexes" is not prohibited, nor are special rights for women "based on the existing difference in the situation of women and men." In fact, affirmative action is considered essential to address the disparities that still exist between the sexes. Although the quota system that was implemented in 1987 to promote equality between the sexes is the most explicit recognition of the need for preferential treatment to address existing inequities, the original act made a good beginning in this direction by, for example, encouraging businesses to set targets for the numbers of women they employ and giving women special benefits related to pregnancy, childbirth, and nursing.

The Equal Status Act's work-related provisions are obviously of key economic and professional concern to great numbers of women. Section 4 of the Act explicitly states: "Except in cases where there is an obvious reason for doing so, a job must not be announced vacant for one sex only. Nor must the announcement give the impression that the employer expects or prefers one of the sexes for the position." Section 4 also asserts that men and women must be treated equally in regard to appointments, promotions, dismissals, and layoffs that apply to full-time, part-time, and temporary employment. However, domestic employees who work in private homes are not covered by the Act. Not surprisingly, the bulk of the Ombud's workload consists of reports and complaints from women about employers who have allegedly denied them the same workplace opportunities that men have received. When these complaints seem justified, the Ombud tries to convince the employers to respond with the appropriate action, such as hiring or promoting the women, and when employers will not correct an injustice voluntarily, she will refer cases to the Appeals Board for further action.

Although the principle of equal pay for work of equal value was endorsed by the Norwegian government as long ago as 1959 when it established the Equal Pay Council to advocate and implement equitable pay policies and practices, the fact that women still tend to be paid less than men has become increasingly acknowledged since the Equal Status Act took effect. The Ombud has therefore rigorously tried to enforce the concept of pay equity and, for example, has ruled that providing male nurses with clean shirts, jackets, and trousers while expecting female nurses to provide their own uniforms and to wash their own aprons is a violation of the Equal Status Act. [*Women's Status in Norway*, p. 14.] However, she has acknowledged the difficulty of enforcing the concept of equal pay for work of equal value primarily because the meaning of the term is still unclear and there is no accepted system of evaluating the similarities and differences between men's and women's jobs in a labor market that is still largely sexually segregated. Nevertheless, some progress has been made in this direction over the years. For example, female laboratory technicians are now granted equal pay with male biological engineers and the Ombud has tried to win the same wages for head nurses as for head engineers.

LABOR MARKET STILL SEGREGATED

Additionally, some government agencies, including the Ministries of Culture and Scientific Affairs, Environment, Foreign Affairs, and Justice and the Police, the Norwegian Railway Authority, and the Norwegian Post Office, have developed affirmative action plans to train women for and increase their representation in some traditionally male occupations. Unfortunately, however, the kind of affirmative action that has been employed in the labor market seems more symbolic than real, in contrast to the very effective quota system that has dramatically increased the numbers and roles of women throughout the political system. In fact, Norwegian women are frustrated by their notable lack of success in achieving equity within the labor market. They complain that while the large majority of women have become wage earners, the labor market is still very segregated, with the top jobs still belonging to men. [*Policies and Strategies for Women in Norway*, pp. 46-47, 50.]

Education is another area with major impact on the status of women because the kind of jobs for which young women are trained during their school years determines their future in the workplace. Here, too, women are trying to undo the traditional inequities of sex stereotyping. Section 6 of the Equal Status Act explicitly states: "In respect of admission to courses, schools and studies, and of other efforts designed to promote recruitment to a particular trade or profession, when circumstances otherwise are approximately equal, it shall be possible to give priority to one sex if it is the case that this will help in the long run to regulate any imbalance between the sexes in the trade or profession in question." Sex quotas that affect admission to educational institutions have long been a fact of life in Norway, primarily to benefit men in environments like teacher training colleges where women applicants were traditionally in the majority. However, admission to educational institutions can only be based on sex quotas when there is an unequal distribution of women and men and the quota system is designed to correct the imbalance. [*Norwegian Equal Status Act with Comments*, Equal Status Ombud, Revised edition 1989, pp. 10-11.]

The act also mandates that books, audio and video tapes, films, and other teaching aids that are used in educational institutions must promote the principle of equal status. In 1981, soon after the act was implemented, the Ministry of Church and Education established a Secretariat for Equal Opportunities in Education, which developed a comprehensive program to promote equity in the schools including offering courses about sex equity for teachers on all levels, providing incentives for women to apply for top teaching and administrative positions in schools, and commissioning new textbooks with a more equalitarian point of view. [*Women's Status in Norway*, p. 13.]

More recently, in 1987, to further implement the intent of the Equal Status Act and to integrate the concept of equal status into every aspect of public policy, all of the government ministries established action programs that involved examining their laws, regulations, and management practices to see their implications for the status of women. [*Women in Norwegian Politics*, p. 19.] In general, although the act has not proven to be a panacea that automatically provided equal pay, status, and opportunities to Norwegian women, it has provided a legal framework for introducing affirmative action in favor of women and restricting preferential treatment of men. Its implementation, impact, and considerable success can largely be attributed to close cooperation between the women's movement and women who have achieved positions of power in the legislative and administrative branches of the Norwegian government.

DECADE OF THE WOMEN

During the 1980s, Norwegian women gained representation and power to a degree previously unknown not only in their own country but also in any other. An unprecedented number and proportion of women, including a prime minister, were elected to national, regional, and local office. Largely as a result of the Equal Status Act, women took on a major role in Norway's political and professional life. According to *Women in Norwegian Politics,* a pamphlet published by the Norwegian Royal Ministry of Foreign Affairs, "The 1980s have been characterized by the fact that the women who had gained strength from organizing in the 1970s started to integrate women's demands into the framework of the establishment." [p. 3.]

The most visible and tangible result of women's rise to power in the 1980s was the large number of women who were elected to office on all levels. By the time of the 1985 election, Norwegian women had nearly 20 years of experience in running major political campaigns. This time, the Equal Status Council called a meeting of the women's organizations to discuss strategies for electing more women that could be underwritten with public financing. The council also provided the women's campaign with free space in the office that it shared with the Ombud, an arrangement that has persisted during subsequent elections. In 1987, the theme of the women's campaign was "Equal Representation." Women in all of the political parties demanded, "Every other candidate on the slate, a woman and a man—and start with a woman." [*Women's Status in Norway*, p. 5.] They almost got as much as they asked for because in the local elections that year, 4,260 women representatives were elected, bringing their numbers to over 31% of the 13,648 municipal council seats nationwide. Additionally, women won fully 40.5% of the seats in the county councils, for which the elections were held at the same time. This result was particularly encouraging, considering that until the middle of the 1970s, women had held only about 5% of the seats on Norway's 19 county councils. With these election returns, Norwegian women had finally reached the level of representation in government that political scientists consider to be the "critical mass" that enables a minority group to have real influence over political decisions. [*Women's Status in Norway*, p. 4.]

By the 1980s, women in Norway had also achieved considerable power in the various political parties to which they belonged even though the relationship between the various political parties and their respective women's associations differs considerably. Thus, the Women's Association of the Labour Party and the women's groups of the Centre Party and the Christian Democratic Party consist only of women who already belong to those parties. Similarly, the Conservative

Women's Federation is a separate section within the Conservative Party. These groups hold their own meetings and elect representatives to their own governing bodies. In contrast, the Socialist Left Party integrates women's issues into its regular activities although it also has established a number of special committees to deal with women's issues. [*Women's Status in Norway*, pp. 60-67.] But however the role of women is structured in the various political parties, their influence is clear. Except in the far-right Progress Party, women in parties across the political spectrum have taken a leading role in formulating public policies concerning children, women, and the family. Additionally, all of the parties, again except for the Progress Party, have placed equal status and other reforms to improve the situation of women high on their agendas.

MULTIPARTY WOMEN'S COALITION

Beginning in the 1980s, there have been increased contact and cooperation among the various political women's organizations. On the initiative of the Christian Democratic Party's Women's Group, representatives of all the organizations meet on a regular basis to discuss political issues and strategies. This collaboration across party lines, for example, has resulted in cooperative initiatives to bring about changes in the National Insurance System to benefit women and to ensure the rights of unmarried women.

Also during the 1980s, the government initiated systematic planning and introduced new programs to implement the Equal Status Act and to advance equality between the sexes. To coordinate and initiate sex equality measures, a separate Department for Family and Equality Issues was established in the Ministry of Consumer Affairs and Government Administration. During the 1980s, the ministry proposed two Plans of Action for Equal Status which focused on education and employment and were subsequently passed by the parliament. The 1981-84 plan, sponsored by the Labour government that was in power at the time, gave special weight to affirmative action and the use of quotas. The second plan, which covered 1985-89 and was presented by a nonsocialist coalition government, was more sex-neutral but ambitiously tried to integrate sex equality into all aspects of public policy. The plan included 270 provisions and required every ministry to present its own action plan before the end of 1987 and then to implement it during the next two years. As a first step to developing its plan, each ministry had to review all relevant legislation, regulations, and administrative practice to determine whether they needed to be revised to reflect the new emphasis on sex equity. [*Policies and Strategies for Women in Norway*, p. 29.]

As a result of the charge implicit in the 1987 plan, many individual ministries developed innovative projects to promote sex equity and address the concerns of women. One of these new initiatives, the "Dream Municipality," was started in

1987 to develop models for city planning which accommodated women's experiences and needs. Additionally, the Regional Development Fund introduced the Women's Program in 1988 which invested in day-care centers and other projects of particular importance to women. For its part, the Ministry of Environment published a Cookbook for Grassroots Planning that encouraged women to exercise the rights they had gained through recent planning and building legislation and gave concrete recipes for the kinds of initiatives they could develop. The Ministry of Culture and Science created a women's archive in the Norwegian Broadcasting Company to promote women's studies and research on women's issues and to increase the number of women in higher education and research. The Secretariat for Women and Research was established in 1977 and a research program to Promote Equal Status and Equality between the Sexes is one of many projects now being implemented. Additionally, the ministry promoted a number of qualified women lecturers to professors, thereby acknowledging the barriers that women have faced in rising to the rank of professor in the male-dominated university system. [*Policies and Strategies for Women in Norway*, p. 30.]

The new programs benefited rural women as well as urban and academic ones. Because many rural women were moving to towns and urban areas and only a few of them had exercised their right as the eldest child to take over the family farm, which they had gained through a 1974 amendment to the Allodial Act, the government encouraged women to use their right to inheritance and adopted the slogan, "Without women there will be no rural Norway." It also funded an Action Plan for Equal Status in Agriculture through an agreement on prices and subsidies between the state and the agricultural organizations. [*Policies and Strategies for Women in Norway*, p. 31.]

Because of a growing awareness that men as well as women would have to change their attitudes and behavior before equality between the sexes could actually be achieved, in 1986 the Ministry of Consumer Affairs and Government Administration established a committee to discuss the role of men, to change their attitudes in regard to sex equity, and to develop measures for reform. The committee has published reports on such subjects as men and caring, how boys become men, men's children and women's divorces. [*Policies and Strategies for Women in Norway*, p. 32.]

The Equal Status Council, which had played a pioneering role in regard to sex equity since it was established in 1972, remained active during the 1980s. In 1987 and 1988, the council focused on labor market issues with special focus on equal pay and working hours.

While many of the new programs were initiated on the national level, some significant efforts were also taking place at the grassroots. During the 1980s, work continued to establish Equal Status Committees for all of Norway's municipal councils and by 1988, despite considerable resistance, 317 of Norway's 454 local authorities did have equal status committees. These committees, a fourth of whose members represent one of the women's organizations, are the fruit of continued cooperation among grassroots women, women in the national government, and women in parliament. The committees deal with a broad range of issues and policies and have devoted most of their efforts to increasing the number of women in politics, to providing information about women's issues on the local level, and to improving the conditions of female public employees, as well as women workers in general. Every county also has an equal status committee that primarily deals with equity issues in the county's administration, county committees, boards, and secondary schools. [*Policies and Strategies for Women in Norway*, pp. 34-35.] A recent evaluation of the Equal Status Council recommended that it be responsible for coordinating the activities of these local equality committees.

QUOTAS INSTITUTIONALIZED

Both participants in the Norwegian women's movement and international observers attribute the virtually unrivalled success of Norwegian women in gaining political power to three factors—well-organized political campaigns, the strategy of reordering the placement of candidates on local ballots to facilitate the election of women, and the use of quotas both in the political parties' recruitment and election procedures and in appointments to public committees, boards, and councils. In fact, the widespread institutionalization of quotas throughout the political system often receives most of the credit. Thus, the publication *Women's Status in Norway* notes that "The rapid increase of women in Norwegian politics is to a considerable extent due to the quota system." [p. 5.] And according to Esther Kostel, vice president of the Norwegian Confederation of Trade Unions, "The quota system has had the impact of increasing women's representation even in bodies where such a system has not been introduced. It has been an instrument to give us women a real share of power. We are no longer satisfied with just participating and being heard. What we say must also result in concrete action." ["Union Women on the Move," *International Confederation of Free Trade Unions, Two-Monthly No. 3/1991*, May-June 1991, p. 3.]

Although sex quotas had been utilized occasionally in the past, for example, to encourage men to enter teacher training schools and other courses of professional study where men were under-represented, they did not become a major instrument of change until the 1970s when women used them as the thin edge of the wedge to gain a proportionate share of representation and power. One relatively early move in that direction was provided by a 1973 Labour government initiative directing all government agencies to nominate both a man and a woman to represent them on government boards and committees. Although the initial resolution had little effect, its intent was eventually incorporated into the Equal Status Act and extended to cover municipal and regional committees, as well as national ones. Section 21 initially directed all public agencies to try to ensure that the number of men and women on boards, committees and councils was as equal as possible, with the minimum requirement that both sexes be represented on all committees and that committees of four or more members should include at least two men and two women. In 1988, a new version of Section 21 was implemented which mandated that all public boards and committees include at least 40% of each sex.

Professor Berit Äs still remembers how difficult it was when she belonged to the Labour Party during the 1960s and 1970s for a woman to be elected to important positions in the party. After being suspended from the Labour Party in 1972 for opposing party policy on Norway's membership in the Common Market, she was asked by leaders of the Norwegian steel workers union to form the Social Democratic Party which was somewhat to the left of the Labour Party. In a paper entitled, "Which Positive Actions at This Time in History?" she recounts that, "As a condition for taking on the leadership of this small party..., I required that, if possible, women should be elected to 50% of the posts at each level of the party and that the party bylaws should guarantee that women should be elected to at least 40% of the seats."

Soon thereafter, in 1975, the Liberal Party, which had just elected its first woman leader, voted to change its bylaws so that there would always be at least 40% of "the other" sex on each committee in the party, including the Central Committee. Later that year, Äs was elected leader of a new coalition party of smaller parties and other groups which incorporated the bylaws of the former Democratic Socialists into its constitution, including the requirement that women should be elected to at least 40% of the seats. At that time, the Labour Party still considered the quota mechanism to be very mechanistic and political leaders in the other parties tended to ridicule the concept of quotas. However, the public option polls had begun to indicate that a substantial number of women were changing their preference to the two small "quota" parties because they felt uncomfortable about competing with male politicians for power and wanted the opportunity that the quota system provided to participate in the political process.

The women's favorable response to the quotas had a rapid impact on the policies of Norway's major parties and by the spring of 1976, all six parties with representatives in parliament had either a woman leader or one who championed women's rights. Thus, although the Labour Party did not adopt quotas until 1983, it did increase its emphasis on women's issues and elevated women to at least some positions of leadership. Similarly, although the Farmer's (Center) Party did not change its bylaws to mandate proportional representation by women, it did send letters to its nomination committees advising them to find women candidates for their ballots. For its part, the Christian People's Party quietly decided to nominate men and women successively on their ballots, increasing their representation of women in parliament from one to seven during the next election. And while the Conservative Party declared that the quota principle was unacceptable, its leadership was made to feel very uncomfortable when the party's Women's Association agreed to support a quota system that would entitle women to 40% of party offices. The women were defeated on this issue at the party convention because all the male members voted against them, but they ended up with a partial victory when the leader of the Conservative Women's Association was elected the vice leader of the party. [Äs, p. 9; *Policies and Strategies for Women in Norway*, p. 39.]

One Norwegian observer offered the following explanation for why the advocates of quotas were eventually able to achieve them at a time when men still dominated political life in Norway. Hege Skjeie attributed this success to the strong Norwegian tradition of acknowledging and assisting different social groups, as well as to the competitive spirit of the leadership of the various parties who believed that more women candidates would be likely to attract new voters. Thus, men were willing to reduce their proportion of seats in favor of women in the name of the greater interest of their party. The Conservative Party faced the most serious dilemma in this regard. On the one hand, party leaders felt obliged to acknowledge the demands of the Conservative Women's Federation while on the other hand they were anxious to keep young conservative men from defecting to the right-wing Progress Party, which does not acknowledge women's claim to equity.

After the leading political parties endorsed and implemented a quota system, it was almost inevitable that the concept would be incorporated into the Equal Status Act which had previously been less explicit in its call for equitable representation on political bodies. Thus, Section 21 of the act was substantially amended in 1988 to mandate at least 40% representation of both sexes on committees, boards, and councils appointed or elected by a public agency or institution. Additionally, both sexes must be represented on committees with less than four members. The Ombud who enforces the Equal Status Act is quite diligent about this provision and refuses to make exceptions simply because of allegations that no qualified men or women are available to serve. As a result of this strengthened mandate, women's representation has increased not only in elected bodies but also on the thousands of appointed committees, boards, and councils that permeate Norway's political system. However, some observers note that women are not as well represented on the most important boards, where, for example, key policies concerning economic development and wages are determined. [*Women in Norwegian Politics*, p. 15.]

Predictably, some critics—most of them male—have called the quota system undemocratic and blamed it for favoring the unqualified over the qualified, and for creating conflicts among men and women. In response, the advocates of quotas assert that they are necessary to give women a fair chance, that women are qualified although their qualifications are under-rated by men, and that the tension they may sometimes cause will eventually dissipate. [*Policies and Strategies for Women in Norway*, p. 39.]

According to a recent poll, women are considerably more likely to support the Norwegian quota system than are men, although party membership correlated more closely with support or opposition. Thus, among members of the Socialist Left Party, 100% of the women and 94% of the men supported quotas to help women obtain a more equal proportion of leading positions in their party; of Labour Party members, 84% of the women and 66% of the men supported them; of Liberal Party members, 84% of the women and 90% of the men supported them; of the Agrarian Party, 48% of the women and 28% of the men supported them; of the Christian Democratic Party, 35% of the women and 17% of the men; and of the Conservative Party, 28% of the women and 7% of the men.

Similarly, when asked if they agreed with the trend towards increased equality between women and men, 100% of the women and 92% of the men in the Socialist Left Party agreed, as did 88% of the women and 73% of the men in the Labour Party, 90% of the women and 80% of the men in the Liberal Party, 23% of the women and 22% of the men in the Agriculture Party, 65% of the women and 51% of the men in the Christian Democratic Party, and 64% of the women and 39% of the men in the Conservative Party. [*Policies and Strategies for Women in Norway*, p. 41.]

WOMEN TAKE CHARGE

Despite the fact that men are still a majority in the Norwegian government, the media nevertheless maintain that Norway has "a government of women." And compared to other countries where women are almost always a tiny minority in the political leadership, it certainly seems that way. Thus, as of 1991, Norway not only had a woman prime minister but also eight other women in a cabinet of 19 members. They include the ministers for labour and administration, agriculture, justice, fisheries, health and social affairs, trade and maritime transport, culture, and development cooperation. Moreover, Norway has several women secretaries of state in the Ministry of Foreign Affairs, the Prime Minister's Office, the Ministry of Defense, the Ministry of the Family and Consumer Affairs, the Ministry of Religious Affairs, Education and Research, the Ministry of Local Government, the Ministry of Transport and Communication, and the Ministry of Culture. [*Women and Political Power*, Inter-Parliamentary Union, p. 159.]

Although women are an especially strong presence in Norway's cabinet, they also have significant representation throughout the country's national and local governments. Thus, at the end of 1989, women were 35.7% of the members of the Storting, 40.6% of the representatives on the county councils, 31.2% on the municipal councils, 33% of the members of national boards and committees, and 36% of the members of municipal boards and committees. Additionally, Norway is the only country in the world in which three of the largest political parties have had a woman at their head. Along with the Labour Party, which until recently was headed by Prime Minister Gro Harlem Brundtland, Anne Enger Lahnstein has taken over the small but influential Centre Party that is composed primarily of farmers, and Kaci Kullman Five is the leader of the Conservatives,

Norway's main opposition party. Among them, the parties headed by these three women win the votes of 70% of the electorate.

One of the most remarkable aspects of the political ascendancy of such women as Brundtland, Lahnstein, and Five is that they have been able to maintain at least a semblance of a personal life along with a commitment to government, although the weight of the greater expectations placed upon the maternal role can create psychological stresses.[1] Thus, all three of the party leaders are mothers with a total of nine children among them. In fact, the Storting has installed a changing and nursing room to serve several political mothers with infants.

Brundtland, now leading her third national administration, is the daughter of a doctor who also served as a Labourite member of parliament and defense minister and a mother who worked in the Labour Party's parliamentary group. She consequently grew up in the thick of Labour Party politics and participated in its youth groups from the time she was seven years old. Nevertheless, Brundtland took time off from politics as a young woman to become a medical doctor with a Harvard degree and to have four children before becoming Norway's minister of the environment in 1974 at the age of 35. At the time that she became Norway's first woman prime minister in 1981, only four other women had ever held similar positions—Sirimavo Bandaranaike of Sri Lanka, Indira Gandhi of India, Golda Meir of Israel, and Margaret Thatcher of the United Kingdom. [*Women in Norwegian Politics*, p. 10.] Although Brundtland's first term as prime minister was cut short when the Conservatives won the election later that year, she has rebounded into office time and again, and in November 1990 formed her third government after the coalition of conservatives, Christian Democrats, and centrists disintegrated over the question of whether or not Norway should join the European Community, a move that Brundtland favors. She has been virtually unrivaled as the leader of Norway's largest party, and opinion polls, as well as her political resilience, testify to her widespread popularity.

Not only is Brundtland admired at home, she is also increasingly becoming an international figure. She led the "Brundtland Commission" on environment and development, an independent body initiated by the UN General Assembly. Its blunt and alarming report finally forced the issue of global responsibility onto the international agenda. Because of her record both in Norway and at the UN, Brundtland was among those mentioned as a contender for the office of UN Secretary General. [*Norway Now*, No. 4, May 1991, p. 12.]

Brundtland sees a close connection between her first career as a doctor and her subsequent one as a political leader. As she told *Time* magazine in 1989, "The doctor first tries to prevent illness, then tries to treat it if it comes. It's exactly the same as what you try to do as a politician, but with regard to society." Brundtland also reminisced about her first eight-month stint as prime minister when she sometimes felt as if all of Norway was waiting for her to fail. "In the worst times I always thought," she said, "if I get through this, it will be much better for the next woman."

In fact, she was the next woman when she returned to power in 1986, by which time her gender was less significant than the increasing problems that Norway confronted. As the country continues to grapple with hefty taxes, the collapse in the price of oil, which had previously bolstered its thriving economy, and the ongoing recession that has affected all of Europe as well as the United States, Brundtland has managed to sustain a delicate and usually successful balancing act between financial stability and social responsibility. While she capped wages, devalued the krone, and restricted consumer credit, she also kept her promise to shorten the work week to 37.5 hours, to extend paid maternity leave to 24 weeks, and generally to maintain a comprehensive safety net for Norwegian society. As she once told Gloria Steinem about her cabinet, "The fact that there are eight women around the table will influence the weight put on different aspects of human life." Brundtland also recounted with satisfaction the story of a little Norwegian girl who couldn't understand that a man she saw on television was also the head of a country. [Steinem, Gloria, "Gro Brundtland," *Ms.* magazine, January 1988, p. 75.]

In contemplating her ascendancy to Norway's highest office, Brundtland has remembered that "My parents conveyed a kind of obvious and natural atmosphere of equality. I think many girls find that they are asked to be so equal, they are not allowed to develop those feminine traits which all of us have." But when Brundtland decided that she wanted both a family and a medical career, nobody told her that she couldn't have both. After marrying and having her first child while in medical school, she nursed him between her classes. When her husband graduated a year later, he took over most of the parenting, including taking the baby to and from day care. He is now an editor and newspaper columnist with more conservative politics than his wife's.

Logically, Brundtland began her professional political career with an issue that related directly to both her family life and abortion—that is, women's right to abortion. Her outspoken lobbying in support of choice brought her public recognition in the 1970s and from then on she began to rise through the Labour Party's ranks to her present preeminent role. Brundtland's career has paralleled the successes of the Norwegian women's movement and her own rise to power has undoubtedly increased the self-confidence of other women politicians and bolstered the belief that women can be successful in politics, to the right of center as well as to the left. ["Norway's Radical Daughter," *Time*, September 25, 1989, pp. 42-44.]

Thus, when a coalition of right-wing parties took over the Norwegian government after the 1989 election, they did not reduce the number of female ministers. [*Policies and Strategies for Women in Norway,* p. 6.] In fact, the career of Kaci Kullman Five, who became the leader of Norway's Conservative Party congress in 1991, is vivid proof that women are taking power across the political spectrum. Five led the party's Young Conservative organization at the end of the 1970s, studied political science, and became a Storting representative in 1981, serving as the Conservatives' deputy leader and minister of trade in the last conservative government. Five made history when she became the first sitting member of parliament to become a mother.

Similarly, Ann Enger Lahnstein of the Centre Party does not fit the stereotype of a crusading feminist politician. A nurse and social worker by education, she began her political career by leading an anti-abortion group. Before being elected to parliament in 1985, she was leader of the Oslo branch of the Centre Party, becoming party deputy leader in 1983. She has been a leading opponent of the movement for Norway to join the European Community. [*Norway Now*, p. 12.] It has been generally true that women have a different slant and change the prevailing politics in the three areas of peace and disarmament; pollution and other ecological catastrophes; and policies to promote equal rights between men and women. However, the Norwegian political system has been so permeated by sex equity that these differences may no longer hold. Thus, both Five and Lahnstein may not differ substantially from their conservative male colleagues in regard to the issues of peace and foreign policy or the environment. However, as women who have made their way in a predominantly male arena, they are likely to stand firm on women's rights and the supports that women need to manage their simultaneous roles at home and in society.

HAS POLITICAL POWER BROUGHT THE REFORMS WOMEN WANT?

As Torild Skard has observed, "Changing the basic structures of a patriarchal society is a long and complicated process." [Skard, *International Social Science Journal*, p. 653.] And while 20 years of women in government have unquestionably helped to make Norway more responsive to women's needs and concerns, Norwegian women have not yet become equal partners in the workplace, in their own homes, or in many other aspects of their society. Thus, despite the fact that women have the same educational rights as men, at least on paper, they do not necessarily exercise them and instead tend to follow those courses of study which have traditionally been "women's field." As a result, they then enter into jobs and careers that are still largely segregated by sex. For example, among high school students pursuing an academic course of study, girls still dominate the humanities while boys are in the majority in the natural sciences and technology. Students who are in vocational training courses also tend to separate according to sex with girls training for service and caring jobs in the pink collar ghetto and boys to a great degree choosing training that will prepare them for higher-paying jobs in production. To break this pattern, which clearly dies hard, education and labor market authorities in the Norwegian government have launched various campaigns and projects to encourage girls to choose untraditional professions.[*Women's Status in Norway*, p. 8.]

At the universities where 50% of the students are women, more seem to be venturing into previously male-dominated subjects. Thus, in 1987, 50% of law students and 41% of economics students were women. Additionally, women constituted 45% of the students at the country's agricultural university and 25% at the college of technology. [*Women's Status in Norway*, p. 8.]

Once women leave school for the workforce, their roles are considerably more confined. Although women have increasingly become wage earners, they are usually relegated to more poorly paying and less prestigious areas of the labor market. A Norwegian journalist writing in *Ms.* magazine was disturbingly blunt about the problems that Norwegian women still face despite their success in political life. According to Marina Tofting, "the 1980s have been retrogressive for women's real-life rights. Women are stuck in low- and mid-level municipal and government jobs. In the media, business, industry, and banking, the traditional pyramid persists: most women at the bottom, a token few at the top. The number of female leaders in private business shows signs of decreasing. The salary gap between the sexes has increased." [Marina Tofting, "Norway: The Price We Pay," *Ms.*, January-February 1991, p. 12.]

Similarly, American Noreen Connell, formerly president of New York State NOW, who recently took a feminist tour of the Scandinavian countries, was struck not only by the power that Norwegian women have amassed in the public sector but also by their contrasting lack of representation and clout in such critical areas as the media and the corporate sector. "Almost all the reporters are men," Connell noted, "which makes the Norwegian media even more male-dominated than it is in the United States." Also, as Kris Kissman, a professor at the University of Michigan's Social Work School, has pointed out, "Business and industry have been less willing to recruit women or to take up their issues than the state." [Kris Kissman, "Women Caregivers, Women Wage Earners, Social Policy Perspectives in Norway," *Women's Studies International Forum*, Vol. 14, No. 3, 1991, p. 197.]

Most Norwegian women are employed in the lower-paid service, social and public job sector, and 47% work part-time so they can handle the tasks of caring for children and aging parents. Single mothers of children under 18 account for 7.1% of families, compared with 0.8% of single fathers. According to Marit Tovsen, senior executive officer, the Equal Status Council, women earn on average 80% of what men do, but this figure is based on those working full-time. In fact, women average 30 hours a week paid employment compared with 39 hours for men.

Norwegian women lag behind Sweden in obtaining some of the social supports they need to maintain their dual roles as wage earners and caretakers. Thus, Kissman points out, "Although reproductive policies in Norway, including child-support payments, mothers allowance benefits, child-care and parental leave, are further advanced than in the USA, they lag behind what is happening in other Scandinavian countries. In Norway municipal child-care is available for only 39% of children needing child-care as opposed to 60% in other Scandinavian countries. Parental leave policy has improved in recent years and, beginning in 1993, was to increase to 42 weeks with full pay and one year at 80% pay.

WOMEN'S WORK

Despite or perhaps because they lack adequate social supports, Norwegian women sometimes feel that between their responsibilities in the workplace and their responsibilities at home, their work is never done. Even while 73% of women between 20 and retirement age hold paying jobs, nearly 90% of all caretaking, including child care and care of the elderly, is performed by women [Kissman, *Women's Studies International Forum*, p. 194.] According to a 1990-91 study, women spend an average of 4.4 hours per day doing unpaid work, including housework and caring for their families, compared to the 2.6 hours that men allocated to those responsibilities. Even when women spent as many hours as men outside the home, they still spent twice as much time on unpaid work, with the amount of time spent on unpaid work increasing with the number of children in the household. [*Women's Status in Norway 1990*, p. 2.] Although men have taken on slightly more of these responsibilities over the past decade, women still bear an inequitable burden.

With their critical mass in their country's government, Norwegian women are trying to gain economic and social benefits that will bring their equity in the workplace and the home to a level equivalent to their considerable rights in the political arena. Still, the struggle for better child care, better income support policies, and better pension benefits for women—to name just some of the most pressing issues—is a difficult one in light of the widespread resistance to government spending that has gripped Norway and the other Nordic countries that have prided themselves on a commodious safety net. Kissman pointed to one instance of this struggle when she noted that, "The current debate in the political arena is between those who claim the need to reduce spiraling social-security expenditures, and the need voiced by feminist politicians to raise the ceiling for income-disregard for working mothers who are entering the labor force. Proposals for policy revisions, spearheaded by feminist advocates, would allow mothers to keep a higher proportion of their benefits while in the process of establishing themselves in the labor market." [Kissman, *Women's Studies International Forum*, p. 195.]

Not surprisingly, sisterly solidarity can become strained as different groups of women with various legitimate needs almost inevitably compete for larger shares of a shrinking economic pie. Thus, older women who are worried about the size of their pensions sometimes differ on political priorities with younger women who want comprehensive child-care policies, including shorter work hours, longer parental leave, and day care.

To a large extent, however, the debate over Norway's priorities tends to divide along the lines of gender. As a recent poll has indicated, men and women vary considerably in regard to what they consider to be the most important issues. Thus, 77% of the women mentioned insurance, health, and welfare for the elderly as compared to 57% of the men who are more concerned with foreign and economic policy and defense. Also, while women are more in favor of public welfare, men tend to favor private solutions to health and social problems. No wonder then that the Norwegians have a political gender gap. In 1985, a majority of women voted for socialist parties for the first time and they are continuing to move to the left while men are moving to the right. The differences between the genders also increase with decreasing age. The majority of the youngest women have voted socialist since 1965. [*Policies and Strategies for Women in Norway*, p. 44.] Basically, what Norwegian women want is not a secret—it is a "women-friendly" society which, as Tove Stang Dahl and Helga Maria Hernes point out in their article on *After Equality*, "would enable women to have a natural relationship to their children, their work, and public life . . . . The present status of feminism is thus a struggle for the redefinition of the concept of equality as much as it is the struggle for equal status between men and women, i.e., for women's inclusion in the world of men. We don't want equality at the behest of men and according to their rules." [*After Equality*, pp. 2-7.]

As far as Norwegian women have come in the last 20 years, it may be difficult for them to complete their march towards equity, at least during the next 20 years. While they may have achieved a critical mass in the political arena, they are still a long way from achieving a balance of power with men throughout the whole of Norwegian society. Some experts assert, with considerable evidence, that as women assume a commanding role in politics and in some professions, the men bail out for other arenas where the real power exists. In fact, women still do not head up any large Norwegian companies and, according to a 1987 report entitled *Scenario 2000* that was issued by a Norwegian think tank, when women move into male domains such as medicine, the priesthood and education, the men move on to higher-paid jobs with greater social status. *Scenario 2000* also asserts that politics are becoming less significant and markets more so as economics are increasingly internationalized. According to the report, "Women may be moving from a marginal minority to a marginal majority." ["Women left, right and centre," *The Economist,* March 23, 1991, p. 56.]

Still another report, discussed in *Women in Norwegian Politics*, similarly concluded that "democratically-elected organizations are in decline, benefiting the large corporate organizations, while the power of those elected by the people is diminished." [*Women in Norwegian Politics*, pp. 14-15.] Additionally, Professor Beatrice Halsa of Oppland Regional College asserts in her paper on *Policies and Strategies for Women in Norway*, "Political scientists agree that power has been transferred from parliament and municipal counties to the cabinet and bureaucracy. Power has also been transferred from the political parties to the interest organizations, primarily the big ones in the labor market." [p. 9.]

WHAT DOES IT MEAN FOR THE REST OF US?

While Norwegian women may be encountering problems as they seek to bring the equity they have achieved in the political arena to other sectors of their society, on balance, they have made significant progress in becoming first class citizens as a result of the country's Equal Status Act and other reforms intended to improve their position. But are the advances in this enlightened but small, homogeneous, and affluent nation actually relevant to women who live in other countries which are larger, poorer, have far more varied populations, and/or less democratic traditions? The answer is that the Norwegian example is important to all of us. Although it may not be an example we can follow, it is certainly one we can learn from, not just in terms of how women in Norway acquired their considerable power but also because of the problems they have encountered and the distance they still have to go. Additionally, the women in Norway's government are providing more than just a paradigm. Following in their country's humanitarian tradition, Norway's women leaders feel a responsibility to extend a helping hand to women in less developed countries.

Although the Norwegians have historically been a compassionate people, now that women are in charge of the government, its policy towards assisting developing countries has acquired a feminist twist. As *Women in Norwegian Politics* points out, "The main objective of Norwegian development aid is to contribute lasting improvements in economic, social and political conditions for the populations of developing countries. One of the main guiding principles has been that women are a priority target for Norwegian assistance." [p. 20.]

In 1985, the Norwegian government devised a strategy intended to aim Norwegian assistance more directly to women. As part of this strategy, the Ministry of Development Cooperation has developed action plans that involve researching the most urgent needs of women around the world, the contributions that are targeted to these needs by other organizations, and Norway's ability to increase its aid to women's causes.

Norway also places efforts to improve the position of women at or near the top of its agenda for international affairs, and particularly in environment and development programs, a major concern of Gro Harlem Brundtland and leading women environmentalists, such as Elin Enge. Thus, its government not only supports programs aimed at assisting women but also takes initiatives to persuade international organizations and most especially the United Nations to place more emphasis on assistance to women in their own aid programs. [*Women in Norwegian Politics*, pp. 20-21.] In fact, Norway is particularly active in the UN and its Commission on the Status of Women, encouraging that body to initiate development projects directed at women and regional conferences on women's political issues and the need for equal status. Norway is also urging the UN to make a special effort to integrate programs that help women, their families, and their struggle for equal rights into its goals for the year 2000.

Closer to home, Norway is cooperating with its Scandinavian neighbors to improve the status of and opportunities for women throughout the region. Thus, the Nordic Forum, composed of the ministers of Denmark, Finland, Iceland, Norway, Sweden, the Faroe Islands, Greenland, and Aland, has developed a Nordic Cooperation Program on equality between men and women that focuses on working conditions, social welfare and family policy, education, housing and social planning, and women's participation in politics. As part of this overall program, the Council is sponsoring an action plan for 1989-93 that emphasizes measures to increase women's role in economic development and opportunities for both women and men to combine family life with paid employment.

Additionally, through sustained advocacy and cooperation among women in politics, government, and the women's movement, the Council sponsored a major Nordic Forum in 1988 attended by 10,000 women from all of the Nordic countries. The nine-day forum featured nearly 1,500 activities, including films, plays, speakers, artists, the first Feminist Symphonic Orchestra, and a daily Forum newspaper. And it covered the spectrum of critical issues ranging from peace and security, environment and housing, women in politics and employment, to health, violence, racism, immigrant women, the new international economic order, and even athletes. Participants agreed that the diverse activities and discussions were highly successful in spreading new insights, providing new energy for old organizations and networks, and establishing new contacts among different women's groups throughout the region. [*Policies and Strategies for Women in Norway*, p. 23.]

For women in the United States, the efforts and successes of Norwegian women have special meaning. Some of us may seize on the obvious differences between the two countries, including the United States's much larger population, greater ethnic diversity, more poverty, and far more resistance to quotas, and doubt that it can happen here. However, it is also possible to stress the positive and, for example, to galvanize women throughout the various sectors of our society to run political campaigns on the imaginative and energetic Norwegian model. The dominant theme of the Norwegian success story may well be the ongoing effort among women in politics, the public sector, and the women's movement to overcome their differences for the sake of their common goals. American women are capable of doing the same.

NOTE

[1] Prime Minister Brundtland resigned as party head in 1992 following the death of her adult son.

3

Close-Up: Sweden

In the last 60 years or so Sweden has remade itself from a poor, backward, and at times even famine-ridden country into a prosperous and world-renowned welfare state that provides a secure and comforting safety net for its 8.6 million inhabitants. Perhaps more than any other nation, Sweden, a rich country about the size of California with a relatively homogeneous population, has recognized the social and emotional stresses that accompany technological development and urbanization and has attempted, with considerable success, to minimize their impact. It has thus become the world's foremost model of a democratic country that has tried to minimize inequality and to provide services that will make life more livable into the twenty-first century. To this end, Sweden's government, which was run almost continuously by the Social Democratic Party between 1932 and 1991, developed the world's most generous and most supportive social policies, including child care, family allowances, free medical care for women and children, and a universal pension system.

Additionally, in keeping with the mandate of the country's constitution that, "The community at large shall assure men and women of equal rights and protect the individual's private life and family life," the government has for the last quarter of a century been at least nominally committed to equality between men and women and has tried, through legislation, public education, and various kinds of advocacy to bring such equality closer to reality. [Sidel, Ruth, "What Is to Be Done/Lessons from Sweden," in *Women and Children Last, the Plight of Poor Women in Affluent America*, p. 176, Viking, New York 1986.]

In fact, most formal barriers to women's full participation in Swedish society have been overcome in recent years. According to Birgitta Silen, editor-in-chief of *Inside Sweden*, "In international terms, Swedish women are highly integrated into public life. Formal barriers to sexual equality have been removed. All occupations are open to women. Abortions are freely available, and there is equal pay for equal work. Women and men are equally entitled to paid leaves of absence when they have children (one parent at a time), and there is a law that bans sexual discrimination in the workplace." [Silen, Birgitta, "Women and Power," *Scandinavian Review*, Vol. 76, No. 1, Spring 1988.] Additionally, since the late 1980s, women have constituted between 30 and 40% of the members of the Swedish cabinet, parliament, and county and municipal legislative bodies.

Nevertheless, Sweden is not completely a land of equal opportunity and some striking inequities between the sexes still remain. For example, the country's job market may well be the most segregated in the Western world and women with children, nearly all of whom work at least part-time, also shoulder the lion's share of household and family responsibilities. Women have very little power where it really counts—in the boardrooms of corporations and high offices of the country's powerful labor unions—and only somewhat more on the appointed governmental boards and committees that do the most important work of the public sector. Perhaps most surprisingly in light of the real advances that Swedish women have made in the last quarter-century, the theoretical aspects of feminism have never made major inroads in the national consciousness.

How have Swedish women made so much progress without a militant, large and highly organized women's movement, like those in Norway and the United States? And why has such a movement not developed in that progressive and democratic country? The answer lies partly in Sweden's history, which reveals a strong tradition of very distinct male and female roles, great emphasis on a stable family life, recurrent fears of a shrinking population, an often thriving economy, and deeply rooted class consciousness that tends to overshadow the differences between the sexes.

FROM A POOR, AGRARIAN COUNTRY TO A MODEL WELFARE STATE

Until well into the second half of the nineteenth century, Sweden was a poor agricultural country in which husbands and fathers ruled supreme. In fact, a law passed in 1734 mandated that both married and unmarried women must be cared for by guardians and specified, "A wife's guardian was her husband, an unmarried woman's guardian was her father or brother." The law was modified in 1872 so that unmarried women came of age at 25 but married women remained permanently under the guardianship of their husbands. Not until 1921, the year that women also got the vote, did a new Marriage Code finally grant women equal legal and economic status with men.

As Ruth Sidel pointed out in her book, *Women and Children Last, the Plight of Poor Women in Affluent America,* in which she portrays Sweden as a nearly ideal society, men and women had strictly defined and very different responsibilities as long as Sweden was primarily an agricultural country. In the south of the country where men worked in the fields, women did the cooking, weaving, and other household chores and also cared for the domestic animals. In the north where men spent much of their time hunting and in the forests, the women took care of the livestock. In fact, this traditional distinction between "men's work" and "women's work" may be at least partially responsible for the persistent segregation of men and women into different sectors of the contemporary Swedish labor market. [p. 176.]

Then in 1884, at a time when women's rights were first becoming a major cause throughout the Western world, a few Swedish feminists founded the Frederika Bremer League, a women's rights organization that is still trying to increase the representation of women in party leadership and public life. Additionally, a National Association for Women's Suffrage, composed largely of women from the Social Democratic Party, was established to achieve the vote for women but it pursued its course with a minimum of protest. Eventually it tied the struggle for the women's vote to the movement for universal suffrage for men and women of all economic classes, a demand ultimately included on the agenda of the major political parties. Although the organized Swedish women's movement was relatively minimal at this time and was gradually incorporated into the mainstream political parties, Swedish women did gain certain rights during the nineteenth century, including the right to attend school, to equal inheritance, and to conduct business in their own names. [Gelb, Joyce, *Feminism and Politics: A Comparative Perspective*, p. 146, University of California Press, Berkeley, 1989.]

During the late 1890s and early 1900s, a few women's unions were also established to organize and support the growing number of women who were entering the Swedish workforce. Later, during the 1930s and 1940s, these female trade unions merged with newly created white-collar federations to form the Central Organization of Salaried Employees (TCO) and the Swedish Confederation of Professional Organizations (SACO/SR). In general, however, the Swedish labor movement, which was gaining membership and strength around the turn of the century, showed little interest in organizing women workers and maintained that men and women had "separate natures" and should assume different responsibilities. According to Yvonne Hirdman, professor of women's history at the University of Gothenburg, Sweden, "Men within the unions and the Social Democratic Party . . . were not particularly eager to have women as comrades in production. On the contrary they wanted their women to be wives and mothers at home." [Hirdman, Yvonne, *The Swedish Social Democrats and the Importance of Gender*, p. 2.] This sentiment was expressed in the popular saying that men should work in the "large household" while women were supposed to work in the "small household."

During the period 1880-1920, an influential advocate of separate roles for men and women was Ellen Key, a well-known promoter of free love, family planning, and voluntary motherhood, who maintained that the proper role for women was to create a good life in the home. In books that found a wide audience throughout Europe and in America, Ellen Key also spoke out for the rights of women, for a freer, fuller conception of spiritual and erotic love, and for making divorce a lawful way to end loveless marriages. In a book entitled *The Century of the Child*, published in 1900, Key set forth a philosophy of practical education that drew on Rousseau and Comte and took a strong stand against the common forms of brutality toward children that many still considered "character-building."

But Key was also at odds with many feminists of the period because she echoed prevailing stereotypes about masculinity and femininity and insisted that women's only true fulfillment lay in motherhood. Although she saw women as strong rather than weak, sentimental beings as they were often depicted, she repeatedly argued that they should not try to imitate men in occupations for which they were not suited by nature, nor should they shortchange their children by working outside the home. Instead, Key maintained that social reforms should make it possible for even the poorest women to devote themselves to their children rather than toil in factories or other people's homes. Her advice neatly complemented the widespread view in the socialist labor movement at this time that women's participation in the labor market was an anomaly created by the capitalist system that would be abolished under socialism. [Hirdman, p. 3.] Key also asserted that women who were childless, as she was, should use their maternal instincts and feminine talents in behalf of poor, oppressed people and world peace. Finally, however, during World War I, the fierce aggressiveness of some women in the warring nations shook Key's long-held faith in women's special talent for peacemaking (despite the growth of a strong international women's peace movement) and led her to assert that women should be free to choose their occupations. [Bok, Sissela, *Alva Myrdal, A Daughter's Memoir*, Addison-Wesley Publishing Company, Reading, Mass., p. 70.]

During the 1920s when women already composed close to a quarter of Sweden's 3.5 million-person workforce, they found themselves in an ambiguous and difficult position. Although women wanted and needed to work, they confronted considerable opposition as they took up paying jobs both because of their traditional role as homemakers and the prevalent contention that they were taking jobs away from men who needed them. In 1927 in response to the general uneasiness about the proper place of women in Swedish society, Per Albin Hansson, then chairman of the Swedish Social Democratic Party, which was quickly becoming the major force in the country's political life, wrote an article for the magazine of the Swedish Social Democratic Women's League that posed the question, "What is the use of women?" Hansson answered his own question by saying , "We have come so far that we have been able to begin furnishing the great People's Home. [The term *folkhelm* or home of the people was the common expression for the Swedish welfare state that the Social Democratic Party was in the process of creating.] It is a matter of creating comfort and well-being there, making it good and warm, bright and joyful and free. For a woman, there should not exist a more attractive calling. Perhaps she only needed to catch sight

of it, to be awakened, to come to it with all her eagerness and enthusiasm."
[Hirdman, p. 1.]

When Hansson became Sweden's prime minister in 1932, he put into practice the Swedish model of socialism which, as Sissela Bok points out in her book about her mother, Alva Myrdal, has always been democratic and reformist rather than revolutionary and less concerned about achieving public ownership of major means of production than about resolving the serious problems of unemployment, poverty, low productivity, and labor unrest. Thus, Hansson and his Social Democratic government successfully pursued the goal of improving the quality of life for Swedish citizens—men and women—and to providing the basic necessities for everyone, no matter how old, or poor, or sick they were. [Bok, p. 102.] According to Hirdman, the welfare reforms of the social democratic government of the 1930s were gifts from the social democratic state to the wives and mothers of Sweden that provided them with better houses and easier lives. But these reforms also had another purpose—they stimulated the economy by creating consumers with homes and incomes. [Hirdman, p. 7.]

ALVA MYRDAL—THE MOTHER OF SWEDISH FEMINISM

In fact, one woman, Alva Reiner Myrdal—in collaboration with her husband, economist Gunnar Myrdal—deserves a great deal of the credit for designing the Swedish welfare state and for encouraging women to make their mark on the world, as well as on their families and their homes. She also served as a shining example of the goals she advocated, going on to be the Swedish minister of disarmament, to win the Nobel Peace Prize, and to be named Sweden's most admired woman in national polls for years on end.

Born in 1902, she was the daughter of a businessman who was also a dedicated social reformer. Alva inherited his passion for equality and justice which she primarily directed towards increasing rights. As her daughter has written, Alva wanted to lead a creative life that would enable her to make important contributions to society at large, but without sacrificing the traditional feminine role of wife and mother. But Bok points out, "For such a life she had no models. It was not just that she saw most women as being restricted to domestic roles; the few well-known women she admired for having broken out of that mold led lives that seemed to her too austere, too one-sided. The great women authors and scholars, like those women who had fought for equality and liberty, had almost all been childless and usually also unmarried. For centuries many women scientists, educators, mystics, and poets had either chosen, or been forced to accept, celibacy. In her own time employed women were still routinely fired if they so much as married, let alone became pregnant." [Bok, p. 8.] As Alva herself wrote, "I wanted above everything to be myself—never to be tied to a housewifely existence that would center on a man." [Bok, p. 49.]

As a young girl, she fought for the right to continue her schooling and subsequently determined to study psychiatry so that she could become a *sjalasorjare*—a spiritual guide for souls in distress. But she had to give up that plan once she realized that no institution would provide a girl who "was only going to get married" with a scholarship for years of medical school. [Bok, p. 65.] After marrying the brilliant and ambitious Gunnar Myrdal, she went with him to the United States in 1929 where, as a Rockefeller Fellow, she studied child development and social work with children under the tutelage of noted sociologist Robert Lynd and spent a year traveling to universities, nursery schools, and child development institutes across the country. [Bok, p. 85.]

Back in Sweden in the early 1930s, Alva Myrdal's "interest in women's questions caught fire," according to her daughter. "She sought out women's organizations and began to take part in the debates about women's and children's living conditions—and in turn to a focus on housing policy, working conditions, and the promotion of better circumstances for families. And she combined her concerns for child development and greater freedom for women by setting up a course in the training of parents: 'what I think was the first course of that kind that existed' in Sweden." [Bok, p. 103.]

At around that time, she sketched plans for a collective dwelling that would "free married women for outside work, free them from the slave role in housework." Her design consisted of a large collective building with a thousand apartments, where infants would be cared for by skilled professionals in sunny, hygienic quarters away from their parents, children could play together with the most up-to-date educational equipment, parents would be free to work and pursue other interests, and an intricate system of dumb-waiters would bring food to each apartment from a central kitchen. Myrdal's utopian environment also featured collective reading rooms, sun-rooms, and athletic facilities. [Bok, p. 105.]

Increasingly, Myrdal felt a sense of solidarity with all women, including those mining families and women prison inmates with whom she spoke and worked. In January 1934 she gave a speech entitled "Education for Femininity," in which she declared that "the conventional talk about 'only a girl' stamps a girl child forever, pulls away the foundation for her self-confidence, undercuts from the earliest years her power to act, take initiatives, carry responsibility, and— yes, all those good characteristics we tend to look at as typically 'masculine.' How can we know whether women do not have these traits by nature, when education is systematically aimed at stifling them and at nurturing a deliciously feminine helplessness, shyness, mildness, etc.?" [Bok, p. 113.]

As Professor Hirdman points out, Alva "revitalized the almost forgotten Marxist interpretation of the subordination of women. She emphasized that women must integrate into society, leave the homes, educate themselves, get a job so that they could be 'real' human beings." [Hirdman, p. 8.] In articles and speeches she also spoke of all that society could and should do to lighten the burdens oppressing both women and men. She felt that individuals should increase their knowledge about parenting, new methods of child care, and family planning options but believed that people also needed broad social reforms, including good medical care and decent housing for everyone, study loans, free access to contraceptives, and child allowances.

Then, in 1934, Alva and Gunnar Myrdal wrote their seminal book, *Crisis in the Population Question*, which responded to the Swedes' widespread concern that the number of children being born had declined to 13.6 per 1,000 in 1933, down from 30 per 1,000 during much of the nineteenth century, by asserting, "The population question is going to raise a powerful political demand: that the social conditions in our country be so changed that its citizens will once again desire to bring enough children into the world to keep our people from dying out." Why should parents bring more children into the world, the Myrdals asked, as long as so many families live in dismal apartments with one room, a kitchen, and no bathroom? As long as schooling and working conditions are so poor and there is no money even for the most essential food and clothing? As long as women are forced to choose between confinement at home with their children or childlessness on the labor market? All over the country, discussion groups sprang up to debate the Myrdals' book which proposed broad social reforms to encourage families to have children. In fact, the reforms that the Myrdals proposed included practically all the benefits that came to characterize the Swedish welfare state. [Bok, pp. 117-19.]

As Professor Hirdman points out, "the success of the Myrdals in making the whole of Sweden accept a totally new interpretation of the situation was remarkable." [Hirdman, p. 9.] In the spring of 1935, only a few months after *Crisis in the Population Question* was released, the government created a Population Commission to discuss and plan for incentives to encourage population growth and invited Gunnar Myrdal to serve as a member. Not surprisingly, in light of her sex, Alva Myrdal was only asked to be a consultant even though she was at least as responsible as her husband for developing their innovative proposals for reform. [Bok, p. 127.] According to Professor Hirdman, however, the Myrdals' proposals did not have the impact the couple had intended. She maintains instead that "Their feminist solution: the comrade-marriage, where both parents worked outside the home, where homework and child care were the responsibility of society in collective forms, was too utopian, too far from reality, too threatening to the gender-ideology within the labor movement—and this was the fact both for its women and men—not to mention the other political parties. The issue of women was thus transformed to a 'social' problem, not a democratic one." Hirdman also claims that the new population policies and welfare reforms that improved the quality of life for children, mothers, and families did not free women from the demands of the home but rather led to a modern interpretation of the gender contract that underlined the separate spheres of men and women. It institutionalized married women in their homes, as "the other." [Hirdman, p. 10.]

RIGHTS FOR WORKING WOMEN

Beginning in the early 1930s, Alva became a leader of the newly formed Association for Working Women which advocated equal rights and equal pay for women. And in 1937, she helped to start and subsequently chaired the Swedish branch of the International Federation of Business and Professional Women. Through this organization, she helped bring about a change in the Swedish Civil Service so that women could no longer be dismissed because of marriage, pregnancy, or childbirth. [Bok, p. 141.] In Myrdal's own words, she and other like-minded women had to "make noise to the conservative male school teachers, make noise for equal salaries, for school lunches, for new abortion laws, for collective housing and other reforms....When banks and shops— even the cooperatives—fired women who expected babies, we in the organization threatened to boycott them. That worked right away." [Bok, p. 142.]

Although, by her own admission, Alva had for many years put her husband's and family's interests before her own, by the late 1940s when the two youngest of her three children were in their teens, she struck out on her own. Thus, in 1949, when she was asked to head the United Nations' Department of Social Affairs, headquartered in New York, she accepted the position and became the highest-placed woman in any international organization. [Bok, p. 207.] Myrdal later rationalized her own transition from supportive wife and mother to independent professional in the 1956 book, *Women's Two Lives*, which she wrote with sociologist Viola Klein. The book asserts that women in industrialized nations have time for both family and work taken consecutively because they no longer have just one lifetime at their disposal, but nearly two, measured against the life span of earlier generations, and have also acquired the liberating ability to limit the number of children they bear and care for. As a result, the book maintained, women in their forties whose children are now grown can turn to the labor market (and public life) with as long a career in front of them as young men had at the beginning of their working lives one hundred years before. The authors also expressed the hope that fathers would one day share the responsibility for housework and child care but for the time being placed the entire burden on the shoulders of mothers. Thus, they also advocated training programs for women returning to the labor market and increased employment of older persons. They spoke of the need to improve living conditions to facilitate combining the two roles of family life and work, including establishing more flexible working hours and extended maternity leave, constructing housing designed for working women, lessening the burden of shopping through better distribution of goods, providing nourishing meals in the schools, and creating a network of day nurseries and nursery schools. [Bok, p. 226.]

At this point, when Alva was in her early fifties, her own career really took off and she increasingly turned her attention to concerns that impacted on all humanity, not just women and not just Sweden. Thus, in 1955, she became

Sweden's envoy to India, Burma, and Sri Lanka and when she returned to Sweden in 1961 was elected to the Swedish parliament as part of a Social Democratic slate. During the 1960s when the Cold War was still in high gear, Myrdal focused much of her attention on attempting to minimize the threat of the nuclear build-up by the world's superpowers. And she posed the important question, "This wonderful planet that we have been given . . . should we not be capable of preserving it, guarding its peace, developing its resources to share in justice with our fellow humans?" [Bok, p. 286.] She wanted to help Sweden play a more constructive role internationally in regard to both development and disarmament issues, which she saw as inextricably linked. She believed that governments were squandering resources on armaments and preparations for war that should instead be devoted to social and economic development. [Bok, p. 287.] Because of her growing concern with the need for peace and disarmament, in 1964 she was asked to head a planning group for what, a year later, became the Stockholm International Peace Research Institute (SIPRI). She then chaired the institute during its first year. [Bok, p. 294.]

In 1967, when she was about to turn 65, Alva Myrdal joined the Swedish cabinet as the minister for disarmament, the first and only such post in the world. In response to an interviewer, she noted that she became a cabinet minister twenty-five years after her husband did. "There's not 25 years' difference in our ages, only four. Add 20 for the handicap of being a woman," she said. Ultimately, Myrdal's cabinet position encompassed three domains—disarmament and foreign aid, which she saw as intrinsically related, and church affairs because churches in various countries had become increasingly involved with disarmament and foreign aid. Through her work in SIPRI and subsequently as minister for disarmament, she traveled around the country to speak about disarmament, development and foreign aid, bringing these issues to unprecedented visibility among Swedish voters. [Bok, pp. 295-96.]

But she had hardly forgotten the issues of social welfare and equality between classes and sexes that had stirred her conscience and interest back in the 1930s. Concerned as the 1960s progressed about increasing greed, materialism and dishonesty that seemed to be infecting citizens of Sweden and other industrialized nations, as well as about some new disparities that had developed despite Sweden's comprehensive safety net of social welfare benefits, Alva suggested it was time for the Swedish government to reexamine its progress in achieving the goal of equality. When a government study group was formed in response to her suggestion, she was asked to head it. Clearly, her stature and contribution were now acknowledged to a far greater extent than they had been back in the 1930s when her husband had been the family member who was asked to serve on important committees. In 1972, the study group issued its report entitled *Towards Equality,* which recommended reforms at least as sweeping as those set forth in the Myrdals' landmark 1934 book, *Crisis in the Population Issue.* For its part, *Towards Equality* advocated a vigorous redistribution of income, social and cultural advantages, educational opportunities, and working conditions. It recommended higher family allowances for each successive child in a family, as well as paid parental leave after the birth of a child, to be divided between mothers and fathers as they saw fit. [Bok, p. 298.] Although the report's recommendations ran into considerable opposition, primarily because they were more sweeping and radical than some politicians were willing to accept, they received strong support from Sweden's progressive and far-sighted prime minister at that time, Olof Palme, and subsequently formed the basis for a second round of Swedish welfare legislation in the 1970s.

Myrdal used her next book, entitled *The Game of Disarmament,* to sound a sharp alarm about the dangerous arms race and the precarious "balance of terror" that placed all of humanity at risk. [Bok, p. 301.] In 1980, she was the first recipient of the Albert Einstein Peace Prize designed to honor each year "the person who has contributed most significantly to the prevention of nuclear war and to the strengthening of international peace." And in 1982, four years before Alva Myrdal died, she was awarded the ultimate tribute—the Nobel Peace Prize.

Late in life, she commented in an interview that women needed to agitate for a chance to unfold their personalities and to lead a richer life, while at the same time moving the family and society, men and women alike, "into a new climate, a softer climate where feelings and togetherness can find more room." [Bok, p. 330.]

THE 1960S AND 1970S—GREATER STRIDES TOWARDS EQUITY

Despite Alva Myrdal's exemplary role and the policies she helped to bring about to change the lives of women and increase their influence in Swedish society, feminism and a united women's movement have usually been viewed as confrontational and anti-Swedish in a country that prides itself on consensus and the absence of conflict. In fact, even most women who consider themselves feminists have been at least as concerned with class as they have been with gender. Thus, the women's movement that developed in Sweden in the 1960s— somewhat before feminist movements got underway elsewhere in the industrialized world—was never particularly visible or vehement and generally waged its battles for equity within the major parties and other political institutions. In fact, the National Federation of Social Democratic Women, which had been founded in the 1880s, played a crucial role in bringing the issue of sex equality to the fore during the 1960s. As early as 1960, it formed a study group that later produced a set of policy proposals regarding day care and sex role equality that was later incorporated into the 1969 party program of the Social Democratic Party. [Gelb, p. 151.]

But perhaps the contemporary Swedish women's movement can be said to have really begun when early in the 1960s a journalist named Eva Moberg sparked a national "sex-role" debate by writing a pamphlet entitled *The*

Conditional Emancipation of Women that asked why, just because the woman was the one to give birth, she also should be the one to wash the diapers and cook the meals. If all important behavioral differences between the sexes are socially determined, the debaters argued, there is no reason why all roles except childbearing should not be shared. [Scott, Hilda, "Equality Swedish Style," *Working Woman*, Nov. 1981, p. 21.]

Undoubtedly, the new interest in equality among Swedish women was perpetuated both by the spirit of activism that imbued young people throughout the industrialized world during the 1960s and the rising expectations of young Swedish women who had been raised in postwar prosperity and coeducational schools and now criticized the double morality of democracy, asserting that in spite of their formal rights, women did not really count. These activists wanted real equality on all levels of life—at work, in the family, and in politics. [Eduards, Dr. Maud Landby, "Women's Participation and Equal Opportunities Policies," *Current Sweden*, No. 369, June 1989, Svenska Institutet, Stockholm, Sweden, pp. 14-15.]

By the time of the 1968 Social Democratic Women's League (SDWL) Congress, pressure had built up to the point where women explicitly rejected so-called "freedom of choice," which they considered to be an euphemism for women's double role at home and in the workplace. (This did not have the reproductive rights connotations of the phrase as used in the United States.) In its 1970 program entitled *The Family in the Future: A Socialist Family Policy,* the SDWL clearly expressed the new demands for equality which were based on Alva Myrdal's ideas from the 1930s, as well as those of other feminists, and also placed some new demands on men whom they wanted to become equally responsible for their children. Additionally, the women called for a six-hour working day, one of the reforms Myrdal had recommended back in the 1930s, as a necessary precondition for equality between men and women.

In fact, the ongoing debate about sex roles in Sweden continued to focus on men's roles as directly related to equality for women. Additionally, many Swedish policy makers had long felt that men as well as women suffered from rigid role differentiation. While they believed that women's roles could not change unless men's roles were altered, they also thought that men would benefit from increased contact with children, a greater ability to express their feelings, and more participation in the domestic aspects of daily life. A 1968 Swedish report to the United Nations put it bluntly: "A decisive and ultimately durable improvement in the status of women cannot be attained by measures aimed at women alone." By the end of the 1960s, Sweden had become the first country in the world to put governmental weight behind the conviction that, in order to bring about equality between the sexes, men's roles as well as women's needed to be changed. [Scott, p. 21.]

In general, the trade unions, which have been the driving force behind the Social Democratic Party, the governing party for most of the past half century, and the government itself responded quickly and presumably thoroughly to the women's demands for better benefits and greater equality. It is worth remembering, however, that this rapid response and the consequent enactment of many desired reforms was less an acknowledgment of the validity of the feminists' demands and/or their political clout and more a pragmatic strategy to enable more women to participate in the rapidly expanding Swedish economy at the same time that they continued to run households and raise children. In fact, between 1950 and 1965, the period leading up to the greatest demands for social, political, and economic equity, the percentage of married women with paid jobs climbed sharply from 15-16% to almost 37%. [Eduards, *Women's Participation and Equal Opportunities Policies*, p.13.] And as Joyce Gelb has noted in her book on *Feminism and Politics: A Comparative Perspective*, "Swedish policy regarding women has been viewed as aimed at alleviating labor shortages by bringing women into the workforce, with welfare and other policies directed toward this end rather than toward women's needs and concerns *per se*." [Gelb, p. 163.] Gelb also pointed out, "Unions viewed women as an alternative preferable to continued use of immigrant labor." [Gelb, p. 157.]

RECOGNIZING WOMEN'S RIGHT TO WORK

Once the unions began to change their position on women in the workforce from their traditional ambivalence about women taking jobs away from men to an acknowledgment that women's labor was sorely needed, especially in the expanding and relatively poorly paying public sector, the labor movement began to consider women's issues and women's demands more seriously. Thus, in the 1960s the leading labor organization, LO, transformed its women's council into a Council for Family Affairs composed of six women and five men, an informal quota approach. Similarly, in 1970, the Central Organization of Salaried Employees (TCO) adopted a family policy program including day care, parental leagues, and nontraditional training and education for women to facilitate workforce participation by both parents. [Gelb, p. 157.] Also in 1970, Swedish equal opportunity policy got its start when the Liberal Party demanded that parliament pass antidiscrimination legislation. Although legislation of this kind was eventually passed, the Swedish Trade Union Confederation, the Swedish Employers' Confederation, and the Social Democratic Party were initially opposed to it because they maintained that equal opportunity issues should be settled through negotiations among the concerned parties, in the nonconfrontational Swedish tradition, instead of being regulated by the state.

By the beginning of the 1970s, the public discussion about women's issues had progressed from focusing on the appropriate roles for men and women to how a policy of equity between the sexes could be implemented, and reforms that improved women's position in Swedish society had begun to occur more and more quickly. In 1971 came one of the most important steps toward economic independence for women—separate taxation of married couples. Before that measure was enacted, both married and unmarried couples had paid taxes jointly and because of the progressive taxation system through which taxes increased along with income, women whose husbands' incomes were already counted in the assessment of their taxes had little to gain economically from going to work.

In 1972, the annual congress of the Social Democratic Party gave the party's women members cause for celebration when equal rights for women ranked high on the party's agenda and the party chairman, Prime Minister Olof Palme, declared women's right to work an inevitable principle, making the first statement of this kind within the Swedish labor movement. [Gelb, p.164.] That same year, Palme appointed an Advisory Council to the Prime Minister on Equality Between Men and Women to enhance "free personal development" and to alter sex roles and responsibilities. The council sponsored experimental efforts to place women in nontraditional jobs, to shorten the workday to six hours, and to provide "equality grants" for companies that trained women for jobs traditionally occupied by men. A parliamentary Committee on Equality, appointed in 1976, continued to work on these policies.

In 1974, the government implemented a major program of "parents' insurance" that enabled both fathers and mothers to stay home during their children's first year of life. And the next year, the Social Democratic congress approved a five-year plan to address the problems of working mothers, which featured as a first priority building day-care centers for over 100,000 children. The year after that, the government enacted the first anti-sex discrimination act, creating an equality ombudsman and calling for affirmative action, increased representation by women on public bodies, and efforts to increase recruitment of women in male-dominated positions. [Gelb, p. 164.]

During the 1970s, women also substantially increased their role in the political process. Between 1921 when Swedish women got the vote and the election of 1970, the number of women members of the Riksdag (the Swedish parliament) rose about one per year. But between 1970 and 1973, women increased their share of seats in the Riksdag by 50%, from 14 to more than 21%. During the 1970s, women also entered government jobs in significant numbers. Between 1947, when the first woman was appointed to a cabinet post, and 1973, only five women had been included in the government. Since 1976 the various governments, both socialist and nonsocialist, have had at least 25 women in their cabinets. Although women in Swedish politics have generally worked within their own parties to achieve the policies they want, nuclear power is one issue that led Swedish women to unite across party lines during the 1970s. Although the majority of voters endorsed the expansion of nuclear power in a 1980 referendum, a majority of women voted against nuclear power altogether. [Eduards, p. 3.]

Although women made many advances politically, economically, and socially during the 1960s and 1970s, they hardly achieved parity with men. As

Professor Hirdman has noted, "The demands of women could be positively met as long as they did not radically change the situation of men. What the Social Democrats actually did was to broaden society; to add women, without changing the conditions for men." [Hirdman, p. 16.]

In fact, Swedish women had good reason for calling on men to make a larger contribution to household and family chores. According to a 1976 study on Swedes at work by the Swedish Central Bureau of Statistics, in families where husband and wife were both employed full-time:

- 67% of women did all or practically all the cooking;
- 50% did all or practically all the washing up;
- 80% did all the laundry;
- 53% did all or practically all the shopping; and
- 55% did all the cleaning.

And still another survey of 7,000 women by the Committee on Equality in 1978 indicated that men spent less than half as much time as women in daily routine household tasks. [Gelb, p. 199.] Clearly, Swedish women at the end of the 1970s had a long way to go before they became truly equal to men.

THE 1980S—WOMEN GAIN GREATER POLITICAL POWER

The decade of the 1980s when women significantly increased their participation and power in the political and economic life of Sweden actually got its start a year early with the passage of the Equal Status Act of 1979 which mandated greater equity in the workplace. Additionally, in an innovative effort in 1979, women from the five major Swedish parties—the Social Democrats, the Centrists, the Communists, the Liberals, and the Moderates—joined together across party lines to demand increased representation for women in the political process. [Gelb, p. 141.] Their efforts met with considerable success and, most dramatically, with the introduction by all the parties of the 40/60 principle which signaled their intention to nominate no fewer than 40% and no more than 60% of either sex to their slates of candidates on the national, county, and municipal levels.

As Gelb pointed out in the late 1980s, "Although the structure of women's activities within the parties differ and women's issues are undoubtedly not in the forefront of party leaders' concerns, both in the Social Democratic Party and in the most centrist parties . . . , women have achieved a degree of influence . . . [and] representation of women at various levels of party organization has grown dramatically (although least at the top decision-making level). Nonetheless, virtually all the women party leaders interviewed felt that the concerns of women are often ignored and viewed as secondary by male party leaders." [Gelb, p. 149.] The Social Democratic Party has generally pursued policies to strengthen women's position in the labor market and to encourage men to take on more responsibility for their homes and children while all the parties have stressed the value of women's economic activity, improved working conditions, and a less segregated labor market.

Some parties have been especially active in recruiting and nominating women. Since the 1970s, the Center Party (which represents the country's agrarian interests) had consistently returned the most women to the Riksdag, except in 1988 when the Liberal Party had 43% women, the SDP 40%, the Green Party 45%, and the Center Party 33%. In total, women accounted for 38% of the parliament [Snyder, p. 338.] As of the late 1980s, the Center Party had the largest women's organization in Sweden, with a membership of almost 75,000. When the former foreign minister, Karin Soder, was elected head of that party in 1986, she became the first woman president of a Swedish political party. It is also worth noting that in 1972 the Liberal Party was actually the first of the parties to translate its concern for women's equality into a demand for greater female representation by requiring that a minimum of 40% women be included on all district boards and in all party bodies.

The political parties themselves and their women's organizations have proven to be relatively fertile ground for women who aspire to political office. According to one study, 40% of women M.P.s used the organizational channel provided by women's organizations to advance politically. Additionally, over half the women who became active party members were initially members of the parties' women's groups. And women also said that issues they first brought up in the parties' women's organizations were subsequently raised at meetings of the party itself. [Gelb, p. 154.] While the various political parties share the goal of nominating at least 40% women as candidates for political offices, the level of women both on their slates and actually holding office is generally a little under that level. Thus, in 1991, the Swedish cabinet was composed of 13 men and eight women or 38%, including two undersecretaries of state and ministers responsible for finance, public administration, justice, culture, education, environment, and foreign affairs. Similarly, women are about 42% of county councillors and 34% of the municipal councillors. Of the 349 members of the Swedish parliament, 34% were women as of 1991, more than double the proportion in 1971 but slightly below the 38% representation they had achieved under the SDP government before the 1991 election. Additionally, the speaker of parliament was a woman and 35% of the seats on the Standing Committees, which do most of parliament's important work, were held by women who are best represented on the committees dealing with social welfare questions, cultural affairs and social insurance—issues traditionally considered the domain of women. It is rather unclear, however, how much difference women politicians have made in advancing equity for other women. As Gelb has pointed out, "Once in office, women in government have tended to support party loyalties rather than gender concerns . . . . . Female party leaders' attitudes resemble party dictates more than feminist views, diverging as much as or more than men's attitudes on women-related issues." [Gelb, p. 156.]

While women politicians may not always let their gender determine their positions, women voters do seem to vote differently than men. Although women voters were initially more conservative, since the 1970s when revitalized feminism became a worldwide phenomenon, the gender gap has increasingly tended to favor more progressive policies and candidates. Thus, in the 1985 election, 46% of women and 41% of men voted for the Social Democratic Party. This preference may have stemmed largely from self-interest and indicates support for the public sector where most women are employed and which parties to the right of the Social Democrats are more likely to cut back. [Eduards, p. 4.] Also, in 1986, a majority of women (but not men) favored the use of quotas to increase the number of women elected to the Riksdag and opposed jobs for men first. [Gelb, p. 197.]

Even if women have achieved a relatively strong position in Sweden's directly elected bodies, men still dominate nearly all policy-making bodies that make important economic and political decisions, including political and governmental boards, committees, and panels as well as senior positions in employer and labor organizations. The percentage of women is especially low in senior management positions in the private sector. In fact, government commissions, which are composed of representatives of labor, management, the political parties, and the national government, are where the country's most powerful interests work out compromise solutions to various political problems, which they then submit to the government and parliament to enact as the law of the land. These commissions thus have a pivotal role in Swedish politics but as of 1986, women composed only about 16% of their members. [Eduards, p. 5.]

Additionally, administrative committees on the municipal level, on which women are also under-represented, have a very important role in determining policy and funding priorities for essential local services such as day care. In fact, city councillors who have nominal authority, and of whom women are a large proportion, actually have a less significant role in making these decisions than do the heads of administrative committees.

Because of the clearly inequitable representation of women on both national and local committees with important policy-making powers, both the government and parliament made efforts to correct the problem during the 1980s, beginning with the government's appointment of a commission of inquiry called the Committee on the Representation of Women. In the spring of 1987, the commission published a report entitled *Every Other Seat for Women*, which showed that only 16% of the members of state commissions and boards of government agencies were women. The study also exposed a clear pattern of decreasing numbers of women, the higher up the government hierarchy. Thus, only five of the 82 directors of government agencies and only nine of 83 chairpersons of agency boards were women, with the majority of women participating as deputies or personnel representatives. Of the bodies that nominate the members of agency boards and of committees of inquiry, the political parties had the highest percentage of women, that is, 22%. Of all representatives for the employer and employee organizations, only 11% were women.

Besides presenting such stark evidence of women's minimal role on these important committees, the report also recommended that an equal balance of the sexes be achieved on national directorates, official commissions, committees and boards not later than 1998. The first, interim objective was reaching 30% representation by women by 1992. The report noted that if these targets could not be reached on a voluntary basis, "The question of a possible legal provision should be considered," which was an allusion to potential need for formal quotas, a method of achieving sex equity which has so far not gained much support in Sweden. [Silen, Birgitta, "Women and Power," *Scandinavian Review*, Vol. 76, No. 1, Spring 1988; and *Equality Between Men and Women in Sweden*, p. 20.]

A FIVE-YEAR PLAN OF ACTION FOR EQUALITY

According to Dr. Maud Landby Eduards, a research fellow in political science at Stockholm University, *Every Other Seat for Women* highlighted the question of women's power and influence in a way that had not occurred since the suffrage movement at the beginning of the century, defining women and men as political groups, rather than just as individuals. The report quickly mobilized diverse women's organizations, including those of the political parties and unions, to join together to boost women's representation on government boards, an effort that was supported by the Ministry of Public Administration. [Eduards, "Women's Participation and Equal Opportunities Policies," p. 5.]

In response to the women's demands, in June 1988, parliament adopted a Government Bill on Equality Policy to the Mid-1990s which featured a five-year plan of action to achieve greater equality between the sexes and to increase women's influence in society, along with a reasonable appropriation to finance corrective measures. One of the goals contained in the bill reiterated the recommendation of *Every Other Seat for Women* that the representation of women on public boards be increased to 30% by 1992—a goal that was actually met a year early—and to 40% by 1994. If 30% representation was not reached by 1992, the bill directed the government to consider legislation to bring about more equal representation by men and women. The bill supported this mandate by stating, "A pre-condition of significance for equality is that women and men should share power, influence and responsibility in all fields of society. An even distribution of the sexes in various decision-making bodies is an issue crucial for democracy." [*Equality Between Men and Women in Sweden: Government Policy to the Mid-Nineties*, Summary of Government Bill 1987/88:105, Division for Equality Affairs, October 1988, p. 19.]

Of course, mandating a larger role for women in the political parties, in elective and appointive office, and on governmental bodies does not necessarily mean that women will consequently achieve a greater say in the country's economic and social affairs. In fact, some feminists maintain that when women gain an equitable role in one arena, the real power simply moves elsewhere. Thus, according to Birgitta Wistrand, president of Sweden's venerable and prestigious women's organization, the Frederika Bremer Association, "The power has moved to the trade unions, where there are few women, and to the employers where there are none. And on equality, the employers and the unions have the same point of view." [Scott, Hilda, "Equality Swedish Style," p. 22.]

It must be acknowledged, however, that Swedish legislators are making real efforts to address the inequities in their society. Thus, along with setting targets for placing more women on government boards, the Government Bill on Equality Policy to the Mid-1990s set forth a five-year plan of action that specified concrete goals for equality in various sectors of society, the dates by which these goals are to be attained, and the specific measures for achieving them. The plan covered the role of women in the economy, equality in the labor market, education, and the family and the influence of women, noting that "there are still shortcomings in several important fields:

- the labor market is sex-segregated to a high degree;
- young people choose training on traditional lines;
- men take too little part in the work of the home and in the care of their children;
- women have less power and influence."

In an effort to correct the problems that it recognized, the plan set the following goals:

- women and men are to have the same rights, obligations and opportunities in all the main fields of life;
- every individual should have a job that pays a living wage;
- men and women should share responsibility for their children and for the housework;
- both sexes should to the same extent devote themselves to political, trade-union and other matters of common interest both at work and in the community. [*Equality Between Men and Women in Sweden: Government Policy to the Mid-Nineties*, pp. 4, 6.]

While the bill has a broad scope and is more ambitious than any previous legislation designed to increase women's rights and power in Swedish society, it stops short of promising to put an end to sex discrimination and inequities, stating, "Ultimately, the success of a policy for equality between men and women depends on decisions taken by individuals; on education, occupation, the sharing of the work of the home, etc. In this sense, equality cannot be the subject of political decisions, nor should it be. The aim of all political endeavors must be to determine the framework (employment policy, tax policy, social policy, etc.) within which the individuals make their own decisions and to remove all barriers impeding equal opportunities." [*Equality Between Men and Women in Sweden: Government Policy to the Mid-Nineties*, p. 19.]

CABINET MINISTER FOR EQUALITY

In fact, no special ministry in the Swedish government is responsible for monitoring the status of women. Instead, all ministers are expected to track equality issues in the fields for which they are responsible. However, a cabinet minister for equality affairs oversees an Equality Affairs Division in the Public Administration Ministry which is responsible for developing government policy relating to equality and for coordinating equality issues and activities with the other ministries. The division also initiates projects to help women gain greater equity by, for example, breaking down sex segregation in the labor market. Additionally, a Council on Equality Issues is an advisory body to the minister for equality affairs which includes 27 representatives from women's organizations, the political parties, and the employer and employee organizations. The council meets four times a year to exchange information and discuss equality issues. The division also includes a Commission for Research on Equality Between Men and Women, established in 1983 to identify research needs and initiate and oversee research concerning women's rights. The Commission for Research, which is composed of academicians and representatives of the parliamentary parties, is also responsible for monitoring the status of women researchers and for disseminating relevant information to policy makers, planners and other interested parties.

The Office of the Equal Opportunities Ombudsman was established in 1980 to ensure compliance with the Equal Opportunities Act, which mandates measures to increase equality in the labor force and educational institutions and also attempts to promote equality between men and women in working life by, for instance, developing and distributing public information about the rights of women in the workplace. The Ombudsman's Office is an independent public agency which receives its funding from the Ministry of Public Administration. There is also an Equal Opportunities Commission which has the responsibility of ordering employers to take active measures to promote equality in the workplace when the Ombudsman considers it necessary. [*Women's Political Power*, IPU, 1992.] Moreover, when the Social Democratic government returned to power in 1982 after several years of a more conservative government, it established a Ministry for Equality and Immigration in the Department of Labour with responsibility for improving conditions for women, changing the roles of men, influencing policy, and aiding immigrant women. The ministry has provided courses in nontraditional fields and careers for young girls that will help them to break the pattern of occupational segregation. [Gelb, p. 165.]

MAI BRITT THEORIN—CARRYING MYRDAL'S LEGACY

Perhaps the Swedish politician who best exemplifies the ideals personified by Alva Myrdal—equality for women and a better world for all humanity—is Mai Britt Theorin, a 21-year member of parliament and former Swedish ambassador for disarmament. In fact, Theorin, who comes from a working-class family and was not able to go to college, worked closely with Myrdal and was her protégée.

Like Myrdal, Theorin has long been dedicated to the cause of disarmament and world peace. In a November 18, 1992, interview in New York with Mim Kelber and Nora Lapin, Theorin said that her concern with this issue began when she was a young girl during World War II and Jewish refugees from Austria and Germany were living in her home town of Gothenburg. She thus became best friends with a girl from Hamburg who taught her first-hand about the horrors of war. By the time she was 16, Theorin had found work as a secretary and joined the labor movement of which she soon became a vocal and active member, especially in behalf of women's rights and disarmament. Through her labor movement activities, Theorin became a member of the board of the Women's League of the Social Democratic Party, on which she served for 15 years.

In 1962, Theorin and her husband, with whom she eventually had four children, moved to Stockholm where four years later she was elected to the city council. Then, in 1970, she was elected to parliament, where she has remained ever since. Additionally, she was ambassador for disarmament for the Social Democratic government from 1982 to 1991, when the Social Democrats lost power, and continues as a Swedish delegate to the UN General Assembly. She headed a UN study which recommended that military-related satellites be reassigned to monitor and share global environmental data and that armies be used as environmental protection corps to monitor and repair damage to natural systems, including clean-up of war zones, military bases and surrounding areas.

Theorin credits her political education to her central involvement in the fight against nuclear weapons in Sweden during the 1960s. Following Myrdal's lead, Theorin worked tirelessly with other women in the Social Democratic Party to defeat the party's—and the nation's—male-instigated policy of acquiring a stockpile of nuclear arms. Eventually, the women were able to gain important male allies like Prime Minister Olof Palme and finally triumphed over their opponents who had hoped to enter Sweden into the potentially lethal nuclear arms race. According to Theorin, the women's victory on this critical issue was an essential component in their journey towards political equity and also gave them the experience and confidence to win a subsequent related battle—the fight against nuclear power. Theorin also initiated the formation of World Women Parliamentarians for Peace, which enlists women parliamentarians from all regions to work for peace, disarmament and human rights.

WOMEN AND THE WELFARE STATE

Sweden's social policies and benefits are the most generous and supportive in the Western world. They are especially helpful for single women who are heads of families and for all women in the labor force who would otherwise bear an even greater burden for child care and live in greater poverty than men. (To be fair, however, it should be noted that day care is probably better in France.) Nevertheless, as Gelb points out, these benefits were generally not enacted on the demands and behest of women but rather "to enhance the Swedish family, encourage population growth, and improve the functioning of the Swedish economy . . . welfare, however progressive, is not synonymous with power and the ability to shape one's own status . . . . Thus far, equality has been defined exclusively in male terms." [Gelb, pp. 174-76.]

As mentioned earlier, the Swedish welfare state got its start in the 1930s largely in response to national concern about a shrinking population and the reforms recommended in Alva and Gunnar Myrdal's influential book, *Crisis in the Population Question*. It is worth noting that although the Myrdals argued (and subsequently won) the case for government supports for families on the grounds that these incentives were necessary to increase the birth rate, it seems likely that the Myrdals' primary goal was improving the quality of life for families and especially for women. The reforms that were consequently instituted by the Social Democratic government in 1938 included free maternal and infant health care, a universal government maternity allowance, and a law preventing employers from dismissing women who married, became pregnant or gave birth. As early as 1945, Swedish women were entitled to six months' maternity leave without pay. A universal child allowance paid to mothers until their children reached age 16 followed in 1947. In subsequent decades, further reforms were implemented to narrow income differential and to increase equality between women and men at work and in family life. [Sundstrom-Feigenberg, Kajsa, "Fertility and Social Change among Women in a Stockholm Suburb," *Inside Sweden*.]

PARENTAL LEAVE AND FAMILY BENEFITS

A second spurt of welfare enhancements occurred in the 1970s when fertility rates were again especially low, at the same time that women workers were sorely needed in the rapidly expanding economy. Thus, the new social programs of this decade included a dramatic expansion of public day care facilities and substantial financial supports for families. All families, regardless of their income, began to and still receive a children's allowance for every child up to the age of 16 and up to the age of 18 if a child is still in school. Additionally, to encourage large families, a special supplement is paid for the third child and an even larger one for the fourth. Families with incomes below a certain level are also eligible for a means-tested housing allowance which one out of every three households with children received in 1983. Although two-parent households are still quite prevalent in Sweden with 81% of the children living with both parents, single-parent families receive significant government assistance if the parent without custody does not pay child support. In that case, the national government will fill the financial gap with a "maintenance advance" to the child which the delinquent parent is ultimately expected to repay. And when child support is paid but in clearly inadequate amounts, the government provides a "supplementary allowance" that the noncustodial parent is not expected to repay. [Sidel, p. 180, and *Equality Between Men and Women in Sweden.*]

Since 1974, Sweden has also assisted families with parental insurance which is financed through taxes and employers' contributions to enable either parent to remain at home for up to 12 months after the birth of a child while drawing about 90% of his or her income. In 1989, the leave time and benefit were increased to 15 months of compensation for the parent who stays at home and will be gradually extended to 18 months. The parent receives 90% of her/his pay for the first 12 months, a basic flat rate for the next three months, with the final three months unpaid. [Snyder, p. 332.] The parents can divide up the leave as they wish but both cannot stay home at the same time. They can also postpone using the leave until any time up to the child's eighth birthday. Moreover, Swedish fathers are entitled to an additional 10-day parents' allowance at the time of the baby's birth to help care for the mother and new baby or other children. Additionally, either parent may take up to 60 days of leave per child per year if the child or its regular caretaker is ill.

When the parental insurance plan was introduced in 1974 to encourage fathers to share the responsibilities of parenthood with their wives, the Social Democratic government of Olof Palme launched an advertising campaign portraying men taking care of their children. Despite an intensive campaign, however, fathers have been slow to respond. [Lamb, Michael, "Why Swedish Fathers Aren't Liberated," *Psychology Today*, October 1982, p. 74.] In 1988, one father in five took parental leave during his child's first year but he stayed home for a much shorter period—an average of 41 days—than did the mother. In fact, as of the late 1980s, only 6% of parental insurance benefit periods were claimed by fathers. [Eduards, p. 9, and Sidel, p. 181.]

"Have you met the new Swedish hero?" asked Karin Ahrland, a Liberal Party MP in the early 1980s, who chaired the parliamentary Committee on Equality between Men and Women. "He's the father who takes one month of parental leave to stay home with his new baby. The mother takes the other five," and of course there are no TV interviews for her. [Scott, p. 22.]

However, men's resistance to taking on a traditional women's responsibility is almost certainly not the only or even the major reason why fathers have been so slow to utilize the parental insurance program. While the right or need of women to stay home with their infants is rarely questioned by their employers, men seem to encounter considerable resistance from their employers and even from their fellow workers when they attempt to stay home with their babies, especially for more than a few days or weeks. Because men have not utilized the benefit sufficiently for it to have achieved its basic goal of encouraging more equal sharing of family responsibilities, there has been some discussion of the Equal Opportunities Minister apportioning parental leave according to quotas if fathers do not voluntarily increase their use of the parental leave in the near future.

Since 1979, parents of infant children have also been able to work a six-hour day, a reform which Alva Myrdal advocated in the 1930s. And since 1982, they have received supplemental pension points for looking after children in the home. [Eduards, p. 8.] Additionally, Sweden has a comprehensive and free system of maternal and child health care, including prenatal care and training for both parents for the delivery, family planning advice, well-baby care, and medical care for preschool children. Since the 1970s, health care for mothers and children has been free of charge. Abortion on demand up to 18 weeks, in consultation with a doctor, has been legal since 1975.

During the 1970s, as women entered the workforce in growing numbers, child care became an especially important component of Sweden's comprehensive social safety net and Swedish day nurseries have become among the best day-care facilities in the world. Around 60% of all children up to age six are cared for in public day care facilities such as day care centers and family day care homes.

In addition to benefits related to the country's family policy, Swedish citizens are entitled to a variety of other social insurance benefits including health insurance, sickness benefits, old-age and disability pensions, work-injury insurance, unemployment insurance, and other assistance for the elderly. In addition, "social assistance," which is comparable to public assistance or "welfare" in the United States, is available for individuals who need still more help. But only 5% of the population, most of them childless adults, receive this assistance, which amounts to only 1% of the country's expenditures for social welfare. [Sidel, p.187.] In 1987 the Swedish parliament passed a new Marriage Code that modified the Code of Succession and Inheritance to strengthen the financially weaker spouse's position upon divorce or the death of the other party. The code also contains some provisions about the property of unmarried couples and is most likely to benefit women primarily. In fact, a great many of the welfare reforms, including parental insurance, the right to six-hour work days (without compensation for lost pay) for parents of preschool children, the right to receive points in the supplementary pension system for taking care of children at home, and the strengthening of spouses' rights in the event of divorce or their partners' death, are sexually neutral. But in reality, these reforms are mainly utilized by women. They are a welcome boon to women who suffer from other inequities at home, in the workplace, and in other areas of Swedish society but they cannot in themselves be considered adequate compensation.

WOMEN IN THE WORKPLACE—OFTEN SEPARATE, SELDOM EQUAL

While the traditional role for Swedish women may well have been staying home to take care of the house and the children, the vigorous expansion of both the country's economy and its public sector after World War II created large numbers of jobs for which women were needed in the labor force. While in 1950 women accounted for 15.6% of the labor force, by 1985 the figure was up to 47% and over 84% of all Swedish women are employed, compared to 90% of the men. Married women and women with children were almost as likely to work as those who were single and without family obligations. Thus, the proportion of women who are married or living in a marriage-like situation while holding down jobs rose from 10% in the early 1940s to around 25% in the 1960s, climbing to more than 70% in 1980. [Kajsa Sundstrom-Feigenberg.] Women's participation in the workforce is still increasing, fueled largely by women with small children, at the same time that the number of working men has declined slightly due to a reduction in the retirement age. If housework is included, women with children under 18 who hold full-time jobs have a working week of 74 hours—longer than any other category of people in Sweden. [Silen.]

Unfortunately, while almost as many women as men now belong to the workforce, nearly equal participation does not translate into equal status or equal rights. In fact, although women have the legal right to be employed in all occupations including the armed forces, women's work is very different from men's work in terms of the kind of careers women pursue, the sectors of the economy that employ them, and the hours and conditions under which they are employed. They actually work in far fewer, more poorly paying occupations than do men and also tend to work fewer paid hours because they still retain responsibility for most housework and child care.

Because women in Sweden are relatively well represented in the country's political system and have better child care, health care, and pregnancy benefits than women in most other countries, it may come as a surprise to learn that the country's labor market is one of the most segregated in the industrialized world. Of the 52 occupational fields included in the Swedish government's 1990 survey of the labor force, only five had equal numbers of both sexes while 13 had at least 90% of one sex. And official statistics indicate that one-third of all working women are employed as secretaries, office clerks, nurses or cleaners. In fact, 82% of women work in sex-segregated occupations as employees of the welfare state. [Gelb, p. 43.]

It should be noted, of course, that when women entered the workforce in large numbers during the 1960s and 1970s they were not simply channeled into public sector jobs such as child care, nursing, care of the elderly, and office work because this kind of work was a logical extension of their traditional care-taking roles in the home although their relevant experience and the preconceptions about what constituted appropriate careers for women were certainly contributing factors. Additionally, the public sector which was also expanding rapidly at the same time was also where the jobs were. Because the public sector has grown to the point where it makes up almost two-thirds of the Gross National Product and employs 40% of the nation's workforce, it is also a considerably larger share of the Swedish economy than it is in most other countries. [Gelb, p. 139.]

The government has made considerable efforts over the past few years to overcome this segregation and to bring greater equity into the workplace. These efforts include bringing children into contact with technology as early as their preschool days, training teachers and vocational counselors on equality issues, and using such incentives as recruitment campaigns, vocational training, support groups, and more convenient working hours to encourage women to enter non-traditional occupations. In addition, the Work Environment Fund began a five-year program in 1988 to promote equal opportunity in the workplace.

Swedish women don't just work in different jobs than men do. They also work different hours. Thus, in 1989, 41% of employed women worked part-time in contrast to only 6% of the employed men. According to Dr. Inga Persson-Tanimura of the University of Lund, who studied the changing role of women in the workforce from an economic perspective, some 45% of women hold part-time jobs, in contrast to only 5% of men. And no fewer than 60% of women with children under the mandatory school age of seven were part-timers, compared with 3% of men. These women worked an average of 28.6 hours per week against 41.6 hours for all men aged 25-44. Ironically, in contrast to the mothers, the fathers of small children work more overtime than any other category of employees, perhaps because they are at an age and stage in their careers when they need to demonstrate their ambition and competency to qualify for subsequent promotions. But there is also an economic reason why so many Swedish women work part-time. Although the tax system was changed in the 1970s so that women's incomes are now taxed separately from their husbands', thereby enabling women to retain more of their earned income instead of giving it away in taxes, Swedish taxes are still highly progressive and minimize the advantage of full-time work. The longer women's working hours, the less their economic reward for each additional hour.

In principle at least, equal pay for equal work is the law of the land and pay differentials in Sweden are actually small compared to those in other countries, with women who work full-time earning an average of 80% of what men do. But fairness and legality are not the only reasons why the gap in earnings between men and women is relatively small. Another is the generally small spread between high- and low-earning workers in Sweden compared to other countries where corporate executives, for example, are paid salaries that totally dwarf the compensation of lower-level workers. Additionally, because so many Swedish women work part-time, total female earnings are in fact about half of men's. Women also garner a smaller share of overtime pay and bonuses for shift work.

[Gelb, p. 215.] In 1991, the government appointed a committee to study pay differentials between men and women and to propose remedies.

OMBUDSMAN ROLE

Legislation to promote equity in the Swedish workplace has existed for quite a while. The Equal Opportunities Act or the Act on Equality Between Women and Men at Work was passed in 1980 "with the purpose of promoting equal rights for women and men with regard to employment, working conditions and opportunities of development at work." The act, which is confined to groups not covered by collective agreements that take precedence when they do exist, bans gender discrimination, includes provisions for actively promoting equal opportunity, and establishes the Equal Opportunities Ombudsman and the Equal Opportunities Commission.

As noted earlier, the Office of the Equal Opportunities Ombudsman has the responsibility of ensuring compliance with the act. [Gelb, p. 165.] When the Ombudsman is unable to resolve a situation to the complainant's satisfaction, the Equal Opportunities Commission can order an employer to take specific measures to promote equality between the sexes at a workplace. The first equality ombudsman, a former judge named Inga Britt, received enthusiastic support from many Swedish women for her activism. However, her seven-person staff was hardly sufficient to their large and diverse responsibilities of taking complaints to the Labour Court, supervising employers, and molding public opinion through issuing reports and other educational materials. The ombudsman who may issue injunctions only on employment discrimination initiated by individuals, employee organizations, or by the ombudsman office itself, is constrained by the fact that many women are reluctant to make complaints in a culture that does not value aggressive individualists. Another problem is that the commission does not have the right to request documentation in discrimination cases in the private sector.

As mentioned above, workers who are covered by collective bargaining agreements between labor and management must turn to their unions rather than to government to resolve their complaint of discrimination. In fact, in 1977, the predominantly blue-collar Swedish Trade Union Confederation (LO) and the white-collar Central Organization of Salaried Employees (TCO) signed equality agreements with the Swedish Employers Confederation that covered all workers in the private workforce, banned all discrimination, called for measures to promote equality, and required discrimination cases to go before a tripartite Labour Court. But while this agreement was a theoretical victory for women and equal rights in the workplace, in practice it didn't make much difference. Thus, in the three years between the signing of the equality agreements and 1980 when an amended version went into effect, no cases went to the Labour Court under the

LO-SAF agreement, largely because women who felt that they were the victims of discrimination did not think that justice would be done under the system and also because, with some exceptions, the unions have not so far considered women's rights to be a major priority. [Gelb, p. 165.]

Although the unions officially endorse the concept of equal opportunity for women workers, to a large extent they do not practice what they preach and tend to view class differences as greater than the differences between the sexes. The National Committee on Equality Between Men and Women pointed out that "As the 1970s unfolded, women gradually increased their representation, for the most part filling lower appointive offices in the union branches and local chapters. However, their muscle-flexing has yet to make itself felt in the higher echelons. It is still more common for women to perform assignments as secretaries and treasurers, and for men to be elected chairmen and collective bargainers." [*Step by Step, National Plan of Action for Equality*, National Committee on Equality Between Men and Women, Stockholm, Sweden, 1979, p. 132.] And the pattern of female membership and male leadership did not change very much during the following decade of the 1980s. Thus, of the 2.2 million members of the LO, 43% are women but only 7% of the members of the LO's executive board are women. And of more than a million members of the TCO, 57% are women, but they account for only 18% of the TCO board. Additionally, women make up 38% of the membership of the smaller Swedish Confederation of Professional Associations but only 20% of its board.

Thus, despite the existing government and union remedies for sex discrimination in the workplace, Swedish women do not really have much recourse when they confront inequitable situations. In fact, the concept of affirmative action in employment does not exist operationally in Sweden because there is no timetable set for compliance with the Equal Opportunities Act and because the equality ombudsman cannot over-ride collective agreements and enforce compliance. Additionally, employers who do not comply with the law do not face statutory sanctions. [Gelb, p. 165.] Not surprisingly, then, the act has received a good deal of criticism from Swedish feminists over the years for being excessively cautious and ineffective. According to a former Ombudsman, the gender neutrality of the act will have to be changed to explicit support for women before it can really make a significant impact on workplace discrimination. [Eduards, p. 7.]

Although a new version of the Equal Opportunities Act that went into effect at the beginning of 1992 does not specifically favor women, it does contain a few provisions that strengthen its ability to promote equal rights with respect to employment, working conditions, and advancement at work. Sweden's five-year plan of action for equality contains the goal that at least 10 occupational fields should have even sex distribution by 1992. Whether or not that target is met, Swedish women still have a long way to go before they achieve equal opportunity and equal rights in the workplace.

EDUCATING WOMEN—AND MEN—FOR EQUALITY

Clearly, the severe segregation of the Swedish workplace does not begin the day that a woman starts her first job but much earlier in her life when she begins to prepare for her future career. Thus, it is hardly surprising that boys and girls tend to pursue quite different courses of study once they have received their early educations. In fact, both sexes receive identical educations during their nine years of compulsory schooling, with all students required to take home economics, technology, typing, textile handicrafts, woodworking, and metalwork. However, once students go on to upper secondary school, which 90% of them attend, girls tend to study nursing, humanities, and social sciences and to some extent economics and natural sciences while practically none at all go into technology, woodwork, metal work, motor engineering, or building and construction, the fields that 80% of boys pursue. [*Facts and Figures about Youth in Sweden*, 1991.]

To combat this segregation by sex, the government has been subsidizing summer courses in technology, engineering workshops, and classes in natural sciences for girls and also invites women in nontraditional occupations to speak to schoolgirls about their work. Additionally, in 1991, parliament passed legislation to reform upper secondary schooling and municipal adult education so that in the future, upper secondary schools will be organized into 16 nationally defined programs, which were partially designed to address the problem of divergent courses of study for boys and girls.

More girls than boys go on to college and about 60% of first-year students at Swedish colleges and universities are girls. However, here too, students tend to pursue sex-segregated courses of study with only 21% of the female students studying technical subjects while nursing, preschool teaching, and related subjects attract about 85% women. Women are also 55% of the law students and 43% of the medical students and about half of the students for administrative and economic professions. Although the number of women engineering students has increased greatly during the last few years, women are still only 20% of the students in this discipline. Nearly twice as many women as men graduated from college during the 1980s although most of them tend to end their educations with their undergraduate degrees. [*Women and Men in Sweden, Facts and Figures. Equality of the Sexes, 1990,* Unit for Equal Opportunity Statistics, 1990, p. 34.]

Women are only one-third of the students in postgraduate studies and also are less likely to complete their postgraduate studies, receiving only one-quarter of the Ph.D.s. And while women constitute 25% of the teachers in institutions of higher learning, they are only 15% of lecturers with Ph.D.s and 6-7% of the full professors. However, the proportion of women in all these categories, as well as among undergraduate and graduate students, has increased steadily in recent years. Moreover, women are 60% of the students in adult education courses and 45% of the students in job training programs which often lead to permanent jobs. [*Equality Between Men and Women in Sweden,* Fact Sheet on Sweden, February 1992.]

To remedy the inequities that permeate the educational system and obviously have severe ramifications for segregation in the workplace, Sweden's five-year plan to promote sex equity has the long-term goal that by 1998 neither sex should fill less than 40% of places in both upper-secondary and college courses such as social service, electro-telecommunications, and other studies in which either girls or boys have traditionally filled less than 5% of the places. The incremental goals were that by the fall of 1998 the proportion of the under-represented sex should be increased to 10% and that the under-represented sexes were to make up at least one-fifth of the students admitted to the three-year vocational programs for industrial technology and social services, with the proportion of admissions of the under-represented sex increasing as the years went by. The plan targeted women teachers, as well as students, by mandating that the proportion of women in the most senior positions in the schools must also increase. It specified that at least half of the senior appointments that become vacant in schools should be filled by female candidates as soon as possible and by 1992-93 at the latest. [*Equality Plan,* pp. 14-15.]

THE CHANGING ROLE OF MEN

As far back as the 1960s, the Swedish government had expressed its concern that men had limited their roles to the detriment of themselves and their families. But 20 years later, not too much had changed. Thus, Gelb reported that while men doubled their share of family domestic responsibilities from a minute 7% to 14% from 1974 to 1981, a 1985 survey by the equality minister indicated that sex role differentiation in the home remained marked, with women almost exclusively responsible for laundry, mending, and ironing and disproportionately involved in cooking, cleaning, and washing up and child care. For their part, men tended to engage in repair work, gardening, and car and boat maintenance. [Gelb, p. 199.] Thus, even as more and more women entered the labor force and public life, and presumably had considerably less time to devote to their homes and children, sex roles in the domestic sphere more or less remained the same.

The disturbing persistence of old habits despite the impetus for change was underscored by the finding of another survey that although younger men were more willing than older ones to honor the laws mandating equality, as well as the spirit of the law, they lacked the support of their colleagues in doing so. In response to the perpetuation of traditional male and female roles, in 1983 the minister for equal opportunities appointed a Working Party for the Role of the Male to propose ways to accelerate equality between men and women. To pursue this goal, the committee, which consisted of five women and seven men, organized seminars on such topics as the importance of the role of the father to the role of the male, men in working life, and aggression. [*The Changing Role of the Male, Summary of a Report by the Working Party for the Role of the Male,* Ministry of Labour, Sweden, 1986, p. 1.]

Stig Ahs, the committee's chairman, described the relationship between the role of the male and society as follows: "The point could perhaps be put by saying that we men are the prisoners of a system for which we ourselves are primarily responsible. A system that is not only detrimental to us as men but also postulates a role for women that renders any equality between the sexes impossible. Our male role makes us both oppressors and oppressed." [*The Changing Role of the Male,* p. 2.]

Similarly, a political adviser to the Swedish Ministry of Labor stated, "We are also convinced that men themselves have everything to gain from greater equality between the sexes. Men have a higher suicide rate than women and are more often involved in violence and accidents. They are more commonly affected by heart attacks and other stress diseases associated with the welfare society." [Sidel, pp. 177-78.]

As a result of the committee's conviction that both men and women would benefit from a change in the male role in the workplace, as well as in the home, its report asserted that "no fundamental change can be brought about in working life unless men are prepared to seek employment in the care sector and other occupations where women predominate. There is strong justification for this approach . . . . Many more men are needed in the child care sector to enable children to acquire a realistic appreciation of men and women. The old, the sick, and the handicapped would benefit from being cared for by both sexes." [*The Changing Role of the Male,* p. 13.]

At least partially as a result of the committee's report, the new Swedish Marriage Act that became law in 1987 contains such clauses as, "Spouses shall jointly care for the home and the children and promote the well-being of the family on the basis of joint consultation, . . . each spouse shall individually exercise control over his or her own property and each shall be individually answerable for his or her own debts, . . . [and] spouses shall share the expenses and the discharge of household duties." [*The Changing Role of the Male,* p. 10.]

But perhaps an even more fundamental restructuring of men's and women's roles is needed to bring about true equity in Swedish society. Thus, as Social Democrat Maj-Lis Loow stated in a debate on "Women in the Democratic Socialist Movement" held in Paris in 1988, "equality is not only about women's access to power and to working life. It is also about men's access to sectors which have previously been women's privilege . . . . In order to build an equal society, you have to have equality in decision-making." Time will tell how much of this rhetoric will eventually become reality.

SWEDEN IN THE 1990S

In 1991, Sweden finally fell in with the conservative trend that had overtaken most of the industrialized world during the last decade or so and elected its first conservative prime minister in 63 years. The new prime minister, Carl Bildt, presides over a coalition government of Moderates, Liberals, Center Party and Christian Democrats that intends to lead the country towards the right and to pare down its exemplary welfare system, a model for the entire world. But even before they lost their seemingly perpetual grip on the Swedish government, the stalwart Social Democrats had begun to dilute their traditional adherence to the social welfare in deference to the public mood which, chastened by a drop in Sweden's economic growth to close to zero, the replacement of a traditional labor shortage by rising unemployment, and the high rate of taxation, was increasingly characterized by a sense that government is playing too great a role in people's lives, a feeling of disillusionment with the ability of the state to solve all of society's problems, and serious dissatisfaction with policies that have reigned in Sweden for 50 years.

According to Anders Aslund, Sweden's leading economist, "Sweden is in a very severe recession. There is a crisis in every part of the public sector—health, education, child care, and aged care." [Kaslow, Amy, "The World from Stockholm," *Christian Science Monitor*, Oct. 22, 1991, p. 3.] And the 1990 final report of a Social Democratic study of power and democracy in Sweden, had sounded a similar note of alarm in stating, "The period of Sweden's history which is characterized by a strong public sector expansion, centralized agreements on fundamental questions through an historical compromise between labor and capital, social engineering and central planning is at an end . . . . The present change of times is characterized by individualization and internationalization." [Taylor, Robert, *The Economic Policies of Sweden's Political Parties*, Stockholm, Sweden: Svenska Institutet, June 1991, p. 3.]

Consequently, although in the 1988 election campaign, the Social Democrats had promised to increase the minimum paid vacation from five to six weeks, to guarantee all preschool children over age 18 months an opening in the municipal day care system, and to expand the parental insurance system, with its already generous benefits to employees who stay at home to care for their children, during the course of their next term in office they felt constrained to shelve these election promises and to implement a number of proposals by nonsocialist legislators. Nevertheless, the party which had designed the modern welfare state and led the country for most of the past 50 or so years was now suffering its worst electoral defeats in memory.

For their part, the Moderates and Liberals unveiled a joint economic program called "New Start for Sweden" aimed at "getting the country moving," which advocated more privatization of medical care and child care, greater economic competition, more private savings, and more individual ownership. Its concrete proposals included abolishing the employee investment funds, easing corporate taxes, privatizing state-owned companies, lowering sick pay for employees and raising employee copayments to the unemployment insurance system. Clearly, this "New Start for Sweden," much of which has been adopted as the goal of the country's new coalition government, would substantially gnaw away at the host of benefits and services that have long sustained Swedish women and their families. Of course, some of this move to austerity was virtually inevitable, given the country's economic woes.

But at the same time that the Swedish economy has been contracting and the leadership and role of the government is changing, the move towards more rights and greater equity for women appears to be going ahead. Certainly, there does not seem to be any inclination to turn back from the five-year plan of action for increasing equity between the sexes in the five areas of the economy—the labor market, education, the family, and the influence of women—which parliament passed as part of a 1988 Government Bill on Equality Policy to the Mid-1990s. The plan specified concrete goals that are to be attained by certain dates, as well as the projects, research, and other measures that should be taken to reach these goals and also allocated a substantial amount of money for various projects to further this goal. And despite the overall tendency to minimize the role of government in Swedish society, in 1991 parliament passed another equal opportunities bill that broadened and reinforced the five-year plan of action. It included the new version of the Equal Opportunities Act that was discussed above along with a plan to counteract violence against women and measures to improve conditions for women throughout Swedish society. [*Equity Between Men and Women in Sweden.*]

In fact, although the Social Democrats and their progressive politics may be on the wane, at least for the time being, it does not necessarily follow that women's political and economic rights will decline too. Although it is unlikely that the Swedes will want or need to reduce their ample safety net to any great degree, the exemplary government system of child care and health care may be to some extent replaced by private sector services which may well be more costly and less extensive. Cuts and changes such as those in services used largely by women and children are likely to have a larger negative impact on them than on men. But it should also not be assumed that members of the Conservative, Liberal, Centre, and Christian Democrat parties who have formed the governing coalition are less likely to support equity for women than the displaced Social Democratic Party. Swedish women are not likely to give up the benefits they have won, and they have the political power, numbers and determination to continue their campaigns for even greater equity.

4

Close-Up: Finland

Finland—a small country in the shadow of both the Scandinavian nations and the former Soviet Union—has been an independent republic for only 75 years. But it has a far longer tradition of women's rights. Even when Finland was largely an agrarian society, women worked alongside of men and enjoyed some, if not their fair share of power. And Finnish women have often been ahead of women in other countries in gaining their political rights. Thus, in 1906, they were second only to women in New Zealand and the first in Europe to get the vote. [*Spirit of Finland*, special issue on women in Finland, number 3, 1991, p. 2.] Then the following year, Finland was the first country in the world to elect women to parliament when as many as 19 women won seats. In 1926, Finland's first woman cabinet minister was appointed and by 1991, fully 38.5% of the members of the Finnish parliament were women, the highest percentage in the world.

HOW WOMEN GOT THEIR RIGHTS

The considerable power of Finnish women has economic roots. The country has a long tradition of women working, and not just in the home, in the fields, or in the most menial of jobs. Thus, in at least a few Finnish towns, the widows of merchants were traditionally permitted to continue the trade of their late husbands, and several women led commercial houses and workshops. In the late eighteenth century one-third of Oulu's trading houses were controlled by women and five of the 10 most prosperous commerces were in the hands of women. Women made frequent business trips to Stockholm and took part in the shipping trade together with their male colleagues.

Women were also shoemakers, tailors, butchers and dyers—to name just some of their trades—and they participated in guild activities. And women sometimes established businesses, including restaurants, inns, pubs, and coffee houses. In fact, poor widows and wives with many children were given preference for obtaining permits to sell liquor. The granting of these permits to run what were usually lucrative businesses actually became a form of social welfare for the poor because funds to assist the poor were practically nonexistent. Although women were not allowed to participate in the election of statesmen and members of the magistrate, they did have their say in the selection of less important functionaries such as inspectors and town doctors. In general, however, women had very few opportunities to participate in political decision-making. Society was eager to reap the benefits of their contribution to the economy through taxes, for example, which women with businesses paid equally with men, but it did not give them any rights in return. [*Vocation: Woman*, National Council of Women of Finland, 1988.]

Not until the second half of the nineteenth century did women began to extend their power beyond their place of work and business and to take several significant steps towards gaining social, professional, and political rights. Thus, in 1864, single women obtained majority at 25 along with the right to dispose of their earnings at 15 and to dispose of their property at 21. In 1870, women were allowed to enroll at the university. In 1887, single and divorced women and widows were allowed to vote in municipal elections on the same conditions as men. In 1882, women became eligible to teach in girls' schools. In 1897, they became eligible to practice as physicians. In 1901, they were allowed to enroll in universities and in 1916 to become university instructors.

During the mid-nineteenth century, women also began to create the social infrastructure for the state, including schools, private education, libraries, nurseries and kindergartens, children's homes and summer camps, and training in nursing and social work. These innovations eventually provided the basis for the modern Finnish welfare state and also established women's basic political role as the policy-makers and caretakers of the country's social welfare institutions. [Kuusipalo, Jaana, M. Soc. Sci, *Women's Power in the Finnish Welfare State: Obstacles and Opportunities*, University of Tampere, p. 5.]

AN EARLY ADVOCATE OF WOMEN'S RIGHTS

One of the major figures who helped women win their rights in nineteenth-century Finland was Minna Canth who lived from 1844 to 1897. A woman of great talents and energy, Canth was one of the most popular Finnish playwrights, the sole provider of a large family, a journalist, businesswoman, feminist, herald of new intellectual trends, bold champion of social reforms, and understanding supporter of literary colleagues.

In 1886, she wrote, "It is not a frivolous revolutionary desire, but the hard and difficult life of women and workers which leads them to oppose society as it is now. The reasons lie deep, and they do not want to return to the past . . . . No respect for 'status quo,' 'historical development' or 'political wisdom' can force them to suffer continuous injustice . . . so they should be given the right to participate in lawmaking and thus strive to change the circumstances and actively influence historical development." [*Vocation: Woman.*]

During this fertile period for women, the first three women's rights organizations in Finland were founded. These groups, which represented middle- and upper-class women almost exclusively, included the Finnish Women's Association, which was established in 1884; the Women's Rights League Union, which came into being in 1892; and the Finnish Women's League, which began in 1907. And Finnish women also looked beyond their own borders to link arms with suffragists in other countries. In 1888, two Finnish women, Alli Trygg and Alexandra Gripenberg, who later became the first president of the Finnish National Council, traveled to Washington, D.C. to attend the first meeting of the International Council of Women. [*Vocation: Woman.*]

In 1900, working-class women founded their own umbrella organization, the Working Women's Union, which did not join forces until a few years later with the Social Democratic Party representing working-class men. During its first years, the Working Women's Union set itself the goal of achieving universal and equal suffrage, which was also the aim of the Social Democratic Party. The middle-class women's rights movement, however, advocated the vote only for upper- and middle-class women.

HOW WOMEN WON THE VOTE

At the time that Finnish women—and working-class men—were struggling to obtain suffrage, their country was still a Grand Duchy within the Russian Imperial Empire. In fact, one reason why Finnish women were able to gain the vote at a relatively early time in history was their major role in the 1905 general strike that led the Russian czar to concede to the establishment of a representative political system in Finland. For example, women organized and presented to the committee for parliamentary reform a petition signed by 25,000 of them.

Because women had fought and suffered side by side with men in the national struggle for Finnish independence, their right to vote received more support than opposition in the Finnish senate. As Finnish author Santeri Alkio put it, "if farm-hands are now given the vote, why then should not the same be given to those who bring up our children? The moral vision of women is often higher than that of men; therefore, it must not be feared that they misuse it."

The Russian authorities did not oppose the expansion of Finnish suffrage, considering it a local issue that did not interfere with their goal of keeping

Finland as part of the Russian empire. Thus, in July 1906, Czar Nicholas II signed a bill creating a modern and democratic parliamentary system for Finland and authorizing universal suffrage. [*Vocation: Woman*, p. 16.] Nevertheless, the achievement of women's suffrage was not a total victory. In Finland, in contrast to other Nordic countries, women did not receive the right to vote in municipal elections until 1917.

Still, the right to vote in national elections carried with it some significant power. When the first unicameral parliamentary elections were held in the same year that universal suffrage was achieved, women, who were 52% of the voters, and the working class were the two new important electoral groups and ushered in a period of rapid political change. In the first democratic elections in 1907, 19 women MPs were elected—nine of them from the Social Democratic Party and 10 from the middle-class parties. In fact, many of these first women MPs were activists in the middle-class women's rights movement and/or in the working-class women's movement. [Kuusipalo, *Women's Power in the Finnish Welfare State: Obstacles and Opportunities*, p. 5.]

FINLAND'S FIRST WOMAN CABINET MEMBER

In 1926, Finland got its first woman cabinet minister when the Social Democratic Party formed a new government and Prime Minister Vaino Tanner chose Miina Sillanpaa for the post of assistant minister of social affairs. Sillanpaa is a historic figure in the struggle of Finnish women for equality. A poor crofter's daughter and former maid, Sillanpaa was a founding member of one of the first women's craft unions and helped to found the Working Women's Union. She was very active in the Finnish suffragist movement and in 1906 was one of the women elected to Finland's first democratic parliament. Sillanpaa, who remained in parliament for almost 40 years, concentrated her political work in three main areas: domestic politics, domestic servants' working conditions, and the welfare of unmarried mothers and their children. [Kuusipalo, Jaana, "Finnish Women in Top-Level Politics," published in *Finnish 'undemocracy': Essays on Gender and Politics*, Karanen, Marja (ed.), Finnish Political Science Association, Jyvaskyla, 1990, p. 3.]

FINNISH WOMEN IN THE MODERN ERA

World War II was a period of transition for Finnish women. During the war women had most of the responsibility for farming and industrial production, as well as public life, and their assumption of these traditionally male roles broke down the long-time division of labor between the sexes. Thus, by the end of the war, women composed more than one-half of the industrial labor force.

Moreover, unlike women in most other countries who were forced to retreat to the kitchen when the men came home from the front, Finnish women kept their jobs during the rapid postwar industrialization of the country.

Not only did women remain employed during peacetime, they also found themselves in increasingly strong positions in the country's unions and political parties as a result of their essential role in both the workforce and public life during the war. The women of the Agrarian Party were soon able to found a women's section despite the longtime opposition of the party's male leaders. Women's sections were also formed in the new Finnish People's Democratic League which included the Communist Party and Liberal Party. These women's sections played a major role in encouraging women to go to the polls and in demanding the inclusion of more women in government. Largely due to their efforts, the number of women voters increased after the war. Similarly, in 1948 the proportion of women in parliament rose from 9.5%, which was already higher than in any other Nordic country, to 12%.

Also in 1948, the first woman cabinet member was appointed since Miina Sillanpaa had been named in 1926. This new appointment was related to a real surge in women's representation in the Finnish government in the postwar period. In fact, for the first time, women were represented in cabinet posts with some frequency although only one or two women served at the same time. During the 1950s and 1960s, hundreds and thousands of Finns moved from the country to the cities as industrialization and economic growth commanded the nation's energies. At the same time, a new welfare state was created, providing both social services and jobs. Even though most Finnish women were already employed outside the home, during the 1950s and 1960s, Finns, like other Scandinavians, entered into a heated policy debate about the proper roles for women in both the home and the workplace. It was not until the late 1960s that equality between the sexes was taken seriously on the national level.

HELVI SIPILÄ—A FINNISH AND A WORLD LEADER

Helvi Sipilä, born in 1915 to a prosperous Finnish family, seemed destined for prominence from the very beginning. The midwife at the hospital where Helvi was born told her mother, "Your child will be a leader. When she begins to cry, all the other babies cry and when she stops, they do too." [Sipilä, Helvi,*Woman at the Top of the World*, edited by Irma Kuntuu, Keuruu, Finland: The Otava Publishing Company, 1979, pp. 7-8.]

Sipilä quickly fulfilled the midwife's prophecy by becoming at age 24 only the 38th woman in Finland to be a lawyer. She then embarked on a distinguished career at the same time that she found time to marry and have four children. Between 1954 and 1956, Sipilä was chairwoman of the National Federation of Women Lawyers and she also became president of the International Federation of Women Lawyers, a leader of the Girl Scouts and Girl Guides, and a founder of the Finnish Refugee Council in 1965.

One of Sipilä's most significant roles in facilitating equity for women was as president from 1967 to 1972 of the National Council of Women of Finland (NCWF), which coordinates the activities of the women's organizations and works to improve the status of women. As NCWF president, Sipilä wrote in 1968, "Our target is an increased participation of the Finnish woman in the life and function of society in accordance with her true capacities." She was also instrumental in shaping the NCWF's assertive program for the 1970s which advocated that "Questions concerning the employment of women should be dealt with in such a way . . . as to focus special attention on problems arising from the participation in work of women and especially of mothers, and when decisions are made, experts in these problems should be among the decision-makers." The NCWF also urged that "Women should be given leadership training according to their capacities, and also provided with real possibilities to put this training to use."

In the 1960s, Sipilä began to use her skills and talents on an international level. She was Finland's delegate to the United Nations Commission on the Status of Women from 1960 to 1968 and again in 1971. In 1963-66, she was vice-chair and in 1967, chair of this commission. She was also the UN's special ambassador for Family Planning and the Status of Women. In 1966-67, Sipilä was a member of the Finnish delegation to the UN General Assembly. In 1972, she achieved her highest post when she was appointed assistant secretary-general of the United Nations, the first woman ever to have held this office. Then in 1975, Sipilä became secretary-general of both the UN International Women's Year and the United Nations Conference on Women, the first of three international women's conferences in what became known as the UN Decade of Women.

In her United Nations positions, Sipilä continued to advocate a greater role and increased equity for women. In one major speech she asserted, "If there is no improvement in the status of women, there can be no amelioration of any conditions, even during the lifetime of the next generation. The development of society as a whole is dependent on the quality of the status of its women." [Sipilä, *Woman at the Top of the World*, p. 38.] And in an address to the National Women's Conference in Houston, Texas, on November 19, 1977, she stressed the need for women's leadership in solving international problems in an interdependent world. "The quality of life of all people and the future of humanity depend on the action of hundreds of millions of women," she said. [*The Spirit of Houston*, The First National Women's Conference, Government Printing Office, Washington, D.C., 1978.]

FINNISH WOMEN DEMAND THEIR RIGHTS

In the late 1960s, Finnish women came together to form an organization called Yhdistys (Association) 9 to advocate policies addressing the double burden faced by the increasing numbers of working mothers—women whose work was never done. Yhdistys 9 called for equality for women both in the workplace and in regard to childcare, housework, and other traditionally women's work in the home. The women's section of the Social Democratic Party was also concerned about the status and rights of women and consequently urged the party to form a committee to study women's position. As a result of the committee's work, equal rights for women became government policy with responsibility for implementation given to the Council for Equality Between Men and Women, which was established in 1972. [Sipilä, *Woman at the Top of the World*, p. 7.]

During the early 1970s, Finnish women increased their political and economic power significantly, largely because the Finnish welfare state was developing rapidly and the public sector was growing accordingly. Women thus entered many of the resulting new jobs in health, education, and social welfare and also achieved more cabinet-level positions. Ironically, however, at least some Finnish feminists believe that as women gained more access to power during the 1970s, they gradually lessened their commitment to women's causes and tended to follow the lead of the men in their parties who appointed or could appoint them to high-level positions, including a place in the Finnish cabinet. As Jaana Kuusipalo, a social scientist at the University of Tampere, has pointed out, between the 1940s and the 1960s, the women's sections of political parties had a major role in determining which women would become candidates for governments. But Kuusipalo maintains that "when the significance of the women's sections of political parties diminished in the 1960s and 1970s as the main channel for women's political careers and women began to be recruited into politics through mixed bodies of political parties, it has been the male-dominated leading bodies of political parties which have chosen the suitable women ministers." [Kuusipalo, *Women's Power in the Finnish Welfare State: Obstacles and Opportunities*, p. 2.]

Moreover, feminists maintain that since the late 1960s, the role of the government has been diminished due to the growing importance of informal negotiations on political decision-making among the staff of central government, some top politicians, and the representatives of unions and other interest groups. Because of the increasing prevalence of this kind of political-administrative decision-making, called corporativism, Kuusipalo points out that "the more women were elected or recruited in political bodies, the less important these organs seemed to become in the changing structure."

The cooperation between labor market organizations and the government was institutionalized in 1968 when they signed the first incomes policy agreement. And it has even been argued that employer and labor organizations have actually usurped the legislative power of parliament because of both the comprehensive nature of incomes policy agreements and the increased participation of these organizations in preparing and planning future social and economic policy and legislation. In fact, the last 25 years have been marked by a high degree of consensus among the major coalition parties, the political opposition which was usually the Conservatives, the labor market organizations, and the government bureaucracy concerning Finland's basic direction. [Kuusipalo, *Women's Power in the Finnish Welfare State: Obstacles and Opportunities*, p. 9.]

LEGISLATING EQUALITY

While women may have lost power in some arenas over the past 20 or 25 years, they have also seen at least some of their rights institutionalized during the same period of time. As mentioned earlier, the Council for Equality, established in 1972, is a permanent government advisory council that:
• promotes equality between men and women;
• draws up reforms to further equality in the labor market and in regard to government;
• draws up proposals to develop legislation and regulations to promote equality;
• originates and furthers research, education, and training in the field of equality;
• promotes women's studies; and
• promotes international cooperation in regard to equality.

The council has a chairperson who is a member of parliament and a vice-chair who is also an MP, in addition to 11 members, each with a personal deputy. The members proportionately represent all the major political parties and therefore a cross-section of parliamentary opinion. Members are appointed by the Council of State for three-year terms. The council is linked to the Ministry of Social Affairs and Health and supported by an annual grant. [pamphlet issued by Council for Equality.]

In recent years, the council has focused most of its work on implementing economic equality with the aim of coming as close as possible to pay parity by 1994. This goal is necessitated by the reality that although Finnish women are more highly educated than men and generally hold full-time jobs, they are paid only three-quarters of the wages that men receive. The council also intends to broaden the scope of women's influence and participation, which is still narrower than men's. To these ends, the council is cooperating with labor market, political, and women's organizations, as well as with municipal equality committees and various other government bodies.

The council includes the following subcommittees:
• a research subcommittee that is its expert body on women's studies, equality studies, and research policy;

- a subcommittee concerned with violence against women that will make proposals for action to address the problem; and
- a subcommittee that is examining ways in which men could become involved with equality issues and sponsoring research in this issue.

Moreover, the council publishes a newsletter on women's studies, along with reports, brochures and information sheets that are published by the Ministry of Social Affairs and Health.

In 1987, the Equality Act was passed, largely due to the efforts of the Council on Equality. The law prohibits discrimination by sex, race, nationality, ethnic origin, and religion in general and in working life in particular and requires the government as well as private employers to promote equality. Its goals are to prevent discrimination on the basis of sex, to promote equality between women and men, and, for this purpose, to improve the status of women—particularly in working life. The act does not apply to religion, relationships between family members, or other personal relationships. An equality ombudsperson supervises compliance with the act while an Equality Board deals with cases of noncompliance and advises courts on compensation. It also has the power to prohibit discriminatory practice under penalty of a fine. Additionally, the office of the Ombudsperson is investigating sexual harassment in the workplace. The services of both the ombudsperson and the Equality Board are free. A year after the Equality Act was passed, it was amended to require that each sex should be represented on government committees and municipal bodies by at least 40% of the members. [Snyder, *European Women's Almanac*, pp. 97, 109.]

FINNISH WOMEN LEAD IN PARLIAMENTARY REPRESENTATION

At least to some extent, equality for Finnish women exists in reality as well as in theory. Thus, as of 1991, there were more women in the Finish parliament than anywhere else in the world. Of 200 newly elected MPs, 77 (up 14) or 38.5% were women, the highest percentage anywhere. Additionally, in the new right-wing government, composed of the Center, Coalition (Conservative), and Swedish People's parties and the Christian League of Finland, which was formed in March 1991, seven of the 17 ministers or 41% were women. [*Spirit of Finland*, p. 3.]

The fact that women made such political gains at a time when the government turned right is a clear indication that greater political representation for women is not a left-wing phenomenon in Finland. Indeed, perhaps the most significant result of the 1991 election was that the Social Democratic Party, which had been the leading party in government politics since 1966, lost its leading role, along with 93,000 votes and eight seats. However, the National Coalition Party (Conservative Party) suffered an even greater defeat, losing 141,000 votes and 13 seats. The indisputable winner was the Finnish Center Party, which won 168,000 additional votes and 15 more seats. [Hailo, Martti, *Finland's Parliamentary Elections in 1991* .]

The record-breaking representation for women in Finland's new government made headlines around the world. Thus, *The European* for March 22-24, 1991, noted in an article entitled "Finland Votes for Petticoat Power" that "the dramatic swing in Finland's general election last week which ousted the Social Democratic Party from power after 25 years has led to humourists dubbing the country Amazonia."

FINLAND'S WOMEN MINISTERS

The seven history-making women named to the 17-member Finnish cabinet led by Prime Minister Esko Tapani Aho included:
• Eeva Maija Kaarina Kuuskoski, minister of social affairs and health;
• Marta Elisabieth Rehn, minister of defense;
• Pirkko Hannele Pokka, minister of justice;
• Riita Maria Uosukainen, minister of education;
• Tytti Maria Isohookana-Asunmaa, minister of cultural affairs;
• Sirpa Maria Pietikainen, minister of the environment; and
• Pirjo Maija Rusanen, minister of housing.

In this connection, it should be explained that in the Finnish administrative system, each ministry is headed by either one or two ministers whose function is political, not administrative. Each ministry also has a secretary general who is responsible for continuity as ministers change. The secretaries general have always been men. [Kuusipalo, *Women's Power in the Finnish Welfare State: Obstacles and Opportunities*, p. 10.]

THE QUEEN OF THE POLLS

Perhaps the stellar member of Finland's historic new cabinet is Eeva Kuuskoski, a pediatrician who represents the Turku constituency in southwestern Finland and is considered to be one of the strongest candidates for the Center Party in the 1994 presidential election. In 1991, Kuuskoski was the first minister ever to give birth while in office. She had previously served as first minister of social affairs and health from 1983 to 1987. Although Kuuskoski was interested in politics since she was a child, she only became politically active when she became a student. Kuuskoski was elected to the Turku City Council in 1977 and to parliament in 1979. In 1980, Kuuskoski moved to the Center Party from the Conservative Party because, as she put it, "People do not only have economic needs—they also have cultural and social needs. To my mind, we have to take the whole person into consideration."

Kuuskoski is proud of the support that the Finnish welfare state provides for women. She has said, "The framework created by society, such as daycare and school meals, makes it possible for Finnish women to move forward in a job or a career." But she maintains that "there is still much more to be done . . . . We should have a wide range of alternatives for the family because children should be a joint concern. The father is just as important as the mother."

Kuuskoski lamented that "dialogue with men seems not to be working too well . . . . The work women do is not valued to the extent it should be . . . . The working day for women is already far too long—and men should be taking more responsibility in the home . . . . In politics, too, it is often a question of attitudes. What is a man's and what a woman's role? Surprisingly often, expertise is tied to gender, where women are experts in soft areas such as social and cultural economic matters and men are the economic and financial experts." [*Spirit of Finland*, p. 4.]

In fact, the Council for Equality Between Men and Women has pointed out: "In politics women have mostly pursued social policy issues. They have put forward more proposals than men on matters pertaining to human safety and security, special social groups and minorities, and environmental protection." ["The Council for Equality Between Men and Women," *A Woman in Finland*, p. 8.]

BARRIERS STILL CONFRONT WOMEN IN POLITICS

While there are now more women than ever before in Finland's current government, most are still taking traditional roles. Thus, Kuusipalo noted in her article entitled *Women's Power in the Finnish Welfare State: Obstacles and Opportunities* that "Between the years 1926-1991 a woman has been appointed in the national government 63 times, but 46 of those appointments have been to the head of either the ministry of social affairs or the ministry of education . . . . Recently the woman at the head of the office of the ministry of national defense received also the functions concerning equality politics so she is also a 'ministry of equality.'" [Kuusipalo, *Women's Power in the Finnish Welfare State: Obstacles and Opportunities*, p. 1.] It should also be noted that most of Finland's women ministers have been members of the main coalition parties, primarily the Social Democratic Party and Center Party.

Additionally, Kuusipalo has pointed out: "Alliances between women politicians are extremely important in the countries like Finland, where there are so many political parties (now 17) and quite sharp political cleavages (class conflict, rural-urban confrontation, language and other minorities, etc.). But in Finland, as perhaps in other countries too, women's abilities to build alliances in the political arena are much more difficult the higher up they are in the hierarchy. In the level of the government [the cabinet], women are strongly committed to the politics of their representative party." [Kuusipalo, p. 3.]

Women are even required to follow the party in regard to issues with women's position in society. For example, during a controversy over Finland's day care, the Social Democrats demanded more communal day care centers while the Center Party suggested that women stay home and even receive wages for doing so. The two women ministers of social affairs represented the Social Democratic and the Center parties, and their negotiations over daycare systems were seen as a personal fight between the two of them. In fact, during the 1970s and 1980s, newspapers depicted these women ministers as two quarreling old women. One woman minister remarked that, in contrast, when two male ministers from different parties argue over a political question, their differences are not considered to have personal overtones.

Kuusipalo also noted that the difficulties Finnish women politicians have in building alliances across party lines may be deeply rooted in the past. In fact, it has been argued that in Finland, women's economic and social class has been more important than their gender in explaining their political positions. This phenomenon has been called "hierarchical sisterhood"—sisterhood being split by class differences. In some cases, however, women politicians—at least those belonging to workers' and agrarian parties—have represented both their class and gender interests. Thus, Kuusipalo pointed out that the women ministers from the Center (Agrarian) Party, which represents rural people, considered themselves representatives of rural women, and women ministers from the Social Democratic Party regarded themselves as representatives of working-class women although this clear connection between politicians and their constituencies became less clear during the 1970s and 1980s.

AN END TO SAUNA DIPLOMACY?

One Finnish tradition not consistent with the emerging prominence of women in government is the use of the sauna as a place to conduct important business. The Finnish theory is that taking one's clothes off strips away pretentiousness while the steam in a sauna melts away anger and helps people to reach compromises. Finns have long said the steam bath was the secret weapon of their diplomacy and business life, and important meetings inevitably ended in the sauna. But while the Finnish government's weekly cabinet meeting used to conclude with a group sauna, that tradition had to change when women became ministers in significant numbers because men and women do not steam up together unless they are members of the same family. Consequently, the cabinet's sauna session is now optional. "It has become a bit more informal," says Perti Salolainen, the male foreign trade minister, "and not everyone goes."

Nevertheless, in many parts of the Finnish public and private sectors, the sauna still functions as a kind of old boys network. And many women complain that too much wheeling and dealing is done in saunas—by men-only groups. [*The Economist,* January 9, 1988.]

The wheeling and dealing that goes on in the all-male saunas is only one example of the disproportionate power that men still have in Finland. Women are usually absent from the most important positions and networks where critical political decision-making seems to take place. One significant instance of women's lack of power in corporations, labor unions, and even the highest reaches of government is the composition of the Finnish delegation negotiating Finland's position in the European Common Market. It consists of six men and only one woman who functions as the secretary. [Kuusipalo.] Additionally, only two of the 23 members of the Finnish supreme court are women (8.7%) and only three of 55 ambassadors (5.5%). [Snyder, *The European Women's Almanac,* p. 109.]

WOMEN IN THE WORKFORCE

The role of women in the Finnish economy parallels quite clearly the role they have in politics. That is, in both spheres women are well represented in numbers but lack their fair share of power. In fact, at 48%, women make up almost half the Finnish labor force, one of the largest shares of the workforce of women anywhere in the world. Not surprisingly, however, women earn considerably less than men—an average of 78% for doing the same job as a man even though equal pay for work of equal worth is mandated by the Equality Act. It should also be noted that only 11% of women in Finland work part-time in contrast to other Scandinavian countries where more than a third of the women have part-time jobs. [*Vocation: Woman*, a publication of the National Council of Women of Finland, p. 34.]

Women workers often find themselves in the Finnish equivalent of the United States' "pink collar ghetto." Half of all women workers are junior office staff. Women constitute 72% of junior office staff, 40% of senior office staff and 20% of the managers, 26% in production, research and planning, 59% of teachers and 60% of doctors. [*Spirit of Finland*, p. 11.]

As *Vocation: Woman* points out, "The division of labor in the society as a whole is gender-based. There are distinct areas of men's or women's work. Only a small minority of occupations include both women and men to an approximately even proportion. Moreover, this segregation into men's and women's jobs is a persistent phenomenon: the situation has remained practically the same during the past thirty years. And no wonder since vocational education in Finland is also strongly segregated by gender, preparing, for example, women for health care services and clerical jobs, men for science and technical jobs."

In general, men hold the positions of leadership as well as receive higher wages or salaries, even when women have had more education in the same occupational category. In the trade union movement, as well, women seem to form the grassroots support while men are competing for the leadership positions. [*Vocation: Woman*, p. 7.]

Certain professions, such as those in the corporate world, have few women in other than clerical positions. Sirkka Hamalainen, a director at the Bank of Finland, noted: "Although in the banking world, women have been able to move forward in their careers, there are still too few of them in leading positions compared to the large number of women working in banks."

Hamalainen went on to say, "for example, in negotiations, ideas and proposals put forward by women are not heeded but the same things suggested by a man are listened to. Men have clubs, hunting societies, fraternities, etc. To my mind, various networks would be just as important for women. Information flows very unofficially and familiarity facilitates the whole process."

Hamalainen attributed much of the disproportionate power of men to the fact that, "When their children are small, men can easily overtake women in their career development. How quickly a woman progresses in her career depends to a large extent on how the husband divides his time. Younger, highly educated men seem to be able to divide their time between work and the home. It is encouraging to see that young men are increasingly taking paternity leave on the birth of a child. Well-balanced children are the responsibilities of both parents." [*Spirit of Finland*, p. 5.]

WOMEN AND EDUCATION

The fact that the wage difference between men and women is wider in Finland than in other Nordic countries is especially inequitable considering that for a number of years, the average level of education for women and men has been more or less the same. Currently, young women have a higher level of education than do men of the same age. Since the beginning of the 1980s, more than half of all students at universities and high schools have been women.

Some observers are hopeful that although women still tend to study social sciences and to prepare for the helping professions, more and more of them are beginning to venture into new, traditionally male areas. For example, although the fields of science and technology are still largely dominated by men, the number of women studying in technical colleges and universities has gradually increased so that they now constitute about 20% of the students. Most of the women students study chemistry with far fewer concentrating in electrical or mechanical engineering. [*Spirit of Finland*, p. 7.]

SOCIAL WELFARE AND FINNISH WOMEN

Like women in other Nordic countries, Finnish women and their families enjoy social welfare benefits that could turn their American counterparts green with envy. Thus, in Finland, parental leave lasts about 11 months and fathers increasingly take from one to two weeks' leave after the baby is born. The parents can also agree between themselves that the mother should go back to work and the father look after the baby for the last 170 days of parental leave. The amount of salary paid during parental leave depends on the parents' gross earnings. Mothers also have the right to stay home with their children until they are three years old without losing their jobs although women with higher educations rarely stay home that long.

Almost all Finnish women, regardless of their economic or social background, use free pre- and postnatal services provided by maternity clinics. Children also receive free health care from the maternity clinics until they reach school age at which time they are eligible for free health care and the services of a school nurse, doctor, and dentist. Additionally, as an incentive to increase the birth rate, the state pays families a child benefit of about FIM 300 a month (about US$55) for each child until the age of 17 regardless of the parents' income. As the size of the family increases, so does the amount paid out for each child.

The state provides daycare for all children under three. If there is no room for a child in a municipal day-care center, the mother receives a home-care allowance of about FIM 1500 (approx. US$275), which she can use either to remain at home to care for the child herself or to pay for daycare in a private center. [*Spirit of Finland*, p. 6.]

Yet despite the support that the Finnish government provides to women with children, their burden is not necessarily an easy or an equitable one. Although Finnish men and women seem to share their housework more equally than do their counterparts in most other countries, women still do far more than their fair share. [*Vocation: Woman*, p. 7.] Thus, in regard to their responsibility for their children and their homes, as well as in political life and in the workplace, women in Finland have made notable, even historic, strides towards equity but they have not yet been able to go the full distance.

5

Close-Up: Denmark

When many foreigners think of Denmark, their first image is of a country swamped in pornography, the result of liberalization of laws in 1967. The Danish government's laissez-faire attitude has actually led to decreased consumption of pornography among Danes. It has, however, created a flourishing pornography market for tourists from all over the world.

One might think that a country serving this function would have a negative attitude toward women, resulting in a general lack of political and social standing. This is clearly not the case. Danish women enjoy a social system that is one of the most advanced in the world in terms of legislation on health care, child care, employment and economic rights for women. They also have one of the highest participation rates (33%, as of this writing) in their parliament, which is called the "Folketing." In addition, four of the 19 cabinet ministers are women.

The advanced social legislation and relatively large participation of women in electoral politics raise several questions: (1) What is the relationship between the advanced social legislation and the participation of women in politics? (2) Do women have power as a women's bloc in the Folketing? and (3) What mechanisms have been used to win such a comparatively large percentage of parliamentary seats for women, and will the percentage continue to grow and lead to an equal share of political power? This chapter seeks to provide some insights on these questions by describing the history of the Danish women's movement, social and political legislation for women, the Danish electoral system and women's issues today.

HISTORY OF THE WOMEN'S MOVEMENT

The Danish women's movement can be said to have begun in 1850, when Mathilde Fibiger's book, *The Emancipation of Women*, was published. Written when the author was only nineteen years old and employed as a governess, the book created a tremendous public debate, and Fibiger was subjected to ridicule and persecution. But her book has been credited with influencing passage of a law in 1857 allowing unmarried women to manage their own affairs without a male guardian and making sons and daughters equal heirs.

At the time, obviously, women did not have the right to vote. The Danish constitution guaranteed universal suffrage, with the exception of "servants, women, criminals and children." The National Council of Women in Denmark (DKN) was founded in 1899, with suffrage for women listed first on its agenda. The male leadership of the Social Democratic Party also joined in the fight for women's suffrage. In 1908, suffrage was granted in the municipal elections, and when Danish women finally won full voting rights in 1915, 12,000 women took part in a victory march. The Social Democrats held a separate victory rally. DKN did not dissolve after its victory, but continued as a vital force in the political arena. Today it remains active as an umbrella group for 43 organizations with a total of 1.3 million members. The member organizations include women's groups, the equal status committees of the various political parties, trade unions, professional women's groups within male-dominated professions, women's studies researchers, youth groups, and religious and humanitarian women's organizations. DKN has seats on a number of governmental committees, including the Danish Equal Status Council and the Danish delegation to the United Nations.

Women's political victories began in 1918 when nine women were elected to what was then a bicameral parliament. From 1918 to 1939, women made up between 2.1 and 3.9% of the lower chamber. From 1940 to 1970, their representation rose steadily to 11.8% of the new single-chamber parliament called the "Folketing." Ten years later, 23% of the seats in the Folketing were held by women, with the current percentage at 33%, based on December 1990 elections. The sharp increases following 1970 were the result of a resurgent women's movement.

As in many other Western countries, the 1970s saw the growth of a revitalized Danish women's movement, kicked off by a radical feminist group called the Redstockings. As in other countries, the growing activism resulted, in part, from increasing participation of women in the labor market. This gave rise to greater demands for child care, equal pay and equal opportunity in the economic sphere and liberalization for women in the personal sphere, in regard to sharing of housework and other issues of power relationships within the home. The Redstockings were an outgrowth of the Danish New Left, with a sometimes supportive and sometimes adversarial relationship to the predominantly male-led movement. A favorite slogan of the Redstockings was "no feminist struggle without class struggle; no class struggle without feminist struggle."

In one of many militant actions (April 1970), the mostly young women marched through Copenhagen to Town Hall Square where they tore off padded bras, artificial eyelashes and other female paraphernalia, dumping them in a trash bag carrying the slogan, "Keep Denmark Clean." They cropped their hair short, made speeches around the country, and refused to pay full fare on buses as long as women's pay was so much lower than men's. ["Women in Denmark," *Danish Journal*, 1980.]

The anti-establishment nature of the Redstockings kept them from concentrating on participation in the mainstream political process. But many of their demands entered the public debate and led to increased consciousness in the existing political parties of the need to include women in leadership as well as to enact legislation designed to eliminate inequities affecting women wage earners.

SOCIAL AND POLITICAL LEGISLATION FOR WOMEN

As a result of pressures from women parliamentarians and DKN, an Equal Status Council was appointed by the government in 1975, during International Women's Year. This replaced the Commission on the Status of Women in Society, which had been operative in the 1960s and early '70s. The purpose of the council is to work toward eliminating inequalities in the hiring, training, promotion and working conditions of women and men. It also oversees affirmative action in the public sector and education. The council became statutory in 1978 with passage of the Equal Treatment Act, which provides for equal treatment of men and women in employment, education and other areas. The prime minister appoints the chairwomen of the council, and eight other members are appointed as follows: one member each from the Federation of the Workers Trade Unions, the Danish Employers' Association, the Federation of Danish Civil Servants and Salaried Employees Organizations; three members from the National Council of Women in Denmark (DKN); one member from the Danish Women's Society, the oldest women's organization in the country, with individual membership, that has worked to increase participation of women in politics; and one member representing women's studies. When a lawsuit is brought against an employer under the Equal Treatment Act, the Equal Status Council makes recommendations to the court, which has generally been reluctant to grant exemptions.

Other legislation enacted in the 1970s that affected women were tax-free family allowance payments (1970) for all children under 16; the Termination of Pregnancy Act (1973), providing free abortion on demand for the first 12 weeks of pregnancy; the Social Assistance Act (1974), which provides for day care and recreation centers for children and young people to be subsidized by public municipal funds; and the Equal Pay Act of 1976, which provides for equal pay for equal work although it does not address the issue of comparable worth of traditionally male and female jobs.

Another factor that helped passage of these laws was Denmark's tradition of social legislation. Since the late 1800s, there had been social legislation on the books concerning poor relief and health insurance. Although enacted in a spirit of compassion, these laws often had little bite to them, because they left the details and funding of the programs to local authorities. The local authorities, who were generally the land-holders and the bourgeoisie, were often more interested in cutting costs than in relieving poverty. It was not until the Social Reform of 1933 that effective social legislation was firmly established. The Social Reform program entailed the repeal of all existing social legislation, replacing it with four acts: (1) The General Insurance Act (covering sickness, disability and old-age insurance); (2) The Unemployment Insurance Act; (3) The Accident Insurance Act; and (4) The Public Care Act. Implicit in the Social Reform was an understanding that public assistance was a legal right and not an act of charity. There was also the understanding that, hand in hand with providing assistance to the poor and needy, the Danish government would have a responsibility to prevent social ills from appearing. This gave rise to various sublegislation and programs seeking to guarantee employment for all, to create housing, to regulate the public health and to provide rehabilitation and employment for the disabled, and to provide child allowances to both two-parent and single-parent households. It is not surprising that legislation for women was able to gain a foothold on this foundation.

The actual architect of the 1933 Social Reform was K.K. Steincke, the minister for social affairs at the time. He had been fighting for such reform for years and was able to get around conservative opposition because the Social Democrats and their allies, the Radical Left, were firmly in power at the time. Both of these parties had been active for many years. The Social Democrats had their beginnings in the late nineteenth century, a result of the socialist movement that was sweeping through Europe. Their influence in Danish politics grew steadily until they actually assumed power in the 1920s. The Radical Left Party had been formed in 1905, a split-off from the more moderate Left Party. In the political spectrum it fell between the Social Democrats and the Left Party. The Social Democrats and Radical Left shared many ideas on social programs, women's suffrage and opposition to increased military defense, which was becoming more of an issue in prewar Denmark. The Danish economy was in a state of devastation in the 1920s and it was this charged social atmosphere that allowed the Social Democrats to come to power in 1924. The first Social Democratic prime minister, Thorkild Stauning, was a moderate and was thus able to appeal to the Radical Left Party to support the reforms the Social Democrats were pushing. To this day, the Social Democrats have remained a force in the Folketing by moderating their socialist heritage in the spirit of compromise and political survival. Their presence as a power in Danish electoral politics must be seen as one of the principal causes of the advanced state of women's rights in Denmark.

In addition, reflecting Denmark's tolerant policy on sexual behavior, same-sex couples can register their relationship under the Registered Partnership Act of 1989, which gives them equal legal status with married couples on inheritance, alimony, taxation and rights of permanent residence for foreign partners. However, the law does not allow same-sex partners to adopt children jointly.

THE DANISH ELECTORAL SYSTEM

As has been mentioned, women in Denmark have one of the highest participatory rates in government in the world. The steady and often sharp rise in the percentage of women in the Folketing has been dependent on a number of factors. Among these was the wide-open political debate created by the Redstockings in the 1970s, which had a snowball effect of creating ever-increasing pressures from a diversity of women for greater inclusion in political structures. There was also the nature of the political parties, some of which (such as the Social Democrats) had a history of fighting for women's rights. The shifting alliances of the various parties in their attempts to create coalition governments may have prevented them from becoming entrenched and closed to change. The use of the direct personal vote for a candidate rather than for a party slate has created a higher election rate for women candidates. And the use of quotas for women has been openly discussed and in some cases implemented.

At this point it is necessary to describe the Danish electoral system, which has been called one of the most complex in the Western world: "A former politician has estimated that there are only 40 people in Denmark who actually understand the electoral method. Another has said there are only one or two members of the Folketing itself with a clear grasp of the Danish electoral system." [Snyder, *The European Women's Almanac,* p. 90.]

In general, the Danish electoral system for the 179-seat Folketing is based on a complicated mathematical system of proportional representation. The procedure attempts to achieve proportionality in the distribution of seats among the various political parties, while at the same time trying to preserve a close relationship between candidates and election districts. This results in there being two kinds of seats, four different geographical levels of importance for holding the elections, three different ways in which the candidates may be nominated in the districts and a number of complex ways to designate the persons chosen.

Danish elections are controlled by the political parties. Although in theory candidates may run as independents, there would be no way for them to be elected as such. Therefore, it is entirely up to the parties whom they will put forward as candidates, and in what order they will be listed on the ballot. Parties already represented in the Folketing automatically have the right to nominate candidates and receive public funds for their campaign. New or unrepresented parties must collect signatures equalling 1/175th of the votes cast in the previous election to qualify for these rights. In practice, this has been easy for any serious organization to do. As many as 13 parties have thus been able to put up candidates in an election, although the smallest of these have little chance of actually winning seats in the Folketing.

Voters may cast their ballots in several different ways. They may vote for a party by putting a mark next to the party's name, or they have the option of casting personal votes by putting a mark next to a specific candidate's name. It is possible to vote for a candidate in one's own district or for any candidate in the larger county (metropolitan constituency). The sometimes partly alphabetical, seemingly random listing of candidate names under a party heading on the ballot is carefully calculated by the parties to use the various nominating procedures, which are important in deciding the outcome of the election. The three nominating methods are: (1) to list candidates on the ballot in order of party preference; (2) to put forward a single candidate in each election district; and (3) parallel nomination in which candidates are put forward at the county/metropolitan constituency level only, which ends up giving the most clout to the personal, as opposed to the party vote. The various parties, depending on their situation, favor one or a combination of these nominating procedures. The Social Democrats, for example, who have the largest number of seats in the Folketing, although not enough to allow them to be part of the current coalition government, favor parallel nomination, with its emphasis on the personal vote. In general, however, it may be said that the personal vote has only a small influence on which candidates are eventually elected, with the real power being almost completely in the hands of the parties. Yet the personal vote option has certainly helped some women get elected.

As if the nominating procedures are not complicated enough, the tabulation procedures are even more obscure. The seats are distributed on three different levels. The modified Sainte League method is used, which calls for the party votes being successively divided by a series of mathematically determined figures, until all but 40 of the seats have been distributed among the parties. Full proportionality is not achieved this way, because many of the smaller parties are eliminated in the process. The final forty seats are distributed with an eye to rectifying this, although a threshold rule, stating that a party must have received at least 2% of the total votes, eliminates the smallest parties. This threshold is still a generous one, compared with the Federal Republic of Germany's 5% threshold, and it increases the chances of the small parties to win one or more seats in the Folketing.

We can see by this electoral system, then, that the power is with the parties, and that women's political power depends on the extent to which the parties actually promote them within the party structure and nominate them as candidates. Although the tabulation procedure and the low 2% threshold help smaller parties win token seats in the Folketing, the reality is that a fledgling Women's or

Feminist Party would have a tough go of it. According to Birgitte Husmark, a member of the Folketing from the Socialist People's Party, there is no prospect of forming a Women's Party. "It's not a country for issue parties, because the issues are covered by one or several parties," she says. Her own party, for example, allies with the Radical Left Party, "which is not radical and not left" on certain environmental issues. [Personal interview, October 2, 1991.] Although the Social Democrats are much closer to them in general on the political spectrum, the Socialist People's Party and the Social Democrats often take very different stances on environmental issues. While the Social Democrats have the largest number of seats in the Folketing (69), the nonsocialist parties have united as a coalition since 1982 to create a minority government. Currently only two parties, the Conservatives and the Liberals, with 30 and 29 seats in the Folketing respectively, share control of the government ministries. The prime minister, Poul Schluter, is a Conservative. Four of the 19 cabinet ministers are women: the ministers for industry and energy (Conservative), health (Liberal), social affairs (Liberal) and cultural affairs (Conservative). Only one of these ministries, Industry and Energy, falls outside what may be considered the traditionally female areas of interest. And it is interesting to note that a conservative woman was given this ministry, making it less likely that women's issues *per se* will be on the agenda.

The distribution of the 59 women in the Folketing among the eight parties as of the 1990 elections is as follows:
• Social Democrats have 71 seats, 24 held by women;
• The Conservatives have 30 seats, with 7 held by women;
• The Liberals have 30 seats, with 9 held by women;
• The Socialist People's Party has 15 seats, with 6 held by women;
• The Progress Party has 12 members, with 4 held by women;
• The Centre Democrats have 9 seats, with 5 held by women;
• The Radical Liberals have 7 seats, with 3 held by women; and
• The Christian People's Party has 4 seats, with only 1 held by a woman.

Four additional seats in the Folketing are reserved for representatives from Greenland and the Faroe islands. None of these seats are held by women.

With an overall percentage of 33% women and percentages of women MPs in each party ranging from 23% (Conservatives) to 55% (Centre Democrats), cross-party coalitions on women's issues seem to be a possibility. It is unlikely that a woman would break sharply with her party to ally with women from other parties on an issue her party strongly disagreed with as the backing of her party is crucial at re-election time. Of the eight parties only three—the Centre Democrats, the Progress Party and the Christian People's Party—have not established women's branches. Even without a women's branch, the Centre Democrats still felt it appropriate to give five of their nine seats to women.

Women actually have a lower rate of electoral success in municipal elections: The most recent figures show women held 26.2% of city council seats and 29.4% of departmental council seats. The Socialist People's Party has the largest percentage of women (36.6% of its council members), followed by the Radical Left (33%) and the Social Democrats (28.8%).

At least two of the parties, the Social Democrats and the Socialist People's Party, have internal quotas for women candidates, but these quotas have yet to be reflected in the seats these parties hold. In 1988, the Social Democrats adopted a 40%/60% quota, meaning that no less than 40% and no more than 60% of internal party positions must be held by women. For local elections they have a quota of no less than 30% women. Only one election has been held since these quotas were established, so it is too early to tell how well they will translate into actual seats for women. The Socialist People's Party has had similar quotas for about ten years, but they are a less powerful party than the Social Democrats and, as yet, these quotas have not translated into corresponding percentages of women in their parliamentary delegation.

With the increased use of the personal, rather than party vote, many women choose to vote for a woman candidate from another party if their own party has no women candidates in a particular district. Women's groups such as the Danish Women's Society have campaigned for women to vote for women regardless of party affiliation, with some success. This creates pressure on parties to promote women candidates where a "gender gap" is seen to be a factor in an election.

WOMEN'S ISSUES TODAY

Women in the Danish government in general seem to agree that despite their relatively high participation rate, top political power for women remains elusive. Even within their own party structures, they tend to be relegated to the less important committees or at least to ones seen as less important by the men, such as health, education and cultural affairs. The higher up one gets in the party structures, the fewer women are represented. Decision-making is often done through informal networks within the parties and the Folketing, and women are routinely excluded from these old-boys networks.

Given that the parties are the "king and queen-makers" of political careers, this doubly hinders the progress of women in political participation. The party coalitions created around certain issues in the Folketing complicate interparty coalitions of women, particularly as women are the minority in most of the parties' parliamentary delegations. As a result, men still hold more power at all levels and also in deciding what priority a particular women's issue will be given. Due to the demands of work, child care and housework, as well as the usual social and cultural biases, it is often hard to convince women to run for office, and those who do run have to be given special support.

Pressure from outside women's groups is still very important to advance women's issues and raise their status in Danish society. While the Redstocking movement has splintered, the National Council of Women (DKN) has been able to keep together its many groups and to continue its work in behalf of women.

What are the main issues of concern to Danish women today? Political participation at all levels of government is important to at least 40% of Danish women. Despite the Equal Treatment Act, women are still greatly concentrated in the lower-paying traditionally female professions and there is growing unemployment among women. There is a great need for affirmative action and counseling programs in education to combat the segregation of women and men in certain fields of study. With 58,000 children on a waiting list for public day care, there is general agreement among women's groups that the system must be improved and expanded. The Social Democrats have been fighting for a six-hour work day, something which women feel would expand their ability to be active in politics. The Radical Left and Socialist People's parties are working on environmental issues, many of which are of particular concern to women.

Finally, DKN and women parliamentarians are actively trying to work with women from other countries in international forums such as the Nordic Council and the European Community, as well as with women from Eastern Europe to put women's issues higher up on the agenda in Europe as well as at the United Nations. The recent Danish referendum on the Maastricht treaty formula for European unity, which was defeated by only 50,000 votes, shows that even a country of only seven million people can influence events in Europe. Danish women can play an important role in European politics to the extent that they can influence Danish politics. According to some reports, more women than men opposed Denmark's approval of the treaty because they feared their existing social benefits would be lowered to EEC standards. [Personal interview, Mai Britt Theorin, November 18, 1992.]

Conditions for Danish women as a whole are in a state of flux. Recession, growing unemployment, and the influx of immigrants and refugees in general do not have a positive effect on women's participation in the labor market. It remains to be seen if the percentage of women in government will continue to grow in the face of these downward economic trends, and if growing percentages can be translated into a government in which women share effective equal power with men.

NOTE

Additional sources: Royal Danish Ministry of Foreign Affairs; *DKN-Information*, National Council of Women Newsletter; Inger Langberg, Secretary, DKN; Royal Danish Embassy, Washington, D.C.; Danish Mission to the UN; *The Economist* (London); Inter-Parliamentary Union; *Danish Journal;* and the following Danish parliamentarians: Inge Sogaard, Social Democratic Party; Birgitte Husmark, Socialist Peoples Party; Sonja Albrink, Centre Democrats; and Inger Stilling Pedersen, Christian Peoples Party.

6

Close-Up: Iceland

Iceland has the distinction of being the first nation to elect a woman president, the first (and only) state to elect an all-women's party candidates to its parliament, and the only one in which women held two general strikes to press their demands for equity and women's rights.

A small, rather barren island of volcanic origin, close to the Arctic Circle, it has a population of 259,000 people, more than half of whom live in or near Reykjavik, the capital city, Remarkable for their homogeneity, most Icelanders are descendants of Norwegians and Celts, 95% are Evangelical Lutherans, and 99% are literate. A relatively affluent society, its unemployment rate in 1992 was 1.7% (the lowest of all the European Community nations) and its Gross Domestic Product (GDP) expressed in per capita purchasing power was $15,851.[1] Women, who are 49.8% of the population, have the world's longest life expectancy rate, averaging 80.4 years compared with 74.8 years for men, and one of the lowest infant mortality rates, 5 per 1,000 births. [Snyder, Paula, *The European Women's Almanac.*]

Absent are many of the social ills endemic in other societies, such as extreme poverty, homelessness and high crime rates. One indicator of the pacific nature of life in Iceland is the fact that there is no standing army, despite the highly controversial presence of a NATO base. The murder rate is one per year and the nation's only prison can hold 53 people at most. The government social security system provides people with their basic economic, retirement and health care requirements, although women's organizations charge that programs are inadequate for working women's needs and economic discrimination as well as job segregation persist. The number of women working full-time and part-time outside the home rose from 20% in 1960 to 84% in 1986, and has remained at that high percentage. The highest proportion of working mothers is 95% for those with one child, with the proportion decreasing as the number of children goes up.

According to scholar Richard F. Tomasson, the comparatively respected position of women can be traced back to Iceland's ancient and highly developed culture. Ancient Icelandic laws were particularly liberal and accorded women higher status and more independence than any other European culture of that era. In the tenth century they had the right to own property, were able to divorce and remarry, to vote and to take active roles in political and social life. With the introduction of Christianity, these rights disappeared. [Kaplan, Gisela, *Contemporary Western European Feminism*, New York University Press, 1992, pp. 87-89.]

President Vigdis Finnbogadottir, first elected in 1980 and now serving her fourth term, believes the independent spirit of contemporary Icelandic women has been shaped historically by the North Atlantic island's economy, primarily based on the fishing industry, which requires many of its seafaring men to be away for long periods of time. "It's the women who are the backbone of daily life; they can do everything ashore and this has made them more self-confident," she said. "Icelandic men have great admiration for them." [Personal interview, Dublin, July 10, 1992.]

Other feminists contend, however, that the heavy workload borne by Icelandic women is inequitable and discriminatory. Not only do most women work at full-time or part-time jobs, earning an average of about 61-66% of the average pay for men, but they also assume primary responsibility for the family and housework. The difficulties in balancing these multiple roles are compounded by the fact that the school day is discontinuous, there is a serious shortage of full-time day care, and women have to resort to makeshift arrangements for their children. Single parents (predominantly women) account for 21% of families with children. After-school care is reserved for the 6- to -10-year-old children of single parents, and only 8.9% of children aged six months to five years have full-time child care places, almost all of which are reserved for children of single parents and students. Most child care centers are publicly funded, but there are long waiting lists for municipal childcare facilities, both for two-parent and single-parent families. [Snyder, *The European Women's Almanac.*] These distinct needs of women exemplify the economic and social issues that many Icelandic women feel have not been sufficiently addressed by a political system in which they have not been equal partners.

The public struggle for equality began on January 27, 1907, with the organization of the Women's Rights Association of Iceland (WRAI) by Briet Bjarnheoninsdottir after she had attended several meetings of the International Alliance of Women in Europe. There she met American suffrage leader Carrie Chapman Catt and took back to her homeland the demand for votes for women. The WRAI had two specific objectives: to win women's rights to vote and to run for local councils and parliament; and to work for full equality between women and men, particularly regarding equal opportunity to education. Both goals were achieved within a short period. [Guthnadottir, Jonina, "Women's Rights in Iceland," *International Women's News*, Vol. 85, No. 3, 1990.]

A law passed in 1911 guaranteed equal rights for women to any form of education available in the country at the time, the first legislation of its kind passed anywhere in the world. Women first gained the right to vote in local elections in 1909, and in parliamentary elections in 1915. Women were granted the right to run for political office at the same time, but it was not until 1922 that the first woman, Ingibjorg H. Barnason, won a seat in the Althing, which is the oldest existing parliament in the world. Between 1922 and 1926 women presented separate women's candidate lists in local elections, and four women won seats on town councils. But until the 1980s, inclusion of women in government remained minimal.

Prior to 1982, the proportion of female representatives was only 6% on the municipal level and 5% in the Althing. From 1922 to 1979 a total of 12 women were elected to parliament. As in the other Nordic countries, Iceland's electoral system is based on proportional representation, with parliamentary seats allocated on the basis of the percentage of the vote received by each party's list of candidates. Candidates at the top of the list have the best chance of winning a seat in parliament, with those cherished positions traditionally reserved for men.

The issue of equal pay for equal work became a goal after the first women's trade union was founded in 1914 at the urging of WRAI board members, and in more recent times the goal has become equal pay for work of comparable worth. Although the Law of Equal Pay was adopted in 1961, women still earn on average less than men, partly because the occupations in which they are concentrated have lower wage scales and also because women average a 36.7 hour workweek, compared with 52.2 hours for men. [Snyder, *The European Women's Almanac.*]

WOMEN GO ON STRIKE

While WRAI continued to work on women's issues and also regularly submitted to the parliament critiques of legislation affecting women (a role it still maintains), a radical feminist group emerged in 1968, as similar groups were being organized in the United States and other countries. Called Raudsokkahreyfingin' (Redstocking Movement), it began to focus demands on the parliament and trade unions for more rapid improvement in women's status. As in Denmark, it had as its slogan: "No women's struggle without class struggle, no class struggle without women's struggle." The introduction of militant feminist activity came when, in support of the UN's International Women's Year, they called for a general women's strike on October 25, 1975, and as Gisela Kaplan [*Contemporary Western European Feminism*] described it:

> A most unusual thing happened: almost 90% of *all* Icelandic women literally went "on strike." Housewives went out for the day leaving small children and household chores to their husbands, working women stayed away from their jobs and almost the entire island came to a standstill. Women wanted to show that their society would stop functioning without them and that the injustices and discriminatory practices at the workplace were neither morally nor practically defensible.

Showing a daring creativity in their public protests, the feminists staged another attention-getting event in 1984 when they held a supermarket demonstration. At the time, women were earning only 66% of the average male pay, Iceland was in the grip of a severe economic crisis and the inflation rate was 50%. In large numbers, women "shoppers" walked into supermarkets, picked various items off the shelves and offered to buy them for 66% of the listed price. Supermarket managers and police stood by helplessly while the women protesters filled the aisles, singing, dancing and shouting their demands. A year later, in response to some sexist remarks made by the mayor of Reykjavik, another demonstration, known as the Beauty Queen Action of 1985, was staged. Women, wearing stereotypical heavy makeup and bikinis, walked into the chamber where the municipal council was meeting, and paraded in front of the embarrassed male councillors. Their principal demand was an end to sexism in the media and public life.

On October 24, 1985, feminists called their second general strike, noting that the UN Decade for Women had ended but that the economic, social and political status of Icelandic women was not improving. A major complaint was that the equal pay law was being flouted by employers who were making secret payments to men. The strike brought out 25,000 women in Reykjavik, a fourth of the capital's population, leaving men desperately trying to maintain skeleton services in businesses and offices. Sectors staffed entirely by women, such as primary schools and fish-processing plants, had to close down completely. In Iceland's second largest city so many women turned out that a rally they had planned to hold in a local community hall had to be moved to a larger facility.

Coincidentally, just before the scheduled general strike, the Althing held an all-night session to debate and vote on a Ministry of Transportation bill forcing striking Icelandair female flight attendants, whose pay negotiations had broken down, to return to work. Three women parliamentarians spoke against the bill and finally walked out in protest. After the bill was adopted at 5 A.M. on October 24, it was rushed to President Vigdis Finnbogadottir for her routine signature. Although technically she had the constitutional power to veto the measure, it was totally unexpected that as essentially a figurehead she would do so. In a move unprecedented in Iceland's parliamentary history, Finnbogadottir refused to sign, asking for "time to think things over." (She had already announced that in support of the women's general strike, she would not be in her office that day. Nine women parliamentarians also joined in the strike.)

Finally, according to Gudrun Agnarsdottir, a Women's Alliance parliamentarian, the president was "bullied" into signing the back-to-work bill, under threats that the cabinet would resign. In a public statement, the president said she had asked for a postponement because she felt: "What a pity it was to be signing laws of that kind on that particular . . . precious day." Commenting on her action, Gudrun Agnarsdottir said, "Most women understood her extreme difficulty. I think there was a wave of sympathy from all of us for her." Icelandair's 160 striking flight attendants, instead of going back to work, joined the women's general strike rally, chanting, "We dare, we can, we will." [de Grass, Jan, "Reckoning in Reykjavik," *Herizons*, Winnipeg, Canada, March 1986.]

FIRST WOMAN PRESIDENT

The dilemma of Iceland's precedent-setting woman president exemplified the conflict other Icelandic women were to face later in weighing the constraints of "establishment" political power as against the independent, free-wheeling and often uncompromising style of organized feminist groups. Vigdis,[2] as she is popularly known, was 50 and a single parent when she was persuaded to run for the presidency in 1980, encouraged, she says, by her father and inspired by the 1975 general women's strike, in which she participated. Divorced and mother of an adopted daughter, she came to national attention as co-host of a popular television program and, for four years, as director of a municipal theater, which she closed down on the day of the first women's strike. When friends suggested that she run for the presidency, a limited-power position that had previously been held by an archaeologist, she resisted, but then decided to give it a try.

Although she was not a member of any political party, she launched her campaign on a feminist, pacifist, cultural and nationalist platform. After a hard-fought campaign in which she was attacked as a "leftist" for having participated in an anti-NATO demonstration, she narrowly defeated her three male opponents—all older, married, veteran politicians. Since then, she has won reelection easily three times and is the most popular political leader in the country, particularly among younger women. For her fourth term, she ran unopposed, receiving 93.5% of the vote.

She handles her gender and single parenthood status with self-assurance and humor. Recalling that she was asked how she could host a state dinner for a visiting head of state without having a spouse to sit opposite her, she replied, "I'll have a round table."

In a 1981 interview, she described herself thus: "I'm a pacifist, but I'm not political. I have no political party behind me; I support all people. I cannot think of adapting to a party discipline because I refuse to have my wings clipped. Moreover, when I speak as head of state, I speak about peace. It sounds naive to say you are a pacifist if you don't explain. I don't know any person who *wants* war. That is the absurd thing; nations have armies today to *prevent* war. We have no army, no military whatsoever. Think what could be done if the money that went into militarism went into . . . cultivating the Sahara."

Seeing herself as a conciliator and optimist, she added: "If you believe in a thing strongly enough, it may be possible to reconcile the different approaches to economic and political social systems." A dedicated environmentalist, she believes Icelanders have created a better life for their tiny nation. "We have succeeded in harnessing the strong elements of nature; ice, rapid waters, fire and even lava. We are the only nation in the world that has detoured a lava stream to save a village, and then used the heat to warm the houses that weren't destroyed.

"Foreigners and geologists said we couldn't save the Vestmann Islands when a volcano erupted in 1973, but we refused to believe them. We poured water on the lava day and night until it began to yield. I refuse to turn over to our children this pessimism, this fright of tomorrow. I think we must offer the next generation, without cheating them, a life they can believe in." [Ridenour, Ron, "Vigdis Finnbogadottir," *Working Woman*, November 1981, p. 76.]

In her Dublin interview, she said she had initiated a reforestation movement that was at first ridiculed, but she persisted. "If you plant three birch trees--one for the girls, one for the boys and one for the unborn," she explained, "you are making a contribution to the ecology of the world."

Using her role as inspirational, symbolic leader, Vigdis seeks to compensate for the very real political limitations in her titular position as head of state. She professes to have more political power than another ceremonial president, Mary Robinson of Ireland, citing the annual speech she gives to parliament, her theoretical veto power, and her role in selection of the cabinet and in what she called the "delicate negotiating process" in government disputes.

EQUAL STATUS COUNCIL

While she enjoys the support of the women's movement, the major impetus for improvement in the status of women continues to come from the strength of organized women's groups. After winning the 1961 Equal Pay Act, they won an Equal Status Act in 1976, which was made obsolete by the more comprehensive 1985 Act on Equal Status and Equal Rights of Women and Men. The legislation created an Equal Status Council, whose responsibilities include dealing with complaints about discrimination, taking legal action to enforce compliance with the antidiscriminatory law, and furthering women's political participation by sponsoring conferences, research and publications. The law also distinguishes illegal from legal or "positive discrimination," described as "temporary measures intended to improve the status of women for the purpose of promoting equality." The council consists of seven members selected from the Supreme Court, the Ministry of Social Affairs, employers and trade unions, and women's groups.

As in the other Nordic nations, generous social welfare laws have been enacted to protect women. Under a 1975 act, abortion is available up to 12 weeks because of social circumstances, medical grounds or rape. Generally, abortions are not permitted after 16 weeks unless there are serious medical grounds. Parental leave that can be shared by women and men is provided for up to six months, and adoptive and foster parents can share combined leave of up to five months. During leave, all mothers receive a maternity subsidy and, if previously employed, both parents qualify for a proportion of their pay, determined by their trade union contracts. Government employees receive their full average earnings over the previous year for the first three months of leave, and their full basic salary for the second three months. Central and local government women employees can also extend their maternity leave to a full year, with a proportionate loss of earnings. Allowances are also provided to one-parent families with children under age 16, and direct child benefits are paid to low-income families and to families with children under 18 if one parent is dead or receiving a disability allowance. Although Icelandic women consider the child care facilities inadequate, a 1973 law does establish the joint responsibility of the state and municipal authorities to provide child care services. [Snyder, *The European Women's Almanac*.]

THE WOMEN'S ALLIANCE

Some of these legislative gains came about as a result of a new emphasis in the women's movement on direct participation in the government. By 1981 Iceland did indeed have the first elected woman president in the world, but there were only three women in the 63-seat, multiparty Althing, and only 6% of all municipal government seats were held by women. The Redstocking movement, torn by internal class-based divisions, was becoming ineffective. A handful of feminists in Reykjavik came up with the suggestion to run an all-women's slate of candidates for the city council in the 1982 elections, and a similar proposal came from feminists in the northern town of Akureyri.

The idea was approved at an open public meeting that drew more than 600 women in the capital. Conducting an unorthodox campaign, which included a street carnival and a roving political choir, the women stunned the four existing parties by winning two seats on the city council, and the women in Akureyri also succeeded in electing two women to their municipal council. The women political activists then founded the Women's Alliance which became the basis for the formation in March 1983 of the all-women's party known as Kvennalistinn (Women's List). The Redstockings formally dissolved and its active members joined the new feminist party, which decided to enter a slate for the 1983 parliamentary elections, focusing on three of the country's eight election districts. By running for the Althing, the women also became eligible for the state election funding that goes to all political parties. [Edgar, Joanne, "Iceland's Feminists: Power at the Top of the World," *Ms.* magazine, December 1987.]

Again the Women's Alliance campaign techniques demonstrated the creativity and grassroots nature of the organization. The women raised additional funds for their electoral activities by selling a host of items, from fish, flowers, coffee and cake to posters, cards and nightgowns. They also held bingo game parties and organized flea markets. A group of 20 women boarded a bus and visited women all over the land, in their homes, at work and in their organizations. The Women's Alliance newspaper, *Vera*, campaign literature and media coverage helped get their message out to voters.

No one was more surprised than the three women who won seats in the Althing in 1983. They had no previous political experience. Gudrun Agnarsdottir was a medical doctor specializing in research in virology and immunology and had assumed she would not be elected. The other successful candidate from Reykjavik, Duna Kristmundsdottir, was an anthropologist. The third winner, Kristin Halldorsdottir, from a region south of the capital, was a journalist. This feminist trio plus three women who successfully ran on other party slates joined the three incumbents, who were reelected, thus tripling the number of women members in the parliament.

In the 1987 elections, the Women's Alliance's Kvennalistinn doubled its membership in the parliament to six, helping to bring the number of women up to 13. After the April 1991 elections, there were 15 women parliamentarians, accounting for 23.8% of the 63 members. Kvennalistinn led with five seats, the major conservative Independence Party women won four seats, and the other three parties each elected two women. Women also made gains in local races, accounting for 19% of municipal councillors and 32% of city and town councillors.

Compared with the 100% "quota" of the Women's Alliance, none of the other parties—right, center or left—has adopted electoral quotas for women. However, the Social Democratic Party and the leftist People's Alliance have instituted the 60-40 rule, meaning that no less than 40% and no more than 60% of either sex must be represented at all levels of party organization, with the proviso that there are enough available candidates of both sexes. The People's Alliance, as of 1991, had the highest proportion of women in its central committee, 39.9%. The SDP had 30.8%. Not all members of the SDP central committee are elected, with some holding their positions because they are chairs of local party branches. Parties that have not adopted affirmative action programs have comparatively lower percentages of women as central committee members: the Progressive Party has 24.6% and the leading Independence Party has 15.6%.

The gadfly role played by the Women's Alliance clearly has been an important factor in increasing the number of women in leadership roles within the traditional parties. However, obtaining top positions on these parties' electoral candidate slates remains an obstacle for many women, although partially in response to the feminists, more women are moving into "safe" top positions on the lists. As Salome Thorkelsdottir, an MP from the conservative Independence Party, has observed, Kvennalistinn "has even helped in our party by opening the eyes of men. They can't ignore women anymore." [Edgar, *Ms.* magazine, December 1987.] But so far the ruling coalition has appointed only one woman minister to its 10-member cabinet. She is the minister of social affairs.

Other Women Politicians Are Critical—and Appreciative

While appreciating the political consciousness-raising influence of the Kvennalistinn, some women's rights advocates in the other parties have been critical of certain rules observed by the women's party: all decisions are made by consensus, the leadership function is rotated among their women members in parliament, and no woman officeholder can serve longer than two terms (six to eight years). Critics believe that term limitation works against both the accretion of political experience and the development of nationally known leaders who can count on strong support from voters familiar with their performance and records. Among the critics are President Vigdis, who also has high praise for the women's party. "I adore the Women's Alliance," she said in a recent interview. [Dublin, July 10, 1992.] "They never get excited. They don't act like the men do. They're very serious, very well-prepared. But I disagree with their policy of rotating women officeholders. I think it's very important to have some continuity in parliament." The Kvennalistinn women's response is that their goal isn't political power for a few but a change of policy and process.

In seeking consensus on their tactics in the parliament, the Kvennalistinn legislators consult with their party's membership every step of the way. According to Gudrun Helgadottir of the People's Alliance, this can be very time-consuming. "If I want their support for some issue," she said, "it has to be discussed so broadly that sometimes you get fed up waiting to see if they're going to say yes or no." [Edgar, *Ms.* magazine, December 1987.] But Magdalena Schram, a Woman's Alliance organizer, insists that "such a structure ensures activism among all members, spreads the responsibility, flattens the pyramids of control, and allows for non-members to see the potential for individual growth through joining the party." [*The Commonwealth,* April 1989.]

The fledgling party's devotion to its principles came under an unexpected test after the April 1987 elections when no two parties had enough seats to form a new government. (Iceland has been ruled by various coalitions selected from the four main political parties since World War II.) The conservative Independence Party, together with the centrist Social Democratic Party, were several parliamentary seats short of being able to form a majority coalition government; overtures were made to the Kvennalistinn to join the coalition government, with their six parliamentary seats providing the balance of power. This would give the all-women's party a role in determining government policy and an opportunity to control some ministries to administer policy in a way favorable to women.

To become part of the coalition government, Kvennalistinn would have had to agree with the other two parties on a policy statement outlining, in general terms, the goals of the new government. Although suspicious of being coopted, the women's party agreed to consider the invitation, but only after much internal discussion and agreement on a few key issues on which it said it could not compromise. Parliamentarian Kristin Halldorsdottir said later: "We were ready to take part in the government, but only if it would really matter. We didn't want to be flowers to make the government look good to the world." [Edgar, *Ms.* magazine, December 1987.]

The sticking point proved to be a dispute over the women's demand for support of a bill they had introduced guaranteeing for several thousand government workers, many of them women, "a meaningful minimum wage that would meet the cost of living." Although not opposed to wage increases, the two major parties objected that making this a legislative mandate might trigger a flood of demands for higher pay that would, in turn, lead to inflation. The negotiations broke down.

Explaining the Kvennalistinn position, activist Raeda Flutt said, "We were all the time convinced that we would have had a weak position within that coalition. Also that we would have had minimal chances of realizing our policies and maintaining our working methods of consensus and power distribution within such a traditional and strongly hierarchical structure of government." Unless the women's party had considerably more seats in the Althing, agreed another activist, Sigridur Duna, being a "minority within the majority" would have been difficult: "In the final analysis they can overrule you easily, in spite of all the gentlemen's promises. You will have to go along with things you don't want, and that in the end is much more dangerous to your goals than being able to speak freely in the opposition."

Women members of the traditional parties disagreed with this view, seeing it as an unwillingness to assume responsibility. "I think they lost courage," said Gudrun Helgadottir of the People's Alliance. "They should have tried to make compromises as we all have to do. After all, they are only six and the Independence Party eighteen. How in heaven could they dream of being able to tell them what to do?" (Edgar, *Ms.* magazine, December 1987.]

Although the most recent elections reduced the number of Kvennalistinn women in the Althing to five, the Women's Alliance party has been successful in advancing women's issues and initiating legislation designed to raise their status. Resolutions passed in the legislature function as a call to action, requiring the government, for example, to undertake an investigation or prepare legislation. As a first step in addressing income inequality between the sexes, the party representatives in the legislature won adoption of a resolution requiring comparative wage statistics to be compiled according to gender, which had not been done before. Armed with the new data, the women had proof of the disparities between male and female income and were able to press more convincingly for measures to eliminate de facto discrimination in the labor market.

Women from the other parties see this as one issue around which all women can unite. There are, however, differences in perspective on pay inequity and other issues among the women of the various parties. The most advanced position is taken by the Women's Alliance, which supports a reevaluation of women's work across the board, identifying discrimination not only within industries but between them as well. The women's party introduced a resolution that would recognize work done in the home as comparable to experience in the wage labor market. This would mean that homemakers who are recent entrants or returnees to the workforce would not necessarily be hired at the lowest end of the pay scale.

Disagreements in Degree among Women Politicians

The women's party also introduced a number of proposals to extend paid maternity leave from three to six months. Disagreements emerged between the women of different parties on this issue, based not on objections to the bill but on whether to accept compromise proposals. The Women's Alliance felt that nothing less than six months at full pay was acceptable. Eventually a bill was approved allowing for six months leave, although at less than full pay, and another party took the credit for this advance. In this instance, women had a similar objective and the dispute over whether to compromise illustrates the fact that there are still not enough women to influence policy without the significant cooperation of other parties. On the other hand, it demonstrates that having women in office gives them greater opportunities to influence the political agenda and the decision-making process.

Another resolution passed on the initiative of the women's party dealt with the way rape cases are handled, and resulted in significant reforms in how rape cases are investigated and treated. Still another resolution that was approved called for more extensive screening of women for breast cancer, and mammograms are now routinely available to women.

While on such issues the women's party representatives can count on support from their female colleagues, the party's overall perspective on the nation's foreign, domestic and economic policies is not shared by all the women of the other parties. The Women's Alliance opposition to military alliances, including Iceland's participation in NATO, does not have the support of most of the other parties, including its women members. The women's party takes the position that all issues are women's issues since they are half the population. The broad scope of the Women's Alliance platform, firmly rooted in a global feminist ideology, is expressed in its 1987 policy statement:

We form our policy from the point of reference of women. We rethink every-thing and take nothing for granted, not even our own existence as a political entity. In our policy we emphasize the demands of women for equal rights on our premises, where women's experiences and our resulting set of values are evaluated equally on their own merits and we reject equality which involves hav-ing to mold ourselves to the standards that men set in order to become equal.

We believe strongly in the distribution of power and decentralization which empowers people to influence their own lives and surroundings. We are strong supporters of environmental protection on a national as well as a global scale, and closely connected with this attitude is our pacifist policy which opposes militarism and all its various manifestations . . . .

At the beginning we often came across the question why we have no men on the list of candidates. The answer is that we think that it is essential for women to represent and carry out a policy which has its roots in and is nurtured by the expe-rience and culture of women. We will not improve the very poor female rep-resentation within the decision-making process by putting more men into repre-sentative roles. However, although our policy and program is for women, it is not therefore against men. We believe that what is good for women and children, whose main advocates we are, is also good for men. It is simply good for people.

We have also been asked what is our advice to women in other countries. We find that each country has its own special circumstances, culture and traditions. This means that women have to find their own way within the situation they find themselves in. There is no right way. However, the conditions of women are so similar all over the world, as far as our status and roles within society are concerned, that there are no foreigners in the land of women. We have indeed much more in common than what separates us.

Therefore we can learn from each other's experiences. We have to support each other if we are to enter and survive as women within the present political system, not to mention if we want to do so on our own terms. To be able to be supportive we must believe in ourselves and in other women, believe in our sisterhood.

Whether or not the Women's Alliance Party will be able to increase its num-bers in parliament and broaden its electoral support, its radical vision of a nation guided by women's values has already inspired and energized thousands of women, strengthened the role of women from all parties in the Althing, reshaped the debate on national issues, and influenced policy—a remarkable legacy from a tiny nation to the women of the world.

NOTES

[1] Based on 1992 prices and using 1992 dollars and international parity formulas determined by the Organization for Economic Cooperation and Development (OECD), comprising 19 European states, Canada, the United States, Japan, Australia and New Zealand.

[2] Surnames are almost always expressed as daughter of the father, but last names are not considered that important. The phone book is alphabetized by first names, and the president is listed therein as Vigdis.

7

Close-Up: Germany

Over the course of more than eight tumultuous decades of struggle for equality, the position achieved by women in the Federal Republic of Germany's parliament (Bundestag) is the highest-ever level of representation. Since 1980, two parties have instituted a system of affirmative action, whereby the female candidates at the national level comprise a fixed percentage. This quota system has led to increased participation by women from the Social Democratic Party and, until recently, from the Green Party, and has exerted pressure on the other parties at least to present an image of concern for women's issues and an interest in fielding female candidates.

Although the women's movement in the newly unified Germany has benefited from the quota rules adopted by these parties, a great deal of discussion continues on the role of this mechanism. To explore the extent to which quotas have aided in opening political opportunities previously closed to women, it will be useful to delve into the evolving political atmosphere in Germany. The 1918-33 period of emerging democratic institutions serves as one orientation point for women's participation in politics. Very little continuity is evident between the Weimar period and the second important stage of female political development, that of the movements of the late 1960s and 1970s. This chapter will focus on tying together these two disparate periods in order to look at the historical context of the women's movement and at the current political environment in Germany. The improved representation of women in parliament does not lend itself to a systematic study of policy outcomes, due to the dramatic social and economic changes occurring in the wake of the Federal Republic of Germany's absorption of the German Democratic Republic (East Germany). It will be valuable for policy-making aimed at women's political development, however, to provide an overview of the use of quotas to achieve women's political goals.

HISTORICAL BACKGROUND

The achievement of equality has been approached variously by the multi-factioned women's movement in Germany. Some women considered the right to vote and participation in political life extremely meaningful steps in their quest for equality. In the minds of others, enfranchisement for German women was a questionable achievement in what was to become their vision of radical social change: There was more at stake than simply gaining the right to serve as accessories in the existing male political system.

In the early twentieth century, social structures were in a formative stage, and women sought political goals within the shifting alignments of a Germany emerging from monarchy. The Social Democracy movement which arose as a response to the conditions of industrialization helped to focus some women's groups on gaining the right to vote and stand for political office. When the Social Democrats won control in 1918, they granted women the vote, and 36 women were elected to the 467-member Constituent National Assembly of January 19, 1919.

In the struggle of German women, as in all the world's female suffrage efforts, gaining the rights to vote and stand for public office was part of a fundamental progression toward moral revitalization and improved social standards. The suffrage victory culminated a nearly 30-year struggle, during which women were at times divided and weak, working against nearly insurmountable discrimination and the legacy of Wilhelmine Germany. The movement was hindered until 1908 by a law forbidding women to assemble for political purposes. Pressuring parties to include the demand for female suffrage in their programs was not the main occupation of all women's groups, with some believing that other goals were more achievable, or of more immediate importance. From diverse points on the political spectrum, various groups pursued their aims through such efforts as calling for an end to state-regulated prostitution, seeking reform of the Criminal Code's Section 218 prohibiting abortion, and opposing or supporting World War I. [Evans, Richard, *The Feminist Movement in Germany 1894-1933*, London, 1976.] Worldwide nonpartisan solidarity among suffrage movements had a great impact. German suffrage leaders were heavily influenced by the English suffragists, whose members were frequent guests at meetings in Berlin, Munich and Hamburg, the main centers of suffrage movement activity from 1908.

It is not surprising that in this atmosphere of flux the many different women's associations were divided within and among themselves about the meaning of equality. By the time women actually stepped into public office and stood to gain from their political roles in 1918, disunity and uncertainty were plaguing the women's movement as a whole. Entry into the Weimar parliament depended not on direct democratic selection of candidates, but rather on party nomination and proportional representation. Parties obtained parliamentary seats in the Weimar system based on electoral percentages, and they filled their allotted seats with candidates from the lists they had compiled. Women were positioned on these lists, albeit in very low numbers, mainly to attract female voters. Some newcomers to parliament were torn between loyalty to their sex and commitment to parties with less concern for women which more closely represented their political views. Most of the women, who comprised 9.6% of the total number of representatives in the first parliament, however, were active members of the women's movement.

The Weimar constitution had just been fashioned, and the newly elected Constituent Assembly approved the new constitution after many amendments, on July 31, 1919. The document contained one provision, Article 109, that codified the equality of men and women. The paragraphs relating to women's representation in the civil service are clearly meant to ensure nondiscrimination, but in practice, many posts were designated for men.

For Marie Juchacz, the first woman to speak in a German parliament, the entrance of women into the Reichstag meant the solution to the "women's question." [Weiland, Daniela, *Geschichte der Frauen Emanzipation*, ECON, Düsseldorf, 1983.] This concept, referred to repeatedly throughout the history of the women's movement, is a catch-all for the political and social problems faced by a variety of groups of women in different contexts. Juchacz's speeches were highly enthusiastic about the new positions being achieved by women in 1919. She declared political life to have benefited from a new feminine perspective provided by the contributions of women parliamentarians, despite their small numbers.

Article 109 in the Weimar constitution, guaranteeing "fundamentally" equal rights and duties for men and women, presented a troubling prospect for the achievement of equality. Not only did its hedging language lay a legal foundation for unequal treatment, but it also served as a point of disunity for the women's movement efforts. Those, including Juchacz and Marie-Elisabeth Lüders, who attempted to change the article met with opposition from most of the bourgeois women parliamentarians who considered such a change a move toward extreme equalization.

One of the first moves toward instituting quotas was an outgrowth of the SPD party convention of June 1919. There, Marie Juchacz proposed that the party's executive committee should include at least two women. In the following years, her proposal was not implemented, and her concern about the lack of female representation among the party elite proved valid, as women entered parties whose platforms did not reflect women's concerns. Again in 1925, some interest was raised in the SPD about the prospect of using quotas to strengthen the voice of women in the party. Overall, the issue was hardly considered of importance in the face of virulent inflation, and a crisis of control which continually had to be remedied by resorting to emergency powers. [Flanz, *Comparative Women's Rights and Political Participation in Europe*.]

Many women rejected the doctrinaire facets of social democracy that were dominant in Weimar politics. The benefits of quotas within the SPD would have been questionable, considering the limitations of women with regard to real political influence. Women working within the male-dominated parties reflected the collaborative approach of the traditional women's movement. Their presence at state and local levels was minor, and women were never admitted to the higher party positions. [Koonz, Claudia, "Conflicting Allegiances: Political Ideology and Women Legislators in Weimar Germany," in *Signs*, Vol. 1, 1976, p. 668.] They attended primarily to matters of education, social security and culture. [Feist, Ursula, "Die Unterrepräsentanz von Frauen im politischen System der Bundesrepublik," in *Vater Staat und Seine Frauen*, Centaurus, Berlin, 1990.] Overall, a program for promoting women's interests failed to emerge from the participation of women in parliament.

One of the biggest successes of the Weimar period was the elimination of policies that until 1900 had barred women from higher education. In terms of real influence and advancement, however, the period was a grim one. Women were allowed into the Weimar parliaments only with the consent of male party functionaries who generally put forth a conservative concept of women's roles and family structures. Over the course of the entire period, the 112 women members of the parliament spoke less often than their male colleagues, had less power and generally felt themselves alienated from the political culture, in which their presence was a type of "tokenism." [Koonz, Claudia, *Mothers in the Fatherland*, 1976, p. 668.] Contemporary feminists, in analyzing the significance of the Weimar period for the progress of women, see it as a brake on the movement's development. Thus, the parliamentary participation failed to meet expectations for improved representation of women's interests.

By 1933, the dissolution of the Weimar Reichstag was complete. The inception of National Socialism and its impact on German women over the 12-year period of Nazi rule will not be discussed in depth here. The role of women during the period was studied by, among others, Claudia Koonz, whose book, *Mothers in the Fatherland,* shed light on the willingness of German women to participate in a system that confined them to traditional female roles of mother and homemaker. Through youth organizations and the dissemination of powerful propaganda, these values and gender roles were imparted with great success. Women were removed from public and civil service, returning to paid employment only after 1941, when the war made it necessary for the National Socialists to revise their labor policies. [Kolinsky, Eva, *Women in West Germany,* New York, 1989.] Though an examination of events in Germany under the Nazis would contribute little to the discussion of quotas per se, it is impossible to comprehend the barriers to be overcome in contemporary society without taking note of the impact of the Hitler regime on social and gender perceptions.

WOMEN IN THE FEDERAL REPUBLIC (FRG)

In postwar occupied Germany, the hope of cooperating with the Soviet Union on the German question was abandoned in 1948. In the Western zone under the control of Allied forces, parliamentary democracy was restored, while the eastern zone came under a new regime imposed by the Soviet Union. Women constituted about 70% of the electorate at the time of the formation of the new Western government. Nevertheless, the women's movement had to wait to reconstitute itself until immediate postwar hardship conditions were at least partially overcome. [Kolinsky, p. 27.]

Once a new parliament was formed, women continued to suffer low levels of representation. The misconceptions about the differences in male and female physical imperatives persisted as a residue of Nazi acculturation. Discrimination was rampant and sanctioned by the provisions of the Civil Code, which had been German law since the turn of the century.

LEGAL FRAMEWORK FOR EQUALITY

This extensive background has important implications for understanding the application and functions of quotas, both potential and actual. The developing legal landscape in the new Federal Republic included many provisions aimed at achieving gender equality and ensuring equal treatment of women. Understanding the legal guarantees will provide a broader context for the examination of measures needed to fulfill the principles embodied therein.

In 1949, the tribunal that convened to formulate the new Basic Law was composed of 66 men and four women. This parliamentary council completed the Basic Law of the Federal Republic of Germany in May of that year, approved by a vote of 53 to 12. The consequences of the gender imbalance in that formative body were severe. It is difficult to speculate about which opportunities were foregone, but it is clear that the battle over constitutional provisions referring to equality was affected by the absence of women. The first person to champion equal rights in the Basic Law was Elizabeth Selbert. When the public outcry went up in 1949 for the inclusion of the principle of equality for men and women, the SPD veteran was the main force ensuring the adoption of the following article:

Article 3 (Equality before the Law)

1. All persons [Menschen] shall be equal before the law.

2. Men and women shall have equal rights.

3. No one may be disadvantaged or favoured because of his sex, his parentage, his race, his language, his homeland and origin, his faith, or his religion and political opinions. [Kolinsky, p. 42.]

Though this wording went quite far beyond the principles embodied in the Weimar constitution, the article falls short of what would have been needed to address many issues of importance to women, such as equal pay for equal or comparable work, discrimination in child custody practices, and the disproportionately male presence in political life. An alternative to the article has been proposed by the <u>Constitutional Commission</u> of the federal and state governments, which says:

> Women and men shall have equal rights. The state guarantees the creation of equal conditions for women in all societal spheres.

* * *

Until 1957, the German Civil Code contained a series of standards requiring women to fulfill household duties before pursuing other employment. The 1949 parliamentary council failed to call for immediate revision of the code, preferring the continuity it provided. The Civil Code provisions concerning women and the family were suspended between 1953 and 1957, after which reforms were finally adopted.

The embedded traditional views of women's roles in the family, parenting and marriage have persisted in West Germany, despite legal reforms. This might be one cause of women's slow progress in gaining major access to political power. Another is the general unwillingness of men in the parliament to translate well-intentioned legislation into real equalizing outcomes. Eliminating separate wage scales for women in the 1950s, for example, did not ensure that the jobs populated primarily by men would not be assigned to higher wage groups. Today, "men's work" is still better paid than that of women. An Equal Treatment Law passed in 1980 added paragraphs to the Civil Code prohibiting this particular type of gender discrimination. This adjustment was the result of intervention by the European Commission to bring the West German government into compliance with the EC standards regarding equal rights in recruitment, appointment, promotion and compensation. Insufficient enforcement of these directives reveals a half-hearted attempt on the part of the West German government to fulfill the European Commission's requirements for eliminating gender discrimination.

If the status of women fails to rise beyond that of second class citizens in the realm of work and family, then it is unlikely that women will find it very easy to acquire access to channels of political participation. The "Catch-22" aspect of this argument, however, can be overcome at least partially by affirmative action, as will be shown below.

WOMEN IN EASTERN GERMANY (GDR)

In contrast to rigidified thinking in the West, women in East Germany had been actively drawn into the workforce by the ruling Communist Party, which claimed to be ideologically committed to the emancipation of women. Its policy on female participation apparently did not extend to the higher party echelons, as very few women were ever represented there. In the 1986 elections, however, women gained 32.2% of the seats in the unicameral legislature. As in other Eastern European nations, they were allowed to share in the essential powerlessness of the parliament. The policy rather was one of expedience, undertaken to prevent massive labor shortages. Women indeed averaged an income 75-80% below that of men, and shouldered most of the domestic burdens, although extensive child care facilities were provided. [Rosenberg, Dorothy J., "Shock Therapy: GDR Women in Transition from a Socialist Welfare State to a Market Economy," *Signs*, Autumn 1991.]

The absence of a significant female presence in top political leadership that characterized both the separate GDR and FRG persists, not surprisingly, in the reunified Germany as well. Though a high level of feminist consciousness had been attained in the GDR, the process of unification reversed or threatened many of the policy gains which had been made, especially in areas such as child care, maternity leave and abortion laws, which were more liberal than those in the West. The women's groups that banded together to form part of the opposition during the time of reunification or "Wende" (change) were intent on remaining separate from the various citizens' groups and democratic initiatives that fielded candidates in the March 18, 1990 elections. The women's groups were formed in the interest of focusing their work on these specifically feminine issues. On the eve of the first "free" elections in East Germany, the largest of the women's groups, the Independent Women's Association (UFV), reluctantly joined the Bündnis '90 coalition of the other roundtable groups that represented an alternative to the established parties. (Bündnis '90 is also known as Alliance '90.)

The citizens' groups, though organized predominantly by women, were not specifically focused on women's issues, and their membership was overwhelmingly male. [Author's interview with Stephan Bickert of Democracy Now, New York, June 15, 1992.] Nevertheless, many of the political goals of the citizens' groups were identical with those of the UFV, such as concern with income equality and the participation of women in various sectors of society. The March 1990 electoral outcome resulted in eight seats designated for the roundtable coalition, but none were filled by women from the UFV. Due to the coalition agreement, the lists of candidates were composed according to a 2:1 formula, and since the coalition won only two seats in each district, none of the UVF candidates were seated. The Independent Women's Association, with its "single-issue" orientation, split from the others, preferring total independence. In the December 1990 national unification elections, the UFV was no longer officially affiliated with Bündnis '90. The consequence of that decision was a migration of some UFV members to Bündnis '90, where they stood a better chance of gaining entry into parliament and could pursue their goals in the context of the multi-issue citizens' movement. This example of a contradiction between gender and political allegiance demonstrates the particular complexities faced by women in political life.

During this period of intensive political organizing among the citizens' groups in preparation for unification, there was never any discussion of adopting a quota rule for increasing female representation. The few who were able to mobilize for this movement were less concerned with the gender composition of the candidate lists than they were with ensuring that the lists could be filled with qualified individuals who were willing to become engaged in politics. Generally, a ratio of 60 men to 40 women characterized the composition of the party members, though the candidates were not selected according to gender. [Interview with Stephan Bickert.] The period was one of incredibly rapid change for the Eastern Germans, who faced three crucial votes within an eight-month period. These crises situations were solved at the expense of women in the drive toward reunification.

EQUAL REPRESENTATION FOR WOMEN IN PARLIAMENT

Although the electorate in Germany is at least 54% female, their representation in the Bundestag, the lower house of the German parliament, has never approached this figure. In 1949, deputies from the 11 West German federal states numbered 70, but only four women sat in the Bundestag. Women in the ten subsequent legislative periods did not comprise more than 10% of those in parliament, until 1987 when the proportion reached 15%. During the first ten periods, the number of female members was about equally distributed among the two main parties, the Christian Democratic Union and the Social Democrats, each of which had a total of close to 70 women representing them over the 38-year period. [Schnitger, Elke, *Frauen und Parlamente*, p. 79.]

The exclusion of women, who clearly represent a sizable portion of the electorate, has been recognized as a serious drawback by at least two of the parties in the Federal Republic. One problem for women in maximizing support for their interests has been the perception that they remain uncommitted to any particular party program. Most female German voters belong to the new middle class, which has not demonstrated a solid party alignment or feminist identity. Nevertheless, in contemporary German politics, parties are expected to be aware of women as a "special interest" group. The established parties are not currently seen as receptive to adjusting the proportion of women in their ranks to match the electorate, or even the party membership. They do tend to fill certain positions with women, but this is done less out of conviction than political expedience. The SPD and the Green parties, as will be shown, made some inroads with quotas.

The German electoral system has been cited as a source of difficulty for women in their efforts to overcome the various barriers to political participation. The upper house, the Bundesrat, is the appointive body through which the various states of the Federal Republic of Germany share in the legislative process, though its powers are minimal. The states are represented by ministers in the state government or by civil servants. Members of the major legislative body, the Bundestag, are chosen in national elections, in which each voter has two votes. The first vote is cast for a specific candidate in the electoral district. The winner of a plurality of these votes represents the district in the Bundestag. However, there are twice as many Bundestag seats as there are electoral districts. To fill the remaining seats, the second vote is cast for a party list of candidates. Under a proportional representation system, the number of seats each party receives is determined by its total nationwide share of second votes. Once the seats won by individual candidates in the first vote have been filled, the remainder of a party's allotment is filled from its candidate list, starting with the top name. If a party fails to garner 5% of the total vote, it will not be delegated any seats.

The first vote for a specific candidate in an electoral district has tended to be more advantageous for women candidates in Germany, although in other nations proportional representation has proved to be more helpful in electing women. In Germany, however, the parties have tended to reserve the safer seats for men, who customarily are placed at the top of the candidates list. As in other countries, Germany's political feminists recognize that positioning women at the top of the lists or alternating male and female candidates can be the key to substantially increasing numbers of women in parliament.

Four of the five parties currently represented in the Bundestag developed in the period from 1945 to 1947 in the German federal states. For the first 17 years of FRG history, the country was governed by a coalition between the Christian Democratic Union and Christian Social Union (CDU/CSU) and the Free Democratic Party (FDP), with the Social Democratic Party (SPD) in opposition. The German Party, a small right-of-center party, also belonged to the coalition under Konrad Adenauer, which began to unravel in 1961. Between 1966 and 1969 a "grand coalition" of the CDU/CSU and the SPD ruled, until the 1969 elections enabled Willy Brandt's SPD to form a coalition with the FDP. This sent the CDU into opposition for the first time. This social-liberal coalition held, despite the loss of a parliamentary majority, until 1982 when the strain of economic crisis and other points of disagreement finally broke the coalition.

With the election of Helmut Kohl in that year, the CDU/CSU coalition with the FDP was formed, and it endured throughout the 1980s. After the 1989 fall of the Berlin Wall and the rapid unification of the FRG and the GDR, December 2, 1990 elections brought the proportion of women to its highest-ever level of 20.5%, though the only major party with an official affirmative action policy is the opposition Social Democratic Party (SPD). [*Das Parliament,* No. 3-4, January 18, 1991.]

The West-based Green Party, weakened by factional splits over political tactics, failed to win 5% of the national vote and lost its seats. However, an East German-based coalition, Bündnis (Alliance) '90 won eight seats, with three going to women, and the East Germany-based Party of Democratic Socialism won 17 seats, eight of them taken by women. These two small parties remain committed to gender balance (approximately equal numbers) in their candidate lists, in contrast to the other parties.

Though the majority of East Germans voted for the CDU in the December 1990 Bundestag elections, the overall 44% CDU representation in parliament is just barely sufficient for the coalition with the FDP to remain workable. Major political debacles over the costs of unification, the economic recession and the issue of reconciling the different abortion regulations in the Eastern and Western parts of the country have dealt severe blows to CDU/CSU popularity.

Adding to the political uncertainty is the potential comeback of the West German Green Party, which in January 1993 announced a proposed merger with Alliance '90, in preparation for 1994 federal and state elections. The merger, which had to be approved by the rank-and-file of both parties, could make the Alliance '90/Greens the country's third-largest party. The party constitution commits it to "human rights, ecology, democracy, social justice and the equality of men and women" and also opposes nationalism, racism, sexism and militarism. A controversial point in the negotiations was the question of quotas for women, which the Greens strongly favored and the Alliance rejected. The two groups pledged to draw up a joint statute on women, acceptable to both sides, by early 1994. While they no longer have representation in the Bundestag, the Greens are coalition partners in the governments of three West German states: Bremen, Hesse and Lower Saxony. Alliance '90 is a government partner in the state of Brandenburg, in former East Germany.

The Greens

Founded in 1979, the Green movement was the outcome of a felt need for an alternative channel of political participation. [Kolinsky, Eva, "The German Greens: A Women's Party?" *Parliamentary Affairs,* January 1988, p. 139.] At its outset, the new social wave wanted to remain removed from the parliament in order to maintain its nonparty status. This desire was at the heart of Green politics. The idea that environmental problems must be dealt with in a comprehensive way soon developed into a massive organizing effort, and a wing of the movement evolved to subject Green ideals to the practical politics against which it was originally interested in protesting. The enthusiasm generated among the grassroots translated into votes from an amalgam of environmental groups such as Greenpeace, women's initiatives, third world groups and citizens rights advocates, all of whom found a home under the Greens.

Under the pioneering leadership of the late Petra Kelly,[1] the Greens decided in 1980 to instill gender balance (equal division) into its candidate lists. Thus, with the entry of the Greens into parliament in 1983, 25 women deputies were added to the Bundestag. While in the past the Greens had rejected the notion of participating in politics, they now were charged with operating in a system against which they had long fought. Over the history of the Green movement, this step has been one of the most controversial and problematic. They brought ideas about women's equality into the political arena that never before had found a voice in parliament. The Greens were the first party to use a quota system to readjust for the under-representation of women in the party, operating on what is termed the "zipper principle," whereby the positions on the candidate lists are occupied alternatively by one man and one woman. This feminist orientation has proven a source of great strength for the parliamentary arm of an "antiparty." Its concept of 50-50 representation also has been adopted by Green Parties in other nations.

In 1985 the party sought to extend this concept to a broader range of social sectors. The imposition of a quota for women in all areas was a radical call for overall equalization in one fell swoop. It generated a great deal of attention, political debate, and discussion of the dilemma of participation: the plodding progress of women toward full, proportional participation would not be achieved until 2017, if the current pace were kept.

Paradoxically, of the 45,000 Green Party members in 1987, only one-third were women, slightly more than the 25% female membership among the other established parties. [Kolinsky, 1988, p. 133.] Despite the fact that the Greens aspire to achieve gender equality through the use of quotas, German women have not shown a great level of support for the party. In fact, the Greens learned some valuable political lessons in the all-German elections in 1990, in which the party won only 3.9% of the vote. Since then, the party has concentrated on strategies for reentering parliament, and, considering significant gains made in subsequent elections in the federal states, there are good prospects as mentioned earlier for their return in the renewed spirit of unity with the eastern groups.

SPD

The Nürnberger party conference of 1980 saw the introduction of a resolution proposing a change in the structure of the Social Democratic Party organization, modeled on the Norwegian 60%-40% rule. At the 1988 party convention in Münster, the SPD instituted a system whereby women candidates are to be integrated by intervals, beginning with 25% and aiming at 40% by 1994. By 1998, these stipulations are to extend to federal, state, local and European electoral slates. In addition, a seat in the party executive is to be reserved exclusively for a woman. These goals were the end result of years of inner-party discussion about the orientation of the SPD toward women. Quotas finally were chosen because of a need to express a tangible commitment where other parties have only nodded in the direction of women. In the December 1990 election, 65 of the 239 winning SPD candidates for the Bundestag were women (27.2%).

Other Parties

The FDP and CDU/CSU have rejected quotas on principle. They have expressed a willingness to implement a plan of promoting women, through general declarations to involve women at higher levels. They deny the need for quotas. [Höcke, Beate, in *Vater Staat Und Seine Frauen*, Berlin, 1990.] Of the 79 representatives the FDP put into office in December 1990, only 16 were women, or slightly over 20%. The results of the election were overwhelmingly positive for the CDU, which ran as the party primarily responsible for unification, but only 13.8% of the CDU deputies are women. CDU parliamentarian Rita Süssmuth is president of the Bundestag, and women make up four of the 20 cabinet members and eight of the 53 ministers.

IMPACT OF QUOTAS

The present gap of women in politics can be closed by the consistent application of quotas. Although women constitute only slightly over 20% of the Bundestag today, the positive changes they engender already are being felt. It must be borne in mind, of course, that as a means toward political development quotas are regarded only as an instrument, not as a goal in themselves.

Despite their narrow application, quotas have already had several positive and wide-ranging effects on German politics. By specifically reserving positions on the candidate lists for women, quotas decrease competitiveness among the qualified female candidates for scarce seats. The result is likely to be more loyalty and support among women for each other.

Slowly, respect for female standards and needs has grown, partly as a result of the women who have proven themselves capable and worthy colleagues in the Bundestag. The most concrete evidence of this process of change is found in the most recent abortion decision. Broad freedom of choice had not been granted to women in West Germany before unification. Paragraph 218 of the German Penal Code categorizes abortion as a criminal offense except in cases of rape, other sexual crimes or psychological grounds. But a recent parliamentary decision to reconcile the differing regulations of Eastern and Western Germany, pending court approval, could make it possible for a woman to make her own choice about whether to terminate her pregnancy in the first three months without penalty. The proposed adoption of the more permissive East German laws on abortion were preceded by lengthy and passionate debate on the part of women over an issue that primarily concerns them, although the decisions have mainly been in the hands of men. In fact, when one parliamentarian from East Berlin, Gregor Gysi, suggested that the decision be left up to the parliament's 136 women, he was met only with laughter.

An unusual political situation developed around the abortion issue. At the point when the 1990 unification treaty was signed, the matter of which law to adopt, the more liberal Eastern or the restrictive Western law, was shelved until a reasonable compromise could be reached. In all, five proposals were submitted, ranging from the very restrictive CDU/CSU proposal narrowing to two the four categories of presently admissible criteria for obtaining the required medical permission, to the FDP suggestion of adopting the East German rule. The decision that was finally taken was the result of the work of a tripartisan commission formed by the SPD, FDP and some CDU members. This unusual defection from the party-line of the CDU caused consternation to the chancellor, as members such as Rita Süssmuth, the Bundestag president, affirmed their loyalty to their sex. The compromise reached by this group also included free distribution of birth control pills to women under 20 years of age, preferential access to childcare for women who choose to give birth, as well as assistance in finding housing and other social welfare benefits.

The public, especially young women, generally favors these support measures to ensure the rights of women to control their own bodies [Feist, Ursula, "Die Unterrepräsentanz von Frauen im politischen System der Bundesrepublik, Gründe und Strategien zur Veränderung," in *Vater Staat und Seine Frauen*, Berlin, 1990, p. 19]. Also, with the help of quotas, the constant pressure for women to prove their right to hold office eases. Other pressures, such as those felt by women legislators during the Weimar Republic to perform in accordance with male standards, are also reduced. No longer do women have to feel beholden to patriarchal patronage.

A greater presence of women in the political arena is clearly a part of social progress. Many seasoned male politicians will, however, necessarily be displaced if the parties successfully put the quota principles into practice. This has been cited as an example of reverse discrimination, and the question has been raised as to whether quotas emphasize quantity over quality. This concern, though valid in the sense that party preferences should primarily be determined by the value and skill of a candidate, fails to acknowledge the need to make more than cosmetic changes in the gender composition of the Bundestag. Political success in Germany has been based on career advancement in male-dominated fields, creating structural barriers that exclude women from influential positions in society. Unless new systems of recruitment are developed, these problems will persist.

RECTIFYING UNDER-REPRESENTATION IN PUBLIC LIFE

The question of whether to utilize quotas does not take into account the overall political environment and whether it is favorable to equality. Nevertheless, the target of quotas is very specific and has in itself an important role: that of reconciling the long-standing inequity in numbers of women in public office. In that realm, quotas are a necessary but not sufficient means toward male/female parity in decision-making bodies—a "top-down" approach to political change. This function is a crucial one, but cannot be meaningful unless taken in conjunction with other, more thoroughgoing measures.

The increasing numbers of women in paid work does not necessarily equate with their social advancement. The large body of civil servants in Germany has since the 1960s seen a rise in the rate of female employment from 25% to 40%, but the positions occupied by women are generally the lower paid positions of lesser authority. The German civil service encompasses teachers, health professionals, ministerial administrators, public works employees, judges and professors. In the highest civil service positions only 19% are female. In 1986 the Ministry for Youth, Family Affairs, Women and Health was set up, and in 1991 it was divided into three different ministries, each headed by a woman: women and youth, the family and the elderly, and health.

Several administrative actions have been taken in response to the growing demands of women for ending inequities in their social and economic positions. In some German federal states, structures providing for equal opportunity counselors began to emerge in 1979 and thereafter. Some states chose the form of departments within ministries, others established more independent units reporting directly to the prime minister.

According to a study by Susanne Seeland, a Berlin feminist/journalist, these structures, regardless of their administrative format, were criticized by women in political parties, unions and women's organizations because they lacked decision-making power, funding and personnel. Between 1980 and 1990 hundreds of positions for equality counselors have been introduced on the regional and local levels, although not all of these positions are full-time.

Tasks of equality units of departments are widespread, Seeland reported, ranging from "screening of all legal drafts concerning women's needs and eventual discriminatory effects, proposals for various political actions to be taken by the state government in favor of women to networking and initiating pilot programs in vocational training. Some are also responsible for research on women and for drawing up an annual report on the situation of women. Most of the units act as counseling and support centers for women who have been discriminated against in the workplace, but they don't have the legal function to file cases in court."

Since the mid-1980s, equality counselors also have been appointed in the civil service, political parties, universities and trade unions, and some private corporations have voluntarily introduced positive action programs and named equality counselors to implement the programs.

Despite the criticisms of the counselors' limited powers, Seeland described the growth and activities of these counselors as part of the dynamic evolution of Berlin's strong and multiform women's movement, which developed hundreds of projects, beginning in the late 1960s, and organized effective political pressure in support of women's needs. Berlin's so-called Red-Green government (a coalition of Social Democrats and the Green Party, 1989-91), she said, "made equality strategies and positive action a political priority area and stressed the objective by introducing quotas into government itself. Out of 12 members of the cabinet, eight were women." [Correspondence with author, October 4, 1992.]

Advances made by women obviously enter into a symbiotic relationship with the progress of the movement at the political leadership level. Though political leadership has long been confined to and defined by the "high politics" decision-makers, whole sectors of society that are excluded from the discussion here also play a pivotal role. If not for the presence of women in the judiciary, the civil service, autonomous movements and women's organizations of academic and professional natures, the women "at the top" would indeed, as they did in Weimar, fail to contribute to the achievement of equality they have sought.

CONCLUSION

The June 25 parliamentary decision on abortion highlights the necessity of bringing gender balance to decision-making bodies, especially those empowered to formulate legislative packages that have a broad impact. Had women been even more under-represented in the parliament, Eastern German women might have come under the more repressive West German law. But more importantly, the 20 defections from the CDU show the classic struggle that was a part of life for political women in Weimar and continues to trouble female legislators today. The conflict was framed by a representative of the Catholic Center Party in 1919: "What shall I represent? The interests of my party or my sex? How can a woman who has fought for so long for the rights of her sex now bow to party discipline and vote against her own instincts?" [Quoted in Koonz, Claudia, 1976.]

The right of suffrage granted to women in 1918 provided a means for politi-cal expression. In twelve years of participation in the Weimar legislature, how-ever, women never emerged from their entrenchment in male-dominated party structures where they were relatively powerless. The achievement of gender equality at the level of German parliamentary politics remains, in many ways, an elusive goal. Some improvements can be made by quotas as one measure of achieving thoroughgoing change in gender relations. The traditional leadership barriers may, however, remain in place despite quotas. For this reason, the active enlistment of women at various levels of society has been and will continue to be of utmost importance.

In order to prevent a polarization and a greater level of tension between the sexes, integration must happen in parliamentary committees working in such areas as finance, research and technology and especially foreign policy, which traditionally have fallen solely under male purview. At this writint, only two of the Bundestag's 23 regular committees are headed by women. There is a tendency to cordon off domestic social issue areas and delegate them to women, while barring their entry into other realms. It is foreseeable that these stigmas and others can be overcome by the concerted efforts towards equal representation taken by some of the parties.

Quotas have indeed played a major role in the progress of women in German society. Relative to the situation at the beginning of the century, women have made massive strides in the levels of representation. One concrete benefit derived from quotas is clear: for a party to survive in Germany today, it must be concerned with the inclusion of women. The awareness of the importance of women's representation has reached a high level, for which at least the debate about affirmative action, if not actual quotas, is partially responsible. Every party must be concerned with the placement of female politicians in leadership positions in order to maintain a favorable public image. Once these accomplishments are matched by progress in state, local and mayoral races, it may be time to reevaluate the necessity of quotas that fall short of equal division.

Of course, in this improved environment, it is hoped that affirmation and support will replace criticism and pressure. In the upcoming period of consolidation, in which women's issues are becoming lost among the "more pressing" questions of the day, such as economic crisis, European Union and asylum seekers, women have to ensure that they do not regress again through disinterest into the old patriarchal structures. Just four years ago the goal of the Greens to put more women into politics seemed extremely difficult if not impossible to implement; there were apparently not enough women party members who aspired to hold public office, nor was there an active national feminist organization pressing for increased political power for women. Now the progress appears more sustainable. Whether this vision of cooperation between the sexes evolves depends ultimately on how people of both genders adjust to the "new politics" of equalized leadership, and upon the overall process of societal growth and development.

NOTE

[1] The murder of Petra Kelly in October 1992 deprived the international women's movement of a brilliant leader and outstanding advocate of women's rights, environmental protection, human rights and social justice.

8

What American Women Can Do to Win Political Equality

The impressive results of the November 1992 elections were seen as a qualitative leap forward for American women in achieving a break-through into the male bastions of political power. More women than ever before were elected to the U.S. House of Representatives and Senate, to state executive offices and legislatures. Success of the widely trumpeted "Year of the Woman" was visible in the refreshing variety of faces and backgrounds of the Ms. Americas going to Washington, D.C. and their state capitols.

Overall, it was a record-breaking year for women candidates: 29 women ran for the U.S. Senate, 11 won their party nominations in mostly hard-fought primaries, and five won seats, including one incumbent; 224 were candidates for the House, 108 won their primaries and 48 were elected. Previously, the largest number of women to win nominations for House seats was 70, in 1990. And a record number of almost 2,500 women ran for state offices in 1992. Although all three women gubernatorial candidates lost, the number of women winning state legislative seats rose to about 20%, and 12 Democratic women and seven Republican women won top state executive jobs, ranging from lieutenant governor to attorney-general, commissioner and treasurer.

The 47 women who won seats in the U.S. House of Representatives included 24 newcomers and 23 incumbents (three incumbents lost), and a quarter of them were women of color, including eight African-American women, three Latinas and one Asian-Pacific woman. In addition, Eleanor Holmes Norton was returned to the House as the restricted-voting representative of the District of Columbia's largely African-American population.

In the Senate, for the first time, an African-American woman, Carol Moseley Braun, an Illinois Democrat, was one of the four female newcomers to the upper chamber, drawing more votes statewide than presidential candidate Bill Clinton. Incumbent Barbara Mikulski, Maryland Democrat, won reelection easily and the only other woman senator, Nancy Kassebaum, Kansas Republican, was not up for reelection. There was another first: Democrats Barbara Boxer and Dianne Feinstein of California became the first pair of women senators to represent a single state and were also the first Jewish women elected to the Senate; California voters also elected seven women to the House, making their state's female representation the largest in Congress. The fourth Senate newcomer, Patty Murray, a Washington Democrat and self-described "mom in tennis shoes," was expected to provide an informal note in the traditional atmosphere of what has been called the most exclusive men's club in the nation. Another first: the Senate male leadership announced they were having a restroom installed for their female colleagues.

A National Women's Political Caucus demographic profile of the successful congressional women candidates described them as "definitely not cookie-cutter politicians," but rather a diverse group representing a wide range of professions and backgrounds. Although 74% are Democrats and 26% Republicans, 91% are pro-choice on the abortion issue. With a mean age of 45, some 15% are under 40 and 23% are over 60; 30% are between the ages 41 and 50, and 32% are between 51 and 60. Challenging the often heard view that women cannot handle simultaneously the demanding responsibilities of family and public office, 68% of the congresswomen are presently married (only 17% are single), and 83% have children.

A case in point was Senator Patty Murray, praised by President Harriett Woods of the National Women's Political Caucus as "just what voters are looking for: an outsider, who is close to them and understands their lives." [The New York Times, September 17, 1992, p. A16.] Murray was a teacher and first-term state senator when she decided to run for the U.S. Senate. A mother of two children, she also cared for her aging parents, cooked several times a week and got into politics via community activism. She says she acquired her name tag 12 years ago when she went to the state capitol to protest budget cuts at community colleges and was told by a male legislator: "You can't do anything; you're just a mom in tennis shoes."

Professionally, the largest percentage (21%) of the congresswomen come from the government/politics/public affairs sector, with 17% each from business and education. Women in the category of community volunteer/homemaker/activist outnumber attorneys 13% to 11%. According to Ruth Mandel, director, Center for the American Woman and Politics (CAWP) at Rutgers University, 22 of the female congressional bloc have held seats in state legislatures earlier in their careers and some have served in city councils or other state and local positions. Estimating that women now compose about 20% of the state legislatures, she told a post-election press briefing: "Many of tomorrow's senators and congresswomen are undoubtedly sitting in state houses today." [National Press Club, Washington, D.C., November 5, 1992.]

Compared with another widely acclaimed "year of the woman" in 1972 when the number of women in the House "soared" from nine to 14 (out of 435 members) and "doubled" from one to two women among the 100 senators, the 1992 electoral victories, both in the numbers of women nominees (108) and women winners (48) in the House and the 11 women nominees and five winners in the Senate, were significantly greater.

Beginning in 1972, the first year in which the newly organized National Women's Political Caucus began promoting women candidates for Congress, the biannual increments in winners ranged from ones, twos and threes, to an actual decline in 1978. Thus, the 1992 gain of 19 House seats and the four-seat gain in the Senate, coming after the modest overall three-seat gain in the election results of 1990 (also called the Year of the Woman), was unprecedented. Yet, after the post-election celebrations came the realization that women had gone from being slightly over 6% of House members to about 11%, and in the Senate from 2% to 6%.[1] It was estimated that even if every female candidate running for election had won, the 103rd Congress would still have been 80% male, a long way from the goal of political equality. The United States remains in the lowest ranks of the world's parliaments when rated for inclusion of women. Clearly, it will take more than a year (more likely decades) to make women equal partners with men in governing our nation or even achieving the political status of women in the Nordic countries, unless extraordinary remedial measures are taken.

THE POWER OF INCUMBENCY AND MONEY

One unusual aspect of the 1992 elections that is not likely to be duplicated in the 1994 and 1996 elections was the large number of open seats available because of near-record numbers of House and Senate male incumbents who retired or chose not to run again and the redistricting of congressional seats, based on the latest U.S. Census data, which forced some incumbents to run in unfamiliar territory.

Despite the widely reported public disaffection with Congress in the wake of various scandals, incumbency remained the most decisive factor in the results of House and Senate races: 93% of House incumbents and 88% of Senate incumbents who ran for reelection were victorious. Aside from incumbent Barbara Mikulski, who won easily, of the four successful women Senate candidates, only one (Dianne Feinstein) was a challenger of an incumbent (a short-term appointee of the Republican governor) and the other three ran for open seats. Among the 48 successful women who ran for House seats, only two defeated male incumbents, 22 won open seats, and 24 were themselves incumbents.

The power of male incumbency and the extremely high costs of electoral campaigns remain the major obstacles to political equality for American women. Under the unusually favorable political atmosphere for women candidates in the 1992 elections, some women were able to raise huge sums of money for their campaigns. Preliminary reports by the Federal Election Commission showed that three of the new women senators were among the nation's top 10 campaign fundraisers. Boxer ($10.3 million) and Feinstein ($8 million), both Californians, were Nos. 1 and 2, and Braun of Illinois ($6.7 million) was No. 7. Whether other women will have similar fundraising appeal and open seat advantages in the 1994 nonpresidential election year remains problematic.

An analysis of the 1992 election campaign shows both the new opportunities and continuing difficulties for women seeking to win electoral office. It is generally agreed that the catalyst for the upsurge of women's political activities in 1992 was the Hill-Thomas hearings and particularly the TV monitor-image in millions of households showing the all-male Senate Judiciary Committee grilling Anita Hill and visibly "not getting it" when she testified on being subjected to sexual harassment by U.S. Supreme Court nominee Clarence Thomas. Adding to women's indignation at this graphic demonstration of their lack of power was a follow-up incident, in which a delegation of Democratic congresswomen (Patricia Schroeder, Colorado; Barbara Boxer and Maxine Waters of California; Louise Slaughter and Nita Lowey of New York; Patsy Mink of Hawaii; Jolene Unsoeld of Washington; and Eleanor Holmes Norton, District of Columbia) attempted to enter a Senate Democratic caucus meeting to protest the treatment of Hill, and were turned away.

The televised national drama was credited with helping Boxer win her bid to switch from her House seat to the Senate, as well as other electoral victories by women candidates. The election of Senator Carol Moseley Braun (D, IL) was assisted by large numbers of cross-over votes from disaffected Republican suburban women, who were also put off by the ultra-right-wing tone of the Republican Party nominating convention and the party's tough anti-abortion platform. [See gender gap data below.]

While describing Anita Hill as "a heroine in the 1992 story of women and politics," Ruth Mandel noted that "neither Anita Hill nor any other single person or event could have given political women a life they did not have. American women stood in readiness for the special circumstances of this extraordinary year. They were prepared for opportunity. This is a 20-year story of building a women's political base—a base of candidates for elective and appointive offices at all levels. Had it not been for the early workshops and pioneering races of the 1970s, had it not been for all the organizing and training and peptalking over the last two decades, there would never have been a solid roster of women ready to move up from local and state levels of political participation."

Columnist Ellen Goodman put it another way: "The ballyhooed Year of the Woman often reminds me of the 'overnight singing sensation' discovered after 20 years of training. The breakthrough came only after a generation of women moved in a slow and grueling pace through the system." [*New York Newsday*, November 10, 1992, p. 86.]

WOMEN'S GROUPS PROVIDE SUPPORT SYSTEMS

From the pioneering July 1971 founding convention of the National Women's Political Caucus (NWPC) in Washington, D.C., when then-Democratic Congresswoman Bella Abzug and Republican Virginia Allen were elected co-chairs, to the present time, an increasingly large community of women's groups has been focusing on recruiting, training, raising funds and campaigning for women candidates, preferably those who support main points in the women's rights agenda. These range from the Equal Rights constitutional amendment, child care, health care, parental leave, jobs and economic equity to abortion rights and an end to sexual harassment and violence against women. Among the key groups are the following:

The National Women's Political Caucus is among the oldest. It is now headed by Harriett Woods, a former Missouri Democratic state legislator and official, who narrowly lost two tries for the U.S. Senate because of insufficient party support and lack of early funding. The NWPC, in preparation for the 1992 elections, actively sought out and encouraged women to run for Congress and state office and raised almost $250,000 to distribute among progressive Democratic and Republican women candidates with the best chances of winning. (The 435 successful House candidates put an average of about $551,000 each into their winning campaigns. They outspent their opponents by more than five to one.) The organization's Democratic and Republican task forces assist in targeting candidates to support or defeat and are active during the quadrennial national party conventions.

The NWPC held 14 campaign skills workshops for women candidates and campaign workers in the 1991 election cycle. It sponsored an information center at the Democratic convention in New York in July 1992 and with other women's groups participated in a convention program showcasing women candidates. Its Democratic Task Force distributed a directory of pro-choice Democratic women and operated an adopt-a-campaign project to provide volunteer support for women candidates. Woods also convened several meetings of an ad-hoc coalition of pro-choice Republican women's groups during 1992 to share information about candidates and plan strategies for the platform hearings and convention. At the Republican convention in Houston, NWPC sponsored a "Showcase of Pro-Choice Republican Women Candidates" that was attended by 13 GOP candidates.

NOW (National Organization of Women), the largest feminist membership organization in the United States, raised about $500,000 to distribute to women candidates through a national political action committee. Its major emphasis was on an Elect Women for a Change campaign, based on a resolution approved at its 1992 convention calling on NOW chapters in areas "where feminist women candidates are running for elective offices to join in supporting a coordinated feminist campaign for all NOW-PAC endorsed feminist candidates rather than working solely on any one candidate's campaign," It enlisted support for its "public organizing meetings and rallies, door to door and telephone canvassing, outreach and election day polling and visibility actions which will build public awareness of the real difference women in office can make."

It also proposed that NOW chapters recruit independent feminist women candidates to challenge the major parties' nominees if both were opponents of women's rights. In Connecticut, former NOW coordinator Lynn Taborsak, after losing the Democratic nomination for Congress to an anti-abortion candidate, ran on a third party line, the Connecticut Party ticket, and lost.

At its June 1992 convention in Chicago, NOW also took a long-discussed step of initiating formation of a national third party, convened by, among others, NOW President Patricia Ireland, Dolores Huerta, of the National Farm Workers Union, and former NOW President Eleanor Smeal, who heads the Fund for a Feminist Majority, which has a gender balance goal of "50-50 by the Year 2001." The new party, called the 21st Century Party—the Nation's Equality Party, is chaired by Huerta, Smeal is its national secretary, and most of its officers are women.

Huerta said the party would provide "a distinctly different platform that will be a conscience to those in political life and expose the shortcomings of the two major parties." She noted that its members would be free to help "candidates of other parties who support feminist issues. The 21st Century Party will stimulate political activity, clarify issues and provide hope and direction for the future." The party mandated that women comprise a minimum of 52% of its candidates and officers.

In practice, both NOW and the Fund for a Feminist Majority followed the strategy of encouraging large numbers of women to run for political office in major party primaries, regardless of their chances of winning nominations. This was in contrast to the policy of NWPC and other women's groups, which preferred to apply more pragmatic criteria. Smeal's organization sent teams of representatives to California, New York, Arizona, Oregon, Tennessee and South Carolina to identify potential candidates. Using mass mailings and a sizable staff, it spread the message that women should "flood" the tickets. With hundreds of women running for office, it contended, some would win, some would lose, and everyone would learn something in the process.

EMILY's List, which takes its first name acronym from the phrase "early money is like yeast," was founded in 1985 by Ellen Malcolm, an independently wealthy Washingtonian who organized a national network of some 22,000 members to raise funds to help give an early start to pro-choice Democratic women candidates. Funds are given only to candidates who can provide polling data and proof of a well-organized campaign as an indication that they have a good chance to win. In a post-election statement, Malcolm reported that EMILY's List members contributed $6,157,523 to House and Senate candidates running in 1992, which she said made the network the biggest contributor to congressional candidates in the election campaign.

Commenting that "The Year of the Woman" had turned out to be "The Year of Democratic Women," Malcolm said: "The number of Democratic women in the House has tripled since EMILY's list began supporting House candidates three elections ago . . . . All the gains in the Senate and virtually all the gains in the House were made by Democratic women candidates. The four new women elected to the Senate are Democratic women. In the House, 21 Democratic and three Republican women make up the freshman class. In total, 36 Democratic and 12 Republican women are in the House of Representatives."

She asserted that by creating a national donor base to support House candidates, "we have revolutionized the process of electing women to the House . . . . Voters often doubt that women candidates can win. But the credibility gap that held women back was dealt a severe blow Tuesday night as voters learned an important lesson. Women can run in the big races and women can win. That lesson will help every woman candidate who runs in the future."

A number of women supported by Malcolm's group lost, including political novice Lynn Yeakel, Pennsylvania Democrat, who challenged incumbent Republican Senator Arlen Specter because of his role in the Hill-Thomas hearings, and Geraldine Ferraro of New York, defeated in a four-way Democratic primary Senate race in which former congresswoman Liz Holtzman and state Attorney General Robert Abrams ran a negative campaign against her. (Holtzman, who had been denied EMILY funds because polls showed her far behind the then front-runner Ferraro, came in last in the primary, and Abrams, after narrowly besting Ferraro in the primary, went on to lose the general election to Republican Alfonse D'Amato, the anti-choice and ultraconservative incumbent.)

But significant numbers of the Democratic women elected to the House and Senate received early funding from EMILY, among them many newcomers. Explaining her selective approach to financial help, Malcolm said: "If we took money and gave it to 150 women equally instead of the 35 we thought could win, then some of those 35 wouldn't win." [*New York Times,* October 12, 1992.]

In one major event, held July 14, 1992, during the Democratic Party nominating convention in New York, the group raised a record-breaking $750,000 for seven women Senate candidates, four of whom won. The evening began with a reception attended by 450 people, mostly women, who each contributed $1,000 or more and were addressed by Ann Richards of Texas and Barbara Roberts of Oregon, two of the nation's three women governors. The event then moved into the hotel's grand ballroom, where almost 3,000 people, including many women convention delegates, were addressed by the Senate candidates and contributed more money.

At an event, held June 25-26 in Washington, D.C., EMILY's List organized a Politics and Policy Seminar for its recommended House and Senate candidates at which they received advice on how to conduct their campaigns, tailor their media messages and deal with issues. Among those briefing them were pollster Celinda Lake, Paul Tully, political director of the Democratic National

Committee, James Carville, key strategist for the Clinton campaign, and other professional political consultants. They were joined by members of the fund's Majority Council, donors who contribute $1,000 or more a year, and by members of Congress at a reception on Capitol Hill, followed by a private dinner with women members in the House Ways and Means Committee chamber. This two-day training program highlighted the dominating, often decisive role money plays in electoral victories and gave the assembled women neophytes a taste of what they can expect as "insiders." Malcolm described the women candidates as "very serious," adding: "They learn and learn. It's like they are trying to pass their S.A.T.'s." [*New York Times*, October 12, 1992.]

Another major money source for women candidates in 1992 was the biparti-san Women's Campaign Fund, headed by Jane Danowitz, which has an esti-mated 10,000 donors. The WCF, founded in 1974, was the earliest group to pro-vide financial support to thousands of women candidates at every political level. In 1992 it gave away more than one million dollars in cash and technical assis-tance to more than 200 women across the country, twice what it contributed in the 1990 elections. Recognizing that women candidates' difficulties in raising enough campaign money have been one of the greatest barriers to their electoral success, WFC says it gives its money early—"six months, nine months, even a year before a primary or general election. Sometimes WCF makes its contribu-tion even before the formal campaign begins. We want women to have the 'start-up' capital they need to get their campaigns up and running." It was the first na-tional PAC to contribute to the eventually successful contests of 10 Democratic women newcomers to Congress from Arizona, California, Georgia, Oregon, Pennsylvania, Texas and Utah.

Observing that "yesterday's women in state legislatures are today's women in Congress, and tomorrow's women in the White House," a WCF brochure states that half of its financial and technical assistance goes to women running at the state and local levels: "Scores of national women leaders—like Governor Ann Richards, Senator Barbara Mikulski, and Congresswomen Barbara Boxer and Susan Molinari (R, NY)—all received WCF support as state and local candidates before they became Governor or members of Congress."

Like EMILY'S List, the WCF says it "carefully targets seats at the federal, state, and local level—seats where women have the best chance of winning. We recruit viable women candidates for these targeted seats from our national net-work of over 2,000 politically active women officeholders and leaders." It re-quires that its candidates support women's rights, including the right to abortion.

Fundraising specifically for Republican women candidates is conducted by the Wish List, which was formed in 1991 and says it has almost 2,000 members. According to its founder and president, Glenda Greenwald, it distributed about $400,000 in 1992 to women candidates who supported abortion rights and were considered able to win. Four of the eight pro-choice Republican women candi-dates supported by the group were successful, and no Republican woman chal-lenger who was not pro-choice won election. Greenwald said in her post-election statement: "Our party has a big job of restructuring to do and prochoice Republican women will be very much a part of that restructuring. We are at the center of the Republican Party and its future." Greenwald was among a number of prominent Republican women who disavowed their party platform's commitment to an unqualified, constitutional ban on abortions.

The firm ultraconservative grip on the Republican convention alienated party women who supported women's rights issues and free choice, but they made no attempt to challenge the platform or debate issues on the convention floor in what was clearly a hostile atmosphere. During the presidential campaign, in a televised interview with TV news star Barbara Walters, President George Bush noted that a lot of women were running and said he hoped they would lose. He was referring to Democratic women candidates, but he did not seize the opportunity to express support for Republican women candidates.

The WISH List advisory board includes Senator Nancy Kassebaum and five incumbent Republican congresswomen: Nancy Johnson, Jan Meyers, Susan Molinari, Connie Morella, Marge Roukema and Olympia Snowe, all of whom were reelected.

Unlike the women in WISH, the loyalist National Federation of Republican Women, founded in 1938, does not challenge GOP public policy positions. It concentrates on identifying and recruiting Republican women to run for state and local offices, provides financial and volunteer support, conducts a two-day training course for Republican women running or considering a bid for public office, and promotes volunteerism and private-sector initiatives at the state, local and national levels. It claims to have 128,000 members in 2,300 clubs throughout the 50 states.

Another group working to elect more women to public office is the National Political Congress of Black Women, cofounded in 1984 by Democratic Party activist Dr. C. Delores Tucker, a former Pennsylvania state legislator, former Congresswoman Shirley Chisholm, and other African-American women. Operating without paid staff, this coalition has organized 42 chapters across the country to press for inclusion of more women in public office and decision-making. In September 1992 it held a summit meeting attended by hundreds of black women, including local, county, state and national legislators, and political aspirants, as well as women involved in the media, education, business, law and society. Among those addressing the meeting was congresswoman Maxine Waters, who said white men "make the rules and regulations to protect themselves. Until we have the audacity to do so, we're on the outside. You have to take the power—they won't give it to you." As a first step, Tucker announced the formation of a multipartisan, multigroup committee to produce a list of the most qualified African-American women for appointment to high government positions. [*Majority Rules! An Independent Newsletter for, and about, Women in Politics*, Vol. 1, No. 6, February 1992.]

WOMEN AND THE DEMOCRATIC PARTY

Under a Democratic Party rule requiring equal division, or gender balance, for all party appointive or elective posts, convention delegates and national committee members, women were highly visible both on stage and on the floor at the 1992 convention. Although candidate Bill Clinton made no nationally televised speeches on women's issues, nor singled them out in the three debates with President Bush and Ross Perot or in his TV commercials, he and his wife, Hillary, an overwhelming favorite among the women delegates, each gave a rousing speech at one of the women's caucus meetings that were held every morning of the convention.

At previous conventions, beginning in 1972, women's caucuses were organized and conducted by the NWPC and other women's rights groups as part of their campaign to gain both platform commitments and equal participation for women. At the 1992 convention, the women's caucus was under the control of the Democratic National Committee (DNC) and the pragmatic emphasis throughout was on unified support for what proved to be a winning ticket that supported abortion rights and other issues favored by the mainstream women's movement and which was also expected to bring large numbers of women into policy-making positions in the new Clinton-Gore Administration.

Another strong expectation was that Hillary Clinton, despite the campaign's clumsy attempt to repackage her into an old-style wife and mother image, would be an activist First Lady in the tradition of Eleanor Roosevelt, who fought for gender balance within the Democratic Party structures. Mrs. Roosevelt was also responsible for getting a record-breaking number of women (50) into the New Deal government by 1935, including the first woman cabinet member, Secretary of Labor Frances Perkins. Sharing the intense desire for defeat of the Bush-Quayle Administration, which had been so hostile to women's agenda issues, some Democratic feminists at the 1992 convention nevertheless felt that in downplaying women's issues, the campaign strategists were ignoring the fact that women were the majority base support of the party.

The Getting It Gazette, an irreverent news sheet published daily during the convention by a collective of feminist journalists, among them the sharp-penned, witty Jane O'Reilly, challenged the Clinton-Gore campaign's downplaying of women's issues and the weakly worded Democratic Party platform. In the *Gazette*'s July 14, 1992 issue, O'Reilly asked whether the people running Clinton's campaign really believed "that we are thrilled by the idea of helping to push this mealy-mouthed platform which they have whittled down to some craven Republican look-alike marketing statement? Who do they think they are talking to when they evade almost every issue we are struggling to solve and duck behind airy regressions about 'mainstream' and 'traditional.'"

O'Reilly said every day women were reading that Clinton and Al Gore were going to "campaign vigorously for votes from minorities, labor groups and other traditional Democratic constituencies." She asked: "What are we? 'The Other?' If so, we are the majority other, and we are not going to wait any more." Another article commented: "Designed to appeal to a broad spectrum of American voters, the platform avoids addressing women, as though we were a fractious special interest group. Can we tolerate our interests being placed, once again, at the margin?"

Pat Reuss, a veteran women's rights activist, wryly described looking for the word 'women' in the platform: "We thought it might be under 'Violence' as in 'Against Women.' Nope. 'Rape'? Nope. 'Battered Women'? Nope. What we got was: efforts are being directed to 'preserving the family unit.' That's nice. And if the 'violence' gets really bad, we can put our children in shelters. We didn't give up hope, though. Certainly 'Women' would be under the ERA. But guess what? The ERA was—oops, we forgot to put that in, said the men. Called it a 'technical error.' Women who don't want to be paranoid realize that sometimes being paranoid is knowing all the facts."

The absence of specific verbal commitments to much of the women's rights agenda was not the work only of male tacticians. Congresswoman Nancy Pelosi, who chaired the Platform Committee, and other women's rights "insiders," as well as the large numbers of women delegates, offered no formal challenges to the platform, joining in the prevailing view that winning came first, and mobilizing support for women's social, economic and political demands would come later. Yet, by being about half the number of delegates, women at the convention were a dramatic reminder that they were there only as a result of earlier hard-fought intraparty battles by women's coalitions.[2]

CBS polls that tracked the composition of both parties' convention delegates over a 20-year period showed that from 1968 to 1988, the percentage of women delegates to the Democratic convention increased steadily, with the exception of the year 1976, while representation at the GOP convention progressed more slowly. Inclusion of women in Democratic conventions was 13% in 1968; 40% in 1972, when the NWPC made its first major impact; down to 33% in 1976, when the moderate Jimmy Carter forces controlled the convention; 49% in 1980 and 1984; and 48% in 1988. Republican inclusions of women delegates were 15% in 1968; 20% in 1972; 31% in 1976; 29% in 1980; 44% in 1984; and 33% in 1988. [*The Public Perspective, A Roper Center Review of Public Opinion and Polling*, July/August 1992, p. 97. For a detailed description of NWPC and other women's rights groups political activities in relation to the Democratic and Republican parties, also see, *Gender Gap, Bella Abzug's Guide to Political Power for American Women*, by Bella Abzug with Mim Kelber, Houghton Mifflin Co., Boston, 1984.]

While assuring women's rights groups of support for their goals, the Clinton-Gore strategists, believing they had their votes locked up, concentrated on wooing centrist voters and particularly white male Reagan Democrats who had contributed significantly to the Republican victories of the 1980s decade. Both Clinton and his wife made appearances with some Democratic women candidates in their local areas. *Putting People First,* the Clinton-Gore paperback book issued after the convention to spell out their plans for change, included a section on women. In general and sometimes specific language, it made commitments on freedom of choice in reproductive rights, as well as on women's rights in the workplace; protection from sexual harassment and violence; "pro-family and pro-children policies," such as parental leave and a child care network; and health care, including legislation "to address deficiencies in the treatment of women's health problems." It also pledged to "hire and appoint more women at all levels of government so that a Clinton-Gore Administration better reflects this country's population." The Clinton-Gore book also emphasized the above-the-party approach evident throughout the campaign: "Our policies," the candidates wrote, "are neither liberal nor conservative, neither Democratic nor Republican. They are new. They are different. We are confident they will work." [Clinton, Bill, and Gore, Al, *Putting People First: How We Can All Change America*, pp. 169-72, Times Books, 1992.]

Except during the convention, no campaign by the Democratic National Committee was evident to bolster women candidates, to commit to the concept of 50-50 gender balance in government or to single out women's economic and social concerns. Fund-raising was largely left to the independent women-run PACs. However, the Democratic Senatorial Campaign Committee (DSCC) agreed to set up a Women's Council, chaired by incumbent Senator Barbara Mikulski, which raised money for the Democratic women nominees for the U.S. Senate. With average donations of about $125 from some 10,000 individuals, mostly women, the council raised more than $1.5 million, divided among the 10 Democratic women nominees. This was a miniscule amount (about $150,000 per candidate) compared with the millions required for each nominee's campaign.

According to DSCC Women's Council director Christine Koerner, post-election fund-raising was already under way for targeted seats where Republican or open seats would be contested in the 1994 elections. She said the council was committed to recruiting and supporting only women candidates. [*Majority Rules!*, February 1993.] A post-election fundraising mailing by the DSCC focused on reelection of incumbent senators (all male, except for Dianne Feinstein) whose terms expire in 1994, and mentioned the possibility of a women candidate for the Tennessee seat vacated by Vice President Al Gore.

One of the few challenges to the DNC's distancing posture came from former congresswoman Bella Abzug, a New York State national committeewoman and the initial driving force behind organized women's equality activities in the party from the 1970s and into the last decade. In preconvention testimony before the party's Platform Committee in Cleveland on May 18, 1992, she called for commitments in the platform "and in the daily life of our party structures and members, to double, triple, quadruple the presence of women in elective and appointive office, from the national down to the local level, with the goal of having fully gender-balanced government by a specific date, the sooner the better." She noted that there was ample precedent for that commitment in the party charter, which provides for equal division within the national committee and in the convention delegations, all party appointed and elective positions.

She recalled that the 1984 convention, which nominated Walter Mondale as president and Geraldine Ferraro as vice president, included in the platform a section on "Political Empowerment for Minorities and Women." It established the goal of doubling the number of minorities and women in Congress by 1988 and said: "We will recruit women and minorities to run for Governorships and all state and local offices. The Democratic Party (through all of its campaign committees) will commit to spending maximum resources to elect women and minority candidates and offer these candidates in-kind services, including political organizing and strategic advice. And the bulk of all voter registration funds will be spent on targeted efforts to register minorities and women."

If the party did do any of those things, she said, "it kept it a secret from those most interested: women candidates in need of party help." In the streamlined 1988 party platform the commitment to women's representation was reduced to a phrase within a longer sentence. It spoke merely of "assuring and pledging the full and equal access of women and minorities to elective office and party endorsement." (In the 1992 platform, as described above, women as a constituency were mentioned only minimally.)

Since 1984, Abzug said, the DNC had failed to seek out, encourage or provide early funding for women candidates. (As noted earlier, this was left to women's groups. The Eleanor Roosevelt Fund, set up in 1982 by the DNC to raise money for women candidates, was nonoperative in the 1992 campaign, except in California, according to a DNC representative.) Abzug also charged that the DNC's caucus of women members, the minority caucus and other caucuses were "kept in the closet, their meetings . . . not even listed in official notices of DNC meetings, and they get no funding with which to function effectively." The only preconvention group activity of the low-profile women's caucus was to publish a training handbook for women candidates, for which it had to raise its own funds. "What does this say about our party's commitment to women?" Abzug asked.

THE NATIONAL PARITY CAMPAIGN

As one solution to the under-representation of women in government, Abzug presented the Platform Committee with a petition being circulated by the National Parity Campaign, which was initiated on May 5, 1992, at a "Women Tell the Truth" conference in New York featuring Anita Hill as the keynote speaker and attended by several thousand women. The conference on sexual harassment and other social, economic and political issues was cosponsored by a broad coalition of area women's organizations—traditional and feminist. The petition, which was still circulating after the election and remains a potentially major focus, calls upon "all political parties to nominate and support *only* women for all open seats until women achieve parity in our government" and said the undersigned "pledge our resources and votes to the many qualified, pro-women's rights women seeking office."

In an accompanying fact sheet, the National Parity Campaign argued that women "do make a difference in elective office." It said: "A government that is overwhelmingly male is not representative of a population that is more than half female. Men, even men with whom we often agree, cannot serve as women's surrogates. We need women leaders with the full range of women's back-grounds, experiences and ideas. We need these women in office to make the de-cisions that affect our lives."

Asserting that "our government was designed by men and operates as a self-perpetuating male political system," the statement said: "The results are now visible. We have seen the hearing rooms of Congress, where men, working on committees that include no women, make judgments, set budgets, establish priorities, debate issues and make decisions that determine the quality of life of every woman in the United States." It cited the following data on the status of American women:

- Although about 57% of females were in the labor force in 1991, women still earned an average 68 cents for every dollar earned by men.
- Women can expect to spend 17 years of their lives caring for children plus an-other 18 years caring for elderly relatives, mostly at their own expense. There are no federal or state laws requiring employers to grant employees paid or un-paid family or medical leave to take care of family members. (President Bush vetoed an unpaid family leave bill in 1992.)
- A majority of Americans over 65 are women, and they get less of everything—social security, public and private pensions, wages and assets.
- In nine out of 10 single-parent families the parent is the mother, yet the family income of single mothers with children is half that of single fathers.
- Women are disadvantaged in terms of health care too. The country's major source of funding for medical research spends 13% of its budget on women's health although women are the fastest-growing group of those infected with AIDS; the death rate from breast cancer is up 24% and women suffer dispro-portionately from other illnesses such as osteoporosis and mental illness. Many medical procedures for women are based on research done entirely with men, such as coronary disease research.

In her testimony stressing the urgency of electing more women to help over-come these examples of women's economic and social inequities, Abzug ex-plained that "the parity campaign focuses on giving women preference in races for open seats because we recognize that the power of incumbency has been one of the major obstacles to electing women to office. Fortunately, mere incum-bency no longer can provide assurance of reelection in this volatile year. Of course, Democratic primaries will continue to be competitive. Anyone who meets the legal requirements has the right to run. But this year and for years to come, the endorsement, support, and early allocation of party funds should go to the many qualified, pro-women's rights women candidates seeking office for the first time, and women seeking reelection must get full party support."

THE GENDER GAP POTENTIAL

A basic argument of political feminists is that because women are a majority of the U.S. population (they outnumber males by 6.2 million) and vote in larger numbers than men, as they did in 1992, their electoral importance should get priority recognition from all political parties, their concerns should get major attention and their inclusion in elected and appointed office should be accelerated until gender balance is reached. In some instances, they note, women's margin of support for a candidate can mean the difference between victory and defeat. But instead, women voters are usually described and treated as though they were just another "special interest" group.

The "gender gap" phenomenon—the difference between the women's and men's vote for a particular candidate—first emerged in the 1980 presidential election. While 54% of all male voters chose Republican Ronald Reagan over Democrat Jimmy Carter, only 46% of women voters did so, a gender gap of 8%, the largest difference between women and men since the Gallup organization began compiling such data in 1952. Only 37% of men voted for Carter, compared with 45% of women. A third party candidate, John Anderson, broke even, winning 7% of the votes of each sex. Women were also showing an increasing tendency to identify with the Democratic Party—more than 40% of all women polled, compared with 33% of all men, called themselves Democrats.

In 1984, at the height of Reagan's popularity, the gender gap narrowed slightly, to 6% in the vote for Reagan and 7% in the vote for Democratic challenger Walter Mondale, with Reagan winning 62% of the male vote and 56% of the female vote. In the 1988 Bush-Dukakis campaign, men voted 57% for the Republican to 41% for the Democrat, while women split 50% for Bush to 49% for Dukakis, gender gaps of 7% and 8%.

The male-female voting difference remained evident in the 1992 election despite the Republican loss of large numbers of both Reagan Democrat males and other groups to Clinton as well as to independent Ross Perot. According to exit polls conducted by Voter Research and Surveys (VRS), a consortium of four major TV networks, Clinton received 45% of the overall vote, Bush 38%, and Perot 19%. Clinton won 46% of the women's vote and 41% of the male vote, a 5% gap; Bush won 38% of the male vote and 37% of the female vote, an insignificant 1% difference; and Perot received 21% of the male vote and 17% of the female vote, a 4% difference. In terms of political preference among women voters, Clinton led Bush by 8%, with women in every age and education category showing more support for Clinton than for Bush. In only one group, homemakers, did Bush outpoll Clinton, 45% to 36%.

The poll analysis also showed a 7% gender gap in party identification: 41% of women identified themselves as Democrats, compared with 34% of men; 34% of women and 36% of men identified with the Republicans; and 26% of women and 30% of men called themselves Independents. Among traditional Democratic African-American voters, 86% of the women voted for Clinton, the highest percentage he received from any group. Overall, 82% of African-Americans supported him.

A post-election analysis, "A Closer Look at the Gender Gap," by Everett Carl Ladd, president of the Roper Center for Public Opinion Research, reported that while the gender gap had closed somewhat in the presidential contest, "the gap this year was large and striking in 10 of the 11 Senate races where a woman faces a man. Women voters are generally less supportive of Republican candidates than are men, and the gender gap refers to this particular difference. In 1992, however, whenever a female candidate faced a male candidate for Senate, she did better among women voters than among men, whatever her party— although it must be noted that there was only one instance in which a Republican woman ran against a Democratic man." [*Christian Science Monitor*, December 4, 1992, p. 218.]

Ladd reported that in the presidential election, the gender gap favoring Clinton was concentrated among young men and women as well as among those with less than a high-school education and with postgraduate training. Among 18- to 24-year-olds, there was a 13% gender gap, with 52% of women compared with 39% of men favoring Clinton. (Among women, only 31% voted for Bush.) Of those with less than a high-school education, 57% of women and 48% of men voted for Clinton. (Only 27% of women in the category supported Bush.) In the ranks of those with postgraduate training, 55% of women and 47% of men favored Clinton, with Bush getting 30% of the women's vote. Single women favored Clinton over Bush by 55% to 29%, and divorced/separated women supported Clinton by 49% compared to 32% for Bush. ["The Polls and the 1992 Election," *The Public Perspective, A Roper Center Review of Public Opinion and Polling*, Vol. 4, No. 2, January/February 1993.]

In the congressional elections, he reported, "women post-graduates went heavily for House Democrats, 62 to 38%, while men with graduate training gave an edge to Republican candidates by a margin of 51 to 49%."

Ladd concluded that "the growth of the women's movement and its increased political activity over the past 15 years seem to have contributed to persisting gender differences in voting (and, as well on various policy questions.) Women's greater entry into the labor force and the sharp rise in single-parent, female-headed households have probably added to the gender gap as well.

"This being so," he continued, "it is not surprising that young women, lacking experience in earlier times when gender differences were not evident politically, show the impact of the new pressures somewhat more than their elders.

Similarly, college training, especially advanced graduation education, is a carrier of the new values."

Thus the Clinton-Gore victory, widely seen as a generational change in political power, owed much of its success to the rising expectations and independence of younger women for whom women in leadership in public life and the professions, exemplified by such women as the senior woman member of Congress Patricia Schroeder (D, CO) and Hillary Clinton, have become role models. The argument that women's votes won the election for Clinton-Gore was made by journalist Deirdre English in a post-election "victory edition" of *The Getting It Gazette* [November 27, 1992.] Using slightly different figures than the VRS data, she wrote:

> Would women have won the election for Clinton even if he had not led among men? Yes, Clinton's lead among women was a decisive 11%. (The women's vote was Clinton 47%, Bush 36%, Perot 17%.)
>
> Would Clinton have won the popular vote if only men had voted? Yes, he would have squeaked by with a four-point lead. (The men's vote was Clinton 41%, Bush 37%, Perot 21%.)

Asserting that six million more women than men voted, she added: "But if, instead, women had given Bush even half of the positive gender gap that they gave to Clinton, it would've meant four more years of Bush-Quayle. That's because the numbers of women voting are greater than the numbers of men."

She noted that "for not-very-mysterious reasons, Democrats have not flaunted the gender gap statistics: they don't want to emphasize their growing debt to women. Clearly the press didn't Get It: mainstream media failed even to raise the issue of choice in the four top-of-the-ticket debates, and now have trouble drawing conclusions from the facts. As of now, women as a bloc can determine both state and federal political outcomes—and they are acutely sensitive to issues like choice, pay equity, family leave and child care, and the need for more women in higher office . . . .

"Women are waking up to their newfound power at the polls . . . . The stage is set for a rapid acceleration in the rate of change—as women realize they can elect more women, and can reward or punish representatives of either gender for their accountability to women's issues."

A post-election study by the Center for the American Woman and Politics [CAWP *News & Notes*, Vol. 9, No. 1] reported that aside from the presidential race, the gender gap also appeared in 22 of the 33 Senate races, two of the four House races and eight of the 12 gubernatorial races where VRS conducted exit polls on election day. In 30 races with a gender gap, women voters supported Democratic candidates in larger numbers than did male voters. In two races, the Democratic candidates owed their victories to female voters—Senator Barbara Boxer of California, who got 57% of the women's vote and 43% of the male vote, and Governor Mike Lowry of Washington state. In five races, including two in which male candidates defeated female candidates, the Republican candidates won because of decisive support from male voters. In those instances, the gender gap favored men.

One of these races was the Senate contest in Pennsylvania between Democrat Lynn Yeakel, a newcomer to politics, and incumbent Republican Arlen Specter, who had become a prime target of women's groups because of the prosecutorial role he assumed in the Hill-Thomas hearings. Specter, drawing on past support from centrist and liberal groups, defeated Yeakel by a narrow 2% margin. He received 56% of the male vote and 46% of the female vote, a 10-point gap, while Yeakel got 54% of the female vote and 44% of males.

The Senate race with the largest gender gap (16 percentage points) was between incumbent Republican Bob Packwood and Democrat Les AuCoin in Oregon, which has a Democratic woman governor, Barbara Roberts. AuCoin received 56% of the women's vote but Packwood won a narrow victory despite getting only 40% of the women's vote. In previous campaigns, Packwood had drawn bipartisan support from women because of his pro-abortion rights voting record, but immediately after his 1992 election victory he was facing an investigation by the Senate Ethics Committee and widespread demands for his resignation after charges by a number of women that he had sexually harassed them broke into the news.

Second in size to the Oregon gender gap were the 14-point leads among women in the two U.S. Senate races in California, where, as noted above, Barbara Boxer's winning margin came from women, while Dianne Feinstein captured 64% of the women's vote and 50% of the male vote. Claire Sargent, an Arizona Democrat, who lost, was the only woman Senate candidate to run in a race without a gender gap. Carol Moseley Braun (D, IL) and Patty Murray (D, WA) each won with 55% of the vote; however, in both races men were about evenly divided between the candidates (splitting 51/49 in favor of the women) whereas women voters showed a clear preference for the women candidates. Incumbent Senator Barbara Mikulski (D, Md.) had an easy victory, winning the highest percentages of support, 76% from women and 66% from men.

Finally, the CAWP revealed, there was a gender gap in two of the three gubernatorial races run by women, but not big enough to elect them. In Dorothy Bradley's (D, MT) contest, there was a four percentage point gender gap; women were about evenly divided whereas men preferred the male candidate, who won. Although there was a seven-point gap in Deborah Arneson's (D, NH) contest, a majority of both women and men voted for her opponent.

The 1992 election results continued a trend evident in earlier congressional elections. Writing in *Ms.* magazine [January-February 1992], Democratic political consultant Ann F. Lewis said that according to exit polls taken during the 1990 elections, "It is only because of the gender gap that Democrats control the U.S. Congress. In contests for the Senate, men voted Republican 53 to 45%, according to *The Washington Post*/ABC survey. But women swung in exactly the opposite direction. We voted Democratic, 53 to 45%. *The New York Times*/CBS

News poll examined House races and found men's votes split evenly in half; women voted Democratic, 54 to 46%." She said:

> Women are the majority of the electorate. Majority, as in power. When men divide their votes evenly, women's votes decide. When women and men vote in exactly opposite ways—our side wins. When women voters get the chance to vote for pro-choice women candidates, the gender gap can look like the Grand Canyon. Ann Richards won the Texas governor's race because she received 59% of the votes cast by women. A majority of men supported her (male) opponent. In Oregon, Barbara Roberts was elected governor with 56% of women's votes, and 40% of the votes from men.

Democratic poll analyst Celinda Lake, of the Greenberg/Lake consulting firm, credited women with electing the first black mayor of New York (David Dinkins) and the first black governor of Virginia (Douglas Wilder). "Women vote more and they vote differently than men," she wrote in *The Women's Political Times* [p.4, Spring 1990.] "In 1988, we saw the first presidential campaign in which men and women differed significantly in their vote with a majority of women voting for (Michael) Dukakis and a majority of men voting for Bush," although the margin was not large enough to elect a Democratic president.

"Women want change," she said. "They are less well served and less satisfied than their male counterparts with the status quo, particularly noteworthy around the economy . . . . [They show] greater desire for government involvement to solve problems facing families. They want help from both the public and private sector . . . 62% of women think federal government should spend more money assuring adequate day care for working parents . . . men 52% and 70% of women (NBC/*Wall Street Journal* September 1988 poll) want to see more government money spent on improving medical and health care." Though women and men show the same level of support for abortion rights, she said, "women are more likely to vote the issue."

As described in detail in the Abzug/Kelber book *Gender Gap* [Chapters 6 and 7], the emerging differences between male and female views on public policy issues—with significant numbers of women expressing more concern than men about preserving the peace, attending the needs of others, promoting the economic and social well-being of their families and children, protecting the environment—are rooted in the socialized nurturing roles traditionally assigned to women. "What is new," it was pointed out, "is that the changing roles and attitudes of women have made them assert that their views should be equally shared by men, and that their ethic of care recognizes the legitimacy of women also caring about themselves as individuals." [p. 117.] Or, as Senator Barbara Mikulski (D, MD) has said, "Women are recognizing that their private values are good enough to be their public values."

More recently, the findings of a major study of American women's attitudes about their lives were reported September 4, 1992, by the Ms. Foundation for Women in New York City and the Center for Policy Alternatives in Washington, D.C. Based on a national public opinion research poll of 1,400 women and in-depth discussions with focus groups, the report, called *Women's Voices*, showed that "despite allegations that family life is deteriorating and women are to blame for it, American women continue to take responsibility for their families and their communities, and are searching for ways to strengthen not just their own, but the nation's families," said Marie Wilson, president of the Ms. Foundation.

According to *Women's Voices,* women have a clear issue agenda for them-selves and their families, and economic concerns are at the center of this agenda. When women were asked which of the issues "you personally worry about the most," women put the economy and jobs at the top of the list (26%), with health care (14%), crime (12%) and education (12%) ranking next in importance. Linda Tarr-Whelan, president of the Center for Policy Alternatives, observed that the data not only demonstrated that "women are bearing the brunt of the recession," but also provide "the work plan for creating a woman's agenda, one that incor-porates the central issues of all American women—health care, equal pay and flex time."

In an accompanying analysis, *Women's Leadership for Change*, Wilson and Tarr-Whelan pointed out that in the past three decades women throughout the nation "have assumed roles that are more complex, more diverse and more de-manding." They cited U.S. Labor Department and Census Bureau data showing that a majority of women are now working outside the home and that women in two-parent families contribute an average of 30% to the household income. "But," they said, "the changes women have experienced are not simply about their jobs; they are about their communities and the institutions in their lives. Women are more politically savvy than at any time in history. They value women's leadership and want more women to hold elective office . . . . In fact, by large margins, women believe that electing more women to national, state and local office is the best way to help them achieve their goals and influence pol-icy."

They described American women as "engaged in the world around them—as concerned parents, dedicated volunteers in civic and religious organizations, voters, political activists and dynamic participants in the process of change. Women are the backbone of the economy, the mainstay of their family and change agents in their communities. The *Women's Voices* poll shows that nearly half of all American women, whether or not they are working outside the home, are engaged in volunteer efforts in their communities giving as much as 20 hours a week to civic, religious, social and political organizations . . . .

"Our data affirm that American women credit the efforts of female trailblaz-ers who have fought to bring equity to women's lives through legislation, public education, and litigation. Latina and African American women in particular ap-preciate the results of these efforts. Numerous national studies have found that

American women believe that the women's movement has helped women become more independent and it continues to improve the lives of women. Women value the presence of other women in elected positions . . . .

"Yet, in the *Women's Voices* groups and the national poll, many women report that they are personally uncomfortable with the term 'feminist,' even while they applaud the goals of the women's rights movement. These results reflect the detailed findings of the Pulitzer Prize-winning reporter Susan Faludi, whose best-selling book, *Backlash*, documents a persistent and expansive campaign on the part of mass media, the religious right and others to undermine the goals of the feminist movement."

QUOTAS, 'BEAN COUNTERS' AND EQUALITY

As is evident from the data presented earlier in this report, negative connotations are no longer attached in many countries to the concept of quotas or the 40%-60% formula to assure gender balance used in Norway or in the repeated statements from the UN male hierarchy that they favor equality for women in decision-making positions. But in the United States, since the 1970s when affirmative action campaigns were first undertaken to overcome economic and employment inequities suffered by women and minorities, the debate has been framed by opponents in pejorative terms of "quotas"—and employment quotas have been equated, sometimes demagogically, with the elevation of presumed incompetents and the displacement of presumably more capable white males by females and minorities. Thus, quotas have been tagged in the United States as "reverse discrimination" by those opposed to any actions providing greater access for women, minorities, disabled, etc. At the same time, critics seeking greater participation by women and minorities in government or employment contend that when numerical quotas are too low, they act as a ceiling against the admission of qualified persons, turning minimum goals into maximums.

In contrast to the terms in which the debate is framed in the United States, as this report has shown, the concept of "positive discrimination"—setting specific goals, timetables and numbers to assure genuine equality between men and women in government and other policy-making and, in some instances, allowing for special mechanisms such as numerical quotas to accelerate the process—is widely accepted in principle (if not always in deeds) in international bodies such as the UN, in international law, in the Council of Europe, and by some 56 political parties in 34 countries around the world.

In the United States, despite widespread and continuing hostility to quota systems, affirmative action policies are nevertheless in place in many governmental, public and private institutions. Real progress, with varying degrees of effectiveness, has been made by both women and minorities in winning employment and higher-ranking positions in professions and occupations once barred to them and even within the political parties despite their continued attempt to dissociate themselves from quotas.

When, as a result of an organized women's campaign, equal division was accepted in the Democratic Party charter (see Chapter 1) for male-female balance in the national committee, state delegations to the national convention and party appointive posts, the party leadership felt it necessary to state in the charter that this was in no way to be construed as the "imposition of mandatory quotas at any level," either directly or indirectly. In their efforts to win back male Reagan Democrats in the 1984 and 1988 elections, party officials were wary of Republican charges that they would seek to impose specific quotas in hiring and continued to reject any mention of quotas as beyond the pale of acceptable policy or practice.

Even after the Clinton victory, the quota issue was raised negatively by the president-elect himself in an angry response to criticisms by some women's organizations that he was not appointing enough women to his cabinet. The criticisms came from Harriett Woods, speaking as chair of the Coalition for Women's Appointments, Eleanor Smeal of the Fund for a Feminist Majority, NOW President Patricia Ireland and many other groups. The coalition had been submitting long lists and résumés of qualified women candidates for cabinet, subcabinet and other high-level jobs in the new administration. At that point (December 21, 1992) more than halfway through his selection process, Clinton had named only two women to the cabinet; he had also made several subcabinet appointments of women, hinting that one of these positions (administrator of the Environment Protection Agency) might be raised to cabinet level.

Asked at a press conference about a letter from Smeal urging him to appoint no fewer than six women to the cabinet, thus breaking what she called the "glass ceiling" precedent of three female cabinet members in the Reagan and Bush administrations, Clinton, in an unusual public display of temper, described the women's request as "amazing" and "astonishing." He called them "bean counters" and accused them of "playing quota games and math games" rather than seeking competent appointees. He also grouped his women nominees with his nomination of several African-American and Latino cabinet members. The following day when he nominated Madeleine Albright as U.S. ambassador to the UN, he said that post too would be designated cabinet-level. Although it was clear that continuing a decades-long upward trend, there would be more women in high-level posts in the Clinton-Gore Administration than in previous administrations, the president-elect's reaction showed that he had expected gratitude rather than demands for more from women's groups and still regarded women as among many "special interest" groups. The goal of *equal* inclusion of women in his administration was not yet an agenda priority.

Spokeswomen for the women's groups reacted with "a mixture of anger and bemusement" to the Clinton attack, *The New York Times* reported the following day. [December 23, 1992, p. A15.] NOW president Ireland wondered why the president-elect singled out women's groups for criticism when, in fact, he had been heavily lobbied on appointment choices by groups of all kinds. Woods said women in leadership circles had received repeated assurances from Clinton staff members that women would be well represented in the executive branch. "Their whole tone was 'Trust us. We are committed. Good things are going to happen,'" she said, but with the first major appointments going mostly to men, women's groups were discontented by what they saw as a growing imbalance and felt they had to step up their pressure. A number of women's organizations sent faxes to Clinton headquarters in Little Rock, Arkansas, urging more female appointments. That pressure would continue despite the Clinton outburst, nor would it dissuade women from working with the Clinton transition team in the appointments process, Woods said. (In a subsequent C-Span TV interview on December 24, Woods asserted she had never asked for quotas, apparently also feeling it necessary to dissociate herself from that word.) Several women speculated that the president-elect "had staged the event to reassure moderate supporters that he could not be manipulated by a radical agenda."

Republican Jeane Kirkpatrick, former U.S. ambassador to the United Nations during the Reagan Administration, commented: "It is a fact that successive presidents find so many different reasons not to appoint specific women to specific positions in specific cabinets. And it is a fact that men always get irritable if they get pressed about this." She favored keeping up the pressure, noting that every president pledged to do better for women than the last, "usually because their predecessor didn't do that well." Kirkpatrick, who had publicly criticized "sexism" at the UN after she left her post there, said there had been "creeping progress" for women on Capitol Hill and her sense was that women across the country were "watching quietly" to see what would happen next. [*New York Times*, December 23, 1992.]

When Clinton announced his remaining cabinet and subcabinet nominations on the day before Christmas, it was shown that he had slightly edged out the Reagan-Bush record in numbers and had named several women to posts previously held only by men. His women appointees were Zoë Baird as Attorney General and head of the Justice Department; Hazel O'Leary as Secretary of the Energy Department; Donna Shalala as Secretary of Health and Human Services, all three major departments. In addition, he spoke of elevating his nominations of Albright as UN ambassador and Carol Browner as administrator of the Environment Protection Agency into cabinet-level appointments. His other top-level appointments were Dr. Joycelyn Elders as U.S. Surgeon General and Laura Tyson as chair of his Council of Economic Advisers. O'Leary and Elders are also African-Americans.

Baird was later dropped when it was publicly revealed that she and her husband had hired an illegal alien couple to care for their child and perform other household duties, and had also failed to pay social security taxes for them. Baird drew little sympathy from the public or from women's groups because of her $500,000 a year corporate salary and lack of identification with women's issues, although there were rumblings about the discriminatory aspects of disqualifying her for doing what large numbers of working women throughout the country were forced to do because of the gross inadequacy of child-care services in the United States.

The rumblings turned into a firestorm when Clinton dropped his second choice for attorney general, Kimba Wood, a highly qualified and widely praised federal judge in New York. Before Woods' appointment could be announced formally, it was revealed that she had employed a child-care worker who was in the country illegally, although at the time it was not against the law to hire her. Wood had broken no laws, had paid social security and all other required taxes, filed the necessary reports and assisted the woman in getting legal status.

Clinton's quick dumping of Wood and his staff's circulation of a report that while a student in England she had applied for an office job at a Playboy Club (she quit after several days) led to charges that the president was practicing a "double standard" that discriminated against women, subjecting them to an additional layer of questioning that male nominees never experienced. Kathleen Brown, treasurer of the State of California, commented: "For every man who has ever been confirmed to a cabinet position, there has never been the notion of disclosure of his housekeeping arrangement, much less how much time he spent with his child. It has never been on anyone's mind. It just doesn't come up for male nominees to think about their pattern of child care as a matter for political disclosure or an FBI search." [*New York Times,* February 7, 1993, p. 22.]

Feminist critics were joined by media commentators, both male and female, who noted the "straining at a gnat, swallowing an elephant" absurdity of the president's disqualifying Wood because of her legal household arrangements while appointing Senator Lloyd Bentsen as Secretary of Treasury and Ron Brown as Secretary of Commerce, whose personal histories of profiting from their corporate connections would have far more ominous implications for objective policy decisions than Wood's or Baird's choice of a babysitter. Other commentators seized on the episode as another occasion for attacking the concept of quotas, and particularly Clinton's desire to find a woman to fill the attorney general post, reportedly at the urging of his wife.

Clinton eventually solved his attorney general problem by naming a 54-year-old woman who had never married and had no children but who, when asked by the press (during a time of heated discussion on the issue of gays and lesbians in the military), professed "a very deep affection for men." She was veteran prosecutor Janet Reno, the mostly liberal state attorney for generally conservative Dade County, Florida. [*New York Times*, p. 1, and National Public Radio, "All Things Considered," February 12, 1993.]

An ironic sidelight to the above controversy is that while the word "quotas" continues to evoke a reflex negative reaction in American political discourse, the concept of gender balance—approximately equal numbers of women and men in appointments to state, county and local boards, commissions and committees— has quietly been gaining approval in some states since 1986. That was when Minnette Doderer, a veteran member of the Iowa legislature and a founder of the

NWPC, led a successful effort by a bipartisan group of women legislators to insert a short sentence into the state Code. The sentence simply stated that it was a "policy of the state of Iowa that all boards, commissions, committees and councils shall reflect, as much as possible, a gender balance."[3]

As Paulee Lipsman of the Iowa House Democratic Research Staff tells the story [personal communication, December 15, 1992], nothing happened until a year later when, with two vacancies on the state board of regents, the governor, at the beginning of the next session, submitted the names of two men for confirmation by the Senate. Those new appointments would result in seven men and two women on the board. Legislators, led by women members, were quick to point out that the governor was ignoring the new gender law. In defense of the governor, a male aide asked the press to name one woman who met the standards of "high stature and credibility" that the governor was seeking in his regents appointments. For the next week, a statewide newspaper, *The Des Moines Register*, printed on its editorial pages a list of approximately 25 women a day (including the wife of the governor's aide) who it believed met the "high stature and credibility" test.

The governor managed to get his two male appointees confirmed, but angry women legislators decided to revise the language in the code adopted a year earlier. They won approval of a law stating: "All appointive boards, commissions, committees and councils of the state established by the Code if not otherwise provided by law *shall* be gender balanced." It also prohibited any appointment or reappointment that would cause the number of members of the board, etc., of one gender to be greater than one half the membership. It allowed for a few exceptions in cases where the pool of qualified appointees for a given board or commission is very small and heavily weighted in favor of one sex.

The women legislators also decided to include the judicial nominating commissions in the gender balance law. The commissions interview potential candidates for judgeships and recommend two names to the governor. Appointments to the commissions are made by the governor and bar associations in each judicial district. These commissions were also required, as of 1987, to be gender balanced.

"And the law has worked," Lipsman reported. "Once the governor began looking, he found many women of 'high stature' and boards and commissions in Iowa are now gender balanced. And with women serving on the judicial nominating commissions, more women are being appointed as district court judges. We even have a woman on the Iowa Supreme Court. Thanks to the persistence of women legislators, with a little help from the news media, it has become clear to all Iowans that there are many qualified women who can, and should, have a role in state government."

The gender-balanced state appointments strategy became the focus of a national campaign initiated in 1988 by Kappie Spencer, then director for Women's Issues of the American Association of University Women (AAUW). The gender balance law held a "real possibility of a breakthrough for women if it could be replicated throughout the nation," she wrote in *News & Notes*, the Center for American Women in Politics newsletter [Spring 1989]. "Since service on appointive boards and commissions is an important route into elective office for many women, there is a potential for a concomitant increase in the number of women in elective office in the next decade."

She cited research by CAWP showing that more than half of the nation's women legislators have held one or more appointive positions in state government and that service in appointive positions is often the route into elective office for both women and men. "It is in these positions where many gather political knowledge and skills, meet the governor and state legislators, become involved in state government and expand their political networks. Here people are also likely to become involved in political parties and to meet the party leaders who are most likely to offer support in elective campaigns," she said.

Spencer also noted that service on the state level is especially valuable for women because they "are too often placed in roles with little visibility and clout and are therefore hidden from view. Service on state boards and commissions helps them to become known and respected for their capabilities and encourages them to think about themselves as candidates for elective office."

In April 1988, her plan "became a project of national proportions practically overnight with the help of Mary Wiberg, president of the National Association of Commissions for Women, and Iowa's then-Representative Sue Mullins, 1988 chair of the Women's Network of the National Conference of State Legislatures," she reported. Their master plan called for a "network of networks"—state alliances among Commissions on Women, women legislators, and state women's organizations working together to attain gender balance laws patterned after the Iowa legislation.

According to the plan, legislation would be introduced and women's state legislative caucuses would promote the concept in statehouses. Commissions on Women would compile statistics on women in state policy-making positions, dispense information on the appointments process and posts to be filled, and maintain rosters of potential appointees. Women's organizations would work within state women's networks or form them if they did not exist, and seek out capable women from their own memberships and communities and memberships who were interested in serving on state boards and commissions. They would also be instrumental in seeking legislative sponsors and lobbying for legislation once it is introduced.

The Gender Balance Strategies plan has been popularized among the network groups described above and distributed to the national presidents of some 60 national women's organizations who comprise the Council of Presidents. It has also become a special campaign of the Fund for the Feminist Majority as part of its project, The Feminization of Power 50/50 by the Year 2000. Their organizing kit reports that studies of board and commission appointments show that without legislative mandates "women rarely reach parity on public boards and commissions and when they do, they are limited to traditional 'women's' areas such as health and social services or library boards." The Fund for the Feminist Majority also notes:

> The studies also found that men are more likely to hold regulatory positions with decision-making power, while women are more likely to hold only advisory positions. Women are less likely to be appointed to salaried positions, and more likely to serve on boards receiving only expenses or no compensation at all.

Since the 1987 Iowa law was adopted, North Dakota has passed a similar gender balance law. Five more states, Hawaii, Rhode Island, Montana, Illinois, and Pennsylvania, plus the city of Tucson, Arizona, and the city and county of Los Angeles, have passed gender balance resolutions that are voluntary, but are preliminary steps to adopting a gender balance law. According to the Fund, at least 15 additional states have introduced or have plans to introduce gender balance measures.

NEW WAYS TO EQUALITY

The above approach, while valid and realistic, is emblematic of the upward osmosis strategy largely pursued by political women's groups in the United States for the past two decades. After 21 years of organized activity to get more women into political decision-making, after the dedicated work of tens of thousands of women's rights advocates, the raising of unprecedented millions of dollars for female candidates, the more favorable climate for women in politics, the continuing influx of women into high-level positions in the professions, the workplace, the universities, the public and private sectors, the overwhelming fact remains that women account for only about one out of five state legislators, three out of 50 governors, 48 out of 435 members of the House of Representatives, seven out of 100 U.S. senators, and two out of nine U.S. Supreme Court justices.

Women, despite being a majority of the population, a majority of those voting, and the base support for the Democratic Party, continue to be regarded as a "special interest" group. Traditional role images are still imposed on them, regardless of whether they are appropriate or welcome. The president-elect's wife had to prove she could bake cookies and look adoringly and silently at her husband as he spoke despite her brilliant career as a lawyer and a children's rights public policy advocate. Her post-election decision to resurrect her maiden name and to be known as Hillary Rodham Clinton drew much criticism, especially when her husband named her to chair his Health Care Taskforce.

As the election results confirmed and what is obvious even without poll findings, women, like men, hold a great diversity of political and personal views and vote for particular candidates for a variety of reasons, not necessarily internally consistent. Other factors, such as economic status, social background, ethnicity, race and color, religious beliefs, and sexual preference, may shape their voting choices. But it is also clear that there is a majority consensus emerging among women voters around the cluster of women's issues discussed earlier that affect their personal life and reproductive choices, work, health, families and participation in decision-making. And the gender gap data showing greater support by women for women candidates point to the growing decisive political power they can exert in future elections.

This consensus is also evident in the voting records of women legislators at every level of government, whether they are Democrats or Republicans. A 1983 study by CAWP, entitled "Women Make a Difference," found women more likely than men to believe that government should take an activist role in solving such social problems as recessions, unemployment and displaced workers, the homeless and women's issues. In the 15 states that failed to ratify the ERA by 1982, it was found that 76% of women legislators (from both parties), compared with only 36% of male legislators, were in favor of ratification. Women legislators from both parties vote strongly for abortion rights, while men vote more frequently for restrictions.

According to a report by the Fund for a Feminist Majority, women in Congress "have been responsible for an array of groundbreaking legislation that addressed issues that had been overlooked, neglected or ignored." Jeannette Rankin, the first woman elected to Congress (in 1917), introduced the first social legislation affecting women and children, which when finally passed in 1921 was called the Maternity and Infancy Protection Act, providing pre- and postnatal care and funding to reduce the mortality rate among women and their newborn infants. The report listed some two dozen bills first introduced by women legislators, ranging from the Fair Labor Standards Act of 1938, the 1944 GI Bill of Rights and the 1963 Equal Pay Act to pension law reform, consumer protection, federal aid to education, child care, medical research and prohibitions on sex discrimination in Title VII of the 1964 Civil Rights Act, the Fair Credit Protection Act and Title IX of the Education Amendments of 1972.

These women, the report said, "whether Democrats or Republicans, shared concern for human welfare, a determination to have government serve the needs of the people, and a dedication to feminism." [*The Feminization of Power in Government*, 1992.]

That tradition continues to be observed under the leadership of the bipartisan Congressional Caucus for Women's Issues, which is cochaired by Democratic Representative Patricia Schroeder and Republican Representative Olympia Snowe. It has an all-female executive committee of House and Senate members but includes male colleagues in its general membership. A caucus statement (10/20/92) said that "while the top issues on the Caucus' agenda, including family and medical leave, women's health research, and overturning the family planning 'gag rule,' remain unfinished business for the 103rd Congress, this year nonetheless saw a record number of bills affecting women become law."

It cited passage of legislation to improve child support enforcement, assist battered women, help women in nontraditional jobs, improve the quality of mammograms and prevent infertility in women. Congress also made it easier for college students with children to obtain financial aid and revised the nation's job training program to ensure that services such as child care are provided for those in training. Many of these initiatives were introduced as part of the Economic Equity Act and Women's Health Equity Act, two omnibus legislative packages introduced by the caucus, and many others had its support. According to Schroeder, "Working as a Caucus has given the women in Congress a strength beyond our numbers . . . . With a record number of women serving in the 103rd Congress, we expect to achieve an even stronger record of success next year." Snowe commented: "From child support enforcement to training for nontraditional jobs to increased research on breast cancer, women's issues became mainstream issues this year. I think we can safely say that issues important to women and families will no longer be relegated to the back burner."

Some congresswomen, however, have expressed private dissatisfaction with the way the Congressional Caucus for Women's Issues operates, saying that its failure to take votes on positions and the inclusion of men dilutes its program and too readily invites compromises on legislation. They favor an all-female caucus, prepared to stake out more advanced positions and to fight for them.

With more male legislators being sensitized to women's concerns, it can be argued that this may translate into significantly greater support from men for female candidates as well as for issues of particular concern to women. If this were to occur, we could expect a narrowing of the electoral gender gap in some races, but this is not likely to happen soon. An alternative approach would be for women's groups to seek to widen the electoral gender gap by educating, registering and getting many more women into the voting booth to elect more women. Among all nations in the world, the United States has one of the lowest voting rates.

According to Curtis Gans, director of the Committee for the Study of the American Electorate, it appeared that 104 million Americans, or 55% of the voting age population, cast ballots in the 1992 presidential election, compared with 50% in 1988 and reversing a 20-year decline since 1972, when 55.2% of the eligible people voted. Gans attributed the increased 1992 turnout to third party candidate Ross Perot's appeal among people who felt disfranchised and had not voted in recent elections. He said preliminary data showed that the Democratic share of the eligible vote rose very slightly, while the Republican share declined, suggesting that Perot caused the overall increase in turnout. [*New York Times*, November 5, 1992, p. B4.]

Those women and men[4] who hold to the vision of increased female political participation in decision-making and government have several options open to them. They can continue to build on the present slow ground-up process of getting more women appointed to commissions, elected to local, county and state office, fielding more women candidates, seeking more party support, raising more money, reforming runaway campaign spending, hoping the incumbent dropout rate will recur or accelerate (not likely), or even trying to persuade some liberal male politicians to submerge their own electoral ambitions to make room for women (absolutely unheard of). .

That is the most likely scenario, and it does indeed include many practical steps that must be taken. It also means that women will have to wait until some time in the next century before the U.S. government accurately mirrors the population and enriches itself with the wealth of experience, insights, dedication and positive social values that many women can bring into leadership and public policy.

Should we have to wait that long? Can we learn anything from the Nordic countries and other nations that have set specific goals and timetables for achieving greater or equal inclusion of women in government?

Direct comparisons with the European nations are difficult because most have multiparty parliamentary systems, proportional representation forms of voting, direct selection of candidates by parties instead of primaries, electoral slates in which the party's positioning of women on the list can determine whether they will win, and comparatively brief and inexpensive electoral campaigns with free access to television and radio.

In contrast, the American electoral scene, particularly in presidential and congressional campaigns, has become a prolonged, money-and-media-driven process in which incumbents have the advantage, party labels do not bind the individual candidate to party loyalty or support for the platform, party machines no longer command the power they once had, though they can still wield considerable influence, and the two major parties usually operate as coalitions of various views, with a third party only occasionally being a factor in the outcome of elections. In individual campaigns, it is the candidate, whether he/she is seeking the presidency, a governorship or a Senate or House seat, who frames the issues, takes personal positions, raises the money, shapes his/her media image, and is responsible for getting out the vote in primary and general elections. Local party clubs and organizations still operate with varying degrees of effectiveness, although in much fewer numbers in recent years, and the overwhelming majority of voters have little personal contact with them.

In the Nordic countries, although the impetus for political gender balance has come from women's organizations, the fight for inclusion of women in political office has been conducted by caucuses within the individual parties and commitments to such quotas as the 60/40 formula have been demanded and in many instances won from the parties, affecting party leadership posts and/or candidate slates. Significantly more women are included in cabinet positions than in the United States, and they are drawn from the parliaments. (In the United States, none of the women chosen for the Clinton cabinet had served in Congress or in any elective position, with the exception of Janet Reno.)

Although the independent U.S. women's movement is the biggest and most active in the world, it is still fighting for *paid* parental leave, family benefits, child care and health care services that are routinely provided in generous terms by Nordic and other European governments. (For example, the 12 member nations of the European Community require paid maternity leave for periods of from 14 to 28 weeks, with pay ranging from 75% to 100% of earnings, and the European Women's Lobby is demanding a minimum of 16 weeks' paid leave.) Nor have American political feminists yet succeeded in getting either the Democratic or Republican Party to make a specific commitment to the goal of 50/50 division in electoral office. It may be argued that neither party can provide a guarantee of gender balance in government and, in fact, the National Women's Political Caucus and other women's groups, with the exception of the Fund for a Feminist Majority and the National Parity Campaign, did not raise this as a specific timetable goal for the parties in the 1992 elections.

But there are interim steps that can be taken to accelerate the process, and they include women's groups making greater demands on the political parties, not only in election years but as an ongoing process. (Although this applies to all parties, the Democrats and Republicans still dominate the political scene and it is within these parties that women will be directing their major efforts, even while experimenting with formation of alternative parties such as the feminist 21st Century Party.)

Democratic and Republican women's caucuses function within the NWPC, as described earlier. In the Democratic Party, under its equal division rule, there are approximately equal numbers of men and women on the Democratic National Committee. An informal women's caucus operates within the DNC, but as Abzug pointed out in her testimony at the Platform Committee hearings, the caucus has a low-profile role, receives no formal assistance from the DNC, and makes few demands either on policy issues or public recognition of its activities. Essentially, it has ceded its potential leadership role within the party to the outside women's groups. Thus, it fails to exert sufficient pressure on the DNC chair and other officials in the national and state party structures to seek out, encourage, fund, train and give preference to women candidates or even to set goals and timetables for achievement of gender balance in government. The National Parity Campaign's proposal that in all open seat elections, the parties should give support only to women candidates is based on the fact that party officials do play a behind-the-scenes role in selecting candidates, encouraging them to run, discouraging others from running, assisting in fundraising and technical assistance and all the other professional services that can lead to victory.

Support for the parity campaign by an invigorated, more activist women's caucus within the Democratic Party and a major public education campaign by the political women's organizations and their support groups, armed with lists of qualified women candidates, could create a sea-change in American politics and public opinion. By convincing national, state and county party leaders to adopt a policy statement committing them to the goal of equal numbers of women and men in elective and appointive bodies, and to implement this by recruiting, funding, training and assisting women candidates for open seats, they could maximize the party's base strength among present and potential women voters and elect significant numbers of women to the House and Senate, extending the victories of 1992 to the 1994 and 1998 elections. They could also apply this strategy to state legislature contests, the branch of government that produces many congressional candidates.

The Republican Party, now on the losing end of the electoral gender gap, could also recoup some of its base support by fielding more women candidates in congressional elections, as it has been doing in contests for state legislatures. According to a report by Professor Wilma Rule and Pippa Norris to the Western Political Science Association's annual meeting (March 21-23, 1991, Seattle, Washington), "The Democratic Party—North as well as South—has been a negative factor associated with fewer women in state legislatures. Competitive or Republican parties have facilitated women's recruitment." Dr. Rule, an adjunct professor of political science at the University of Nevada and a leading authority on electoral systems, attributed women's comparatively low status in the state legislatures (now up to 22%) to, among other reasons, "state or local Democratic Party dominance and lack of party competition." In the past, Rule said, the Democratic Party "has been unfavorable to women's state legislative recruitment," while "competitive or Republican-dominated states have . . . been best for women's election to state legislatures."

As most political observers do, Professor Rule cited the power of incumbency and the high cost of campaigns as major hurdles for women candidates seeking first-time election. Among the factors favoring incumbents, she noted, are the perquisites of office, estimated as worth some $1 million per member each term. These include free (franked) mail to constituents, unlimited free phones and free travel to their districts, enabling them to campaign informally between elections. They also receive large contributions when their formal campaigns for reelection begin, and thereafter. In contrast, women are usually handicapped in fundraising by fewer business and/or professional connections with potential contributors. The large sums raised in 1992 by successful women candidates Boxer, Feinstein and Braun were atypical. Although modest campaign spending reforms were being considered by the 103rd Congress, "big bucks" fundraising was expected to be a continuing obstacle to the election of more women, unless more drastic reforms were adopted. But with party leaders usually committed to reelection of incumbents, such reforms were unlikely to happen without a massive citizens' protest movement.

NEEDED: A U.S. COMMISSION ON THE STATUS OF WOMEN

Another mechanism for strengthening women's inclusion in government elective and appointive posts would be restoration at the national level of a commission on the status of women. This was first instituted in 1961 under the

Kennedy Administration when The President's Commission on the Status of Women, chaired by Eleanor Roosevelt, was established by Executive Order 10980, with a charge to study seven areas: education, private and federal employment, social insurance and tax laws, protective labor laws, civil and political rights and family law, and home and community. Mrs. Roosevelt and Esther Peterson, then director of the Labor Department's Women's Bureau, were the moving force in the commission's establishment, with the assistance of then Vice President Lyndon Johnson. This was followed by formation of a Governor's Commission on the Status of Women in 1962 in Michigan, and within a few years similar commissions were in place in a majority of the states, as a result of a campaign undertaken by the National Federation of Business and Professional Women's Clubs.

In 1963, the Interdepartmental Committee on the Status of Women and Citizens Advisory Council on the Status of Women was established by Executive Order 11126, with Margaret Hickey as its first chairperson. The committee and council sponsored national meetings of the state commissions, issued annual reports on issues affecting women, and made legislative and administrative recommendations. Dissatisfaction with the government's failure to enforce Title VII of the Civil Right Act led during a national conference of state women's commissions in 1966 to the impromptu formation of the independent National Organization for Women (NOW) by Betty Friedan, Dr. Kathryn Clarenbach, Aileen Hernandez and others. This was an expression of the growing militancy among American women that produced what has become one of the most influential movements for social change in U.S. history.

In 1968, the official governmental body dealing with women's issues was the President's Task Force on Women's Rights and Responsibilities, appointed by President Nixon. In the 1970s, with outspoken feminists such as Patsy Mink, Shirley Chisholm and Bella Abzug coming into Congress, the organization of the NWPC and the first-step congressional approval of the Equal Rights Amendment, Republican President Ford appointed a National Commission on the Observance of International Women's Year (1975), which had been designated by the United Nations. Later, the UN expanded this to the Decade of Women, 1976 to 1985, during which it sponsored international women's conferences in Mexico City (1975), Copenhagen (1980) and Nairobi (1985). President Ford also created an Interdepartmental Task Force for IWY consisting of at least two representatives, a man and a woman, from each federal department and agency. They were assigned to examine their department's programs in terms of actual and potential impact on women, and presented their recommendations in formal reports, part of a process that provided a climate more receptive to women's programs as well as women personnel.

Abzug attended the 1975 Mexico City conference as a congressional advisor to the U.S. delegation and in early 1977 the incoming Democratic President Jimmy Carter named her as presiding officer of his newly appointed National Commission on the Observance of IWY. The 41-member multipartisan

Commission (38 women and three men) had the task of of organizing the first (and only) federally funded National Women's Conference, authorized under legislation, based on bills introduced by Abzug, Mink and Margaret Heckler, approved by Congress and signed by President Ford in December 1975 as one of his last acts in office. Abzug, who managed the final bill on the House floor, won a $5 million appropriation for the conference, which was held in Houston in November 1977 after almost two years of planning and preliminary meetings in every state.

Under the guidance of the National Commission, presiding officer Abzug, and executive director Kathryn Clarenbach, the conference was a high point in the growth of the American women's movement. It was attended by almost 2,000 delegates elected at public meetings held in every state over the period of a year, by an additional 18,000 women from the United States and other nations who participated in a host of workshops, seminars and other activities, by First Lady Rosalynn Carter, former First Ladies Betty Ford and Lady Bird Johnson and other dignitaries, and women members of Congress. It received extensive media coverage. The conference delegates, mostly women, of every age, color and class, from every income group, ethnic, racial and religious group, debated and voted on each of 26 planks of a proposed National Plan of Action compiled from recommendations from the state meetings. Only one plank was rejected, Others passed by large majorities, and one calling for equal access to credit for women was adopted unanimously. Three amended resolutions and four substitute resolutions were also overwhelmingly approved. The action plan provided the matrix for a national women's rights agenda on issues ranging from the standard items such as employment, welfare and poverty, education, child care, rights for homemakers and the disabled, sexual preference and reproductive freedom to violence against women, militarism, international affairs and empowerment of women in decision-making. (An ad hoc conference continuing committee, operating on a volunteer basis, has been monitoring implementation of the National Plan of Action on a state-by-state basis for the past decade.)

A serendipitous legacy of the conference was the formation of many new national networks of women organized around a common identity or specific issues and the cross-fertilization of ideas and action proposals that occurs whenever large numbers of women from many different areas, backgrounds and viewpoints get together in one place. The National Commission itself, after presenting its official report to President Carter at a White House ceremony in March 1978, was dissolved and was replaced several months later by a National Advisory Committee for Women (NACW), cochaired by Abzug and Carmen Delgado Votaw and including a broad spectrum of women leaders and several men.

The central mission of the NACW was to advise the president and members of Congress on how the policy changes advocated in the National Plan were to be translated into legislative and executive actions. Its mission, however, turned out to be short-lived. Carter did not meet with his committee until January 12,

1978, seven months after it had been appointed. At the end of the White House meeting, at which the president expressed his unhappiness at a NACW report criticizing the Administration's proposed increases in military spending and major cuts in programs and funding for women and children, Abzug was taken aside privately and told she was being dismissed as chair. A majority of the committee resigned in protest. Carter later transformed the group into The President's Advisory Committee for Women, indicating that its major purpose was to be supportive of his policies. The new committee was specifically barred from an advocacy role on Capitol Hill for women's concerns and the National Plan recommendations.

In 1981, when Ronald Reagan became president, an executive order continuing the committee then in existence was superseded by an order setting up a taskforce with a short-term, more limited assignment to study the legal status of women in various state laws. No subsequent body with a widely mandated commitment to equality and justice for women was created. Thus, for the past 12 years of Republican administrations the only federal-level executive branch body concerned with women's issues has been the Labor Department's venerable U.S. Women's Bureau (set up in 1920), which is mostly confined to programs and problems affecting employed women but which also monitors activities of state commissions on the status of women. The absence in the United States of a federal-level department, commission or committee with a mandate to work for equality for American women contrasts with the practice in almost a hundred other countries.

The 1992 Inter-Parliamentary Union (IPU) study, *Women and Political Power*, found that of 156 nations responding to its survey, 24 possess a Ministry for the Status of Women, while 57 countries have some other governmental body specially responsible for questions relating to the status of women. The survey also showed that 36 of these ministries or bodies devote part of their activities and budget to promoting the political participation of women. As can be seen in this report's description of councils on the status of women in the Nordic countries, Canada and elsewhere, the presence of such bodies can be a powerful force in behalf of women's economic, social and political aspirations.

As the Clinton-Gore Administration takes shape, a major goal of the women's movement should be the appointment of a federal-level Commission on Equality for Women and an Inter-Agency Task Force on Women, with professional staff, budget, and multipartisan membership. In fact, under Public Law 94-167, which authorized the National Commission on the Observance of IWY to hold a National Women's Conference, the commission was directed to "take steps to provide for the convening of the second National Women's Conference . . . to evaluate the steps taken to improve the status of American women."

No such conference has been held. An appropriate time would have been in 1994, a year before the UN's scheduled Fourth World Conference of Women, which meets September 4-15, 1995, in Beijing, China, to review what has been happening to the status of women in the decade since the 1985 UN women's conference in Nairobi. The Forward-Looking Strategies document that emerged from the 1985 meeting, like the U.S. 1977 National Plan of Action, combined a review of the economic, social and political status of women with detailed proposals for what must be done to overcome the persisting barriers to equality for women. Organizing U.S. women's participation in the 1995 conference, in cooperation with the many non-governmental women's organizations that will also be focusing on this event, could be a major and much needed activity for a newly constituted federal commission on women's issues. At present, the task of compiling post-Nairobi progress reports from the various federal departments, agencies and states on the status of American women is being carried out by a State Department woman officer in charge of international programs.

The commission, in addition to providing the nation with an overall evaluation of the current status of women, could also serve as the government's official center to coordinate programs and policies affecting women among the various executive departments and agencies, to work with the Congressional Caucus on Women's Issues, and to make its own recommendations for policy changes and implementation. In doing so, it would be accelerating the presence, visibility and influence of women in government.

BASIC STRUCTURAL CHANGE PROPOSALS

These interim measures could lead to a national campaign demanding basic structural changes in the electoral system to guarantee that we have approximately equal numbers of men and women governing us—not at some remote time, but in the foreseeable future. For example, multimember districts, which have been shown to be favorable to the election of more women in many countries, could be introduced more widely in localities and states, possibly along with proportional representation, which also is a women-friendly voting system. Before 1842, when Congress mandated the single-member district system of elections for the House of Representatives, according to Professor Rule, multimember districts and high turnover of representatives were common. With time, incumbency increased and the number of open seats declined.

Currently, 15 states have multimember districts for election to their state legislatures. A study by Professor Rule showed that in 1989 the 35 single-member district states averaged 12.4% women in their legislatures, whereas the 15 states with multimember districts averaged about 21.6%—almost twice as many. "Thus," she concluded, "single-member districts are a major spoiler of women's state legislative opportunity and eventual congressional chances . . . . Black and Anglo women are favored in states with multi-member legislative districts, and this is likely true for other minority women. When voters have two or more representatives to choose, more women run and are elected." Rule also asserted that minority candidates as well as Anglo women are disadvantaged by runoff primaries requiring a majority vote for winning. A single plurality primary, she said, would give them an opportunity to compete in general elections.

Article 2, Section 4 of the U.S. Constitution provides that "The times, places and manner of holding elections for Senators and Representatives, shall be prescribed in each state by the Legislature thereof; but the Congress may at any time by law make or alter such regulations, except as to fix the places of choosing Senators." Congress used its statutory powers to fix the number of House members at 435, and it has remained this size since 1910. In 1789, the first House of Representatives had 65 members, each representing about 30,000 inhabitants. Today, a House member represents a constituency of about 560,000, and with continued population growth, democratic representation will be further diluted. Some critics of the present system argue for a modest increase of about 150 seats in the House, which could be authorized by statute [See Lind, Michael, "A Radical Plan to Change American Politics," *The Atlantic Monthly,* August 1992.] This would provide new openings for women candidates and other underrepresented categories.

Although there is no doubt as to the constitutional right of Congress to fix the size of the House by statute and to determine the manner in which its members are elected, constitutional lawyers point out that changes in district size might be subjected to constitutional challenges under the equal protection and due process clauses if the changes gave greater weight to some votes compared with others. This might arise in some states which are so sparsely populated that they have more inhabitants than needed for one congressional district but not enough for two. Under current law, Montana has already gone to court to challenge the present apportionment system, which would give the state only one congressional seat, representing 800,000 people. [Lind, Michael, *The Atlantic Monthly,* August 1992.]

Another reform option suitable for U.S. multiparty primaries or general elections is the transfer system in which the second-choice votes of those voting for a party candidate who does not receive above a specified small percentage of support are transferred to another candidate. This could give more power to minority third parties, a process that would be viewed as desirable or undesirable, depending on how it changed the outcome of the election and the political views of the candidate benefiting from the vote transfers. This system was responsible for the election of Mary Robinson as president of Ireland in 1990 in a three-way race [see Chapter 1, p. 34].

Another electoral reform idea has come from the United Kingdom, which, like the United States, is one of the few democratic nations in the world that does not have some form of proportional-representation voting. With women accounting for only 9.5% of the House of Commons, Conservative M.P. Teresa Gorman proposed that adjoining constituencies (akin to U.S. congressional districts) be merged into one, with voters allowed to elect two representatives, a man and a woman. Also, without specifying how equality was to be achieved, Labour M.P. Tony Benn has called for a gender-balanced House of Commons in a bill he introduced that was designed to be the United Kingdom's first written constitution. It also called for abolition of the monarchy. Neither proposal has received much support.

The U.S. Congress could exercise its constitutional right to legislate a Gorman-like change in our laws for House elections, which could apply to all but the six states that are now allotted only one representative. The overall number—435—would remain unchanged. Here too, this change would have to conform to equal protection and due process guarantees under the Constitution and might require a constitutional amendment. The major problem with this approach, as Gorman discovered when her male colleagues refused to consider it, is that it would halve the future number of male representatives, and no male politician is likely to risk voting himself out of possible reelection.

The U.S. Senate is another matter. When the founding fathers wrote in the Constitution that each state should have two senators, the population of our nation was slightly under four million. It is now above 250 million. Doubling the state delegations to four senators, with two seats allotted to each sex, would change the present 100-member, overwhelmingly male club into a 200-member body that would at long last look like America, not like the Senate Judiciary Committee. (Its present seven women members cannot be expected to transform the agenda there or to carry the weight of all the pent-up demands from women for social reform.) A 635-member bicameral Congress would still be a manageable size, somewhat smaller than the 651-member House of Commons or the 662-member Bundestag, and the increased costs could be absorbed partly by cutting bloated staffs and reducing salaries and "perks."

This electoral reform would require a constitutional amendment, which would have to be approved by a two-thirds vote of both houses of Congress and include a statement that a mandatory requirement for gender balance in the Senate would not violate the equal protection or due process clauses of the Constitution. Since it would not reduce the existing number of men in the Senate (indeed, it would guarantee them 100 seats), it could have a good chance of passing Congress and winning approval in the required three-fourths of the states. The legislatures now have more women members than when the Equal Rights Amendment fell short of approval by a narrow margin of three states, in which the presence of just a few more women could have spelled victory for ERA. Analyses have shown that ERA had significantly more support from Democratic and Republican women legislators than from male legislators of either party. A gender-balanced Senate reform that would eliminate direct competition between male and female candidates and at the same time transform the clubby male atmosphere into a more diverse, representative and democratic body might get a positive response from the electorate, both women and men, though probably not in equal percentages.

In the November 1992 elections, voters showed their desire for change by approving congressional term limitation initiatives in 14 states while at the same time returning most incumbents to office. Term limitations, which some legal experts believe would eventually require a constitutional amendment, have been criticized for indiscriminately scapegoating all members of Congress despite their individual leadership abilities and accomplishments and at the same time diminishing their responsibility to their districts by turning them into "lame ducks" in their final terms. Term limitations would restrict the right of voters to reelect representatives and senators of whom they approved. In contrast, an enlarged, gender-balanced Senate would expand the electorate's opportunity to get a Congress that really does look more like America and is more in tune with the needs of the female half of our country.

A U.S. Senate based on equal division would institutionalize what everyone knows: that being and growing up female and living as a female is different from being and growing up male and living as a male, especially in a world ruled almost exclusively by men. It would acknowledge the coexistence of the two sexes, with men and women having an inherent equal right to utilize their individual physical and intellectual capacities, skills and experiences in public life as well as in their private lives. Without romanticizing women or demonizing men, without expecting women candidates to be flawless, morally perfect superwomen, it would recognize their equal right to make decisions about our lives, our society and the future of our planet. It would settle the dilemma of many voters, women and men, who believe there should be more women in office but don't want to oust a male incumbent whose voting record they find acceptable or even admirable. In answer to the oft-heard comment that "I'm not going to vote for a woman just because she's a woman," there would be the alternative for female and male voters of choosing among a number of women candidates, with the assurance that a woman would be elected.

At the same time, a gender-balanced Senate would likely lead to voter acceptance of significantly more women in the House—not as an occasional "Year of the Woman" anomaly but as a normal democratic practice. And we could expect that while the women elected would span a broad range of political views, competence, and personal behavior, just as their male colleagues do, they would also bring to government new perspectives and social priorities needed to deal realistically with the enormous problems facing our nation and the world.

The above scenario for structural reform would, of course, require a national campaign by a coalition of women's organizations and party caucuses to educate the electorate on its validity, to get a constitutional amendment introduced and passed in Congress with the full support of the Congressional Caucus on Women's Issues and, hopefully, the president and the women's commission, if one is set up. It would also require mobilizing women to conduct state-by-state campaigns for ratification. If the amendment campaign were to fall short of the 36 states needed for ratification, at the very least the entire nation would have had its consciousness raised on the deplorable under-representation of women in government. If the amendment were to be approved, we would have at last achieved real political equality for women.

Summing up, a number of short-range and long-range options are available to American women seeking to break through the political glass ceiling. They range from an immediate mobilization for parity in elective and appointive offices by supporting only women for open seats, voter registration of more women and radical reforms in campaign spending laws to long-range mobilizations for such structural reforms as multimember districts and proportional representation voting in local and state elections and a model 50/50 U.S. Senate. All these options, to be successful, will require unified action by the women's movement to let the public know that 48 women in the House and seven women in the Senate is just not good enough and to enlist support for fundamental changes in our presently undemocratic electoral and political system.

Both in the short run and the long run, as Eleanor Roosevelt once said: "It's up to the women." They have the votes, the potential power and the vision of a nation in which men and women together will share in leading a genuinely democratic government into the twenty-first century.

NOTES

[1] Subsequently, in a 1993 by-election, Republican Kay Bailey Hutchison of Texas was elected to the Senate, becoming the seventh woman member.

[2] For a detailed discussion of the women's campaigns within the Democratic Party to achieve gender balance in delegations to the 1972 convention and thereafter and an analysis of the relationship between affirmative action programs and quota systems, see "Women in the Democratic Party: A Review of Affirmative Action" by Bella Abzug, Phyllis Segal and Miriam Kelber, Columbia (University) *Human Rights Law Review,* Vol. 6, 1974.

[3] This demand was first included in the National Plan of Action adopted at the federally funded National Women's Conference in Houston, Texas, in November 1977. Its plank on increasing the numbers of women in elective and appointive office included the following paragraph: "Governors should set as a goal for 1980 a significant increase and, by 1985, equal membership of men and women serving on all state boards and commissions. Concerted efforts should be directed toward appointing women to the majority of State boards and commissions which have no women members."

[4] Although many male legislators and politicians support the goal of increasing the presence of women in government, few have made it a personal cause. A rare exception is retired advertising executive George Dean of Fairfield, Connecticut, who conducts an energetic one-man campaign by writing articles and letters to the editor advocating "50/50 by 2000," speaking at colleges, and working with women's groups. Dean attributes his commitment to his admiration for the late Governor Ella Grasso of Connecticut as well as the state's history of electing outstanding women to Congress and to local government bodies. While men react to his 50/50 appeal by saying it sounds like a quota, Dean says, "Of the thousands of women I've spoken to, none has ever said that. The women say, 'Oh, it sounds like sharing a partnership.'" [Phone interview, 1/12/93.]

Bibliography

Abzug, Bella, with Kelber, Mim. *Gender Gap, Bella Abzug's Guide to Political Power for American Women.* Boston: Houghton Mifflin Co., 1984.

Agonito, Rosemary. *History of Ideas on Woman, A Source Book.* New York: Capricorn Books, G.P. Putnam's Sons, 1977.

Äs, Berit. *Which Positive Actions—At This Time in History.* Norway.

Asia Pacific Women's Studies Journal. No. 1, 1992, Manila, Philippines, Institute of Women's Studies.

Avgar, Amy. "Women, War and Peace." *Na'Amat Woman,* March-April 1990.

Berkin, Carol R., and Lovett, Clara M., eds. *Women, War & Revolution.* New York and London: Holmes & Meier, 1980.

Bok, Sissela. *Alva Myrdal, A Daughter's Memoir.* Reading, Mass.: Addison-Wesley Publishing Company, 1991.

Buckley, Mary, and Anderson, Malcolm, eds. *Women, Equality and Europe.* London: The Macmillan Press, 1988.

Building a Europe without Frontiers: The Role of Women. Report from European Network for Women's Studies Conference, Ministry of Education and Science, Zoetermeer, The Netherlands, November 1991.

Cameron, Averil, and Kuhrt, Amelie, eds. *Images of Women in Antiquity.* Beckenham, Kent, Great Britain: Croom Helm, Ltd., 1983.

The Changing Role of the Male, Summary of a Report by the Working Party for the Role of the Male. Ministry of Labour, Sweden, 1986.

Collection of the Council of Europe's Work Relating to Equality between Men and Women (1950-1988). Strasbourg, 1989.

Cook, Dr. Blanche Wiesen. *Eleanor Roosevelt, Vol. 1 (1884-1933).* New York: Viking, 1992.

Dahl, Tove Stang, and Hernes, Helga Maria. "After Equality." *Scandinavian Review,* 1988.

Das Parliament. Bundeszentrale für Politische Bildung, Bonn, No. 3-4, January 18, 1991.

Eduards, Dr. Maud Landby. "Women's Participation and Equal Opportunities Policies." *Current Sweden.* Stockholm: Svenska Institutet, No. 369, June 1989.

Equal Status Between Men and Women. Norwegian Ministry of Foreign Affairs, April 1990.

Equality Between Men and Women in Sweden. Fact Sheet on Sweden, February 1992.

Equality Between Men and Women in Sweden: Government Policy to the Mid-Nineties. Summary of Government Bill 1987/88:105, Division for Equality Affairs, October 1988.

Evans, Richard. *The Feminist Movement in Germany 1894-1933.* London: Sage Publications, 1976.

Facts about Finland. Helsinki: Otava Publishing Co., 1987.

Feist, Ursula. "Die Unterrepräsentanz von Frauen im politischen System der Bundesrepublik, Gründe und Strategien zur Veränderung." *Vater Staat und Seine Frauen.* Pfaffenweiler: Centaurus-Verlagsgesellschaft, 1990.

Finlay, Fergus. *Mary Robinson, A President with a Purpose.* Dublin: The O'Brien Press, 1990.

Flanz, Gisbert H. *Comparative Women's Rights and Political Participation in Europe.* Irvington-on-Hudson, N.Y.: Transnational Publishers, 1983.

Fund for a Feminist Majority. *The Feminization of Power in Government.* 1992.

Gelb, Joyce. *Feminism and Politics: A Comparative Perspective.* Berkeley: University of California Press, 1989.

Guthnadottir, Jonina. "Women's Rights in Iceland." *International Women's News*, Vol. 85, No. 3, 1990.

Haavio, Mannila, ed. *Unfinished Democracy, Women in Nordic Politics.* Pergamon Press, 1985.

Halsaa, Beatrice. *Policies and Strategies for Women in Norway.* Lillehammer: Oppland Regional College, 1989.

Hirdman, Yvonne. *The Swedish Social Democrats and the Importance of Gender.* Paper presented at New Sweden Seminar on Women and Power, 1988.

Höcke, Beate. *Vater Staat und Seine Frauen.* Berlin, 1990.

Inter-Parliamentary Union.*Women and Political Power.* Document No. 19, Geneva, 1992.
_____. *Symposium on the Participation of Women in the Political and Parliamentary Decision-Making Process, Reports and Conclusions.* No. 16, Geneva, 1989.

Kaplan, Gisela. *Contemporary Western European Feminism.* New York University Press, 1992.

Kissman, Kris. "Women Caregivers, Women Wage Earners, Social Policy Perspectives in Norway." *Women's Studies International Forum*, Vol. 14, No. 3, 1991.

Kolinsky, Eva. "The German Greens: A Women's Party?" *Parliamentary Affairs.* Oxford: Oxford University Press, 1988.
_____. *Women in West Germany.* New York: St. Martin's Press, 1989.

Koonz, Claudia. "Conflicting Allegiances: Political Ideology and Women Legislators in Weimar Germany." *Signs: Journal of Women in Culture and Society*, Vol. 1, No. 3, Pt. 1, University of Chicago, 1976.
_____. *Mothers in the Fatherland.* New York: St. Martin's Press, 1976.

Kuusipalo, Jaana. "Finnish Women in Top-Level Politics." *Finnish 'undemocracy': Essays on Gender and Politics*, Karanen, Marja, ed. Jyvaskyla: Finnish Political Science Association, 1990.
_____. *Women's Power in the Finnish Welfare State: Obstacles and Opportunities*, University of Tampere.

Lamb, Michael. "Why Swedish Fathers Aren't Liberated." *Psychology Today*, October 1982.

Landes, Joan B. *Women and the Public Sphere in the Age of the French Revolution.* Ithaca, N.Y.: Cornell University Press, 1988.

Lind, Michael. "A Radical Plan to Change American Politics." *The Atlantic Monthly*, August 1992.

McDonald, Ian. *Vindication! A Postcard History of the Women's Movement.* London: Deirdre McDonald Books, Bellew Publishing, 1989.

Millan, Betty. *Monstrous Regiment, Women Rulers in Men's Worlds*. Great Britain: The Kensal Press, 1982.

Nissen, Fernanda. *Women in Norwegian Politics*, 1909.

Norwegian Equal Status Act with Comments. Equal Status Ombud, Revised edition, 1989.

Olive, David. *Political Babble*. New York: John Wiley & Son., 1992.

O'Reilly, Emily. *Candidate, The Truth Behind the Presidential Campaign*. Dublin: Attic Press, 1991.

Österberg, Christina, and Hedman, Birgitta. *Women and Men in the Nordic Countries*. Nordic Council of Ministers, 1988.

Phillips, Melanie. *The Divided House, Women at Westminster*. London: Sidgwick & Jackson, 1980.

Pietilä, Hilkka, and Eide, Ingrid. *United Nations and the Advancement of Women*. The role of the Nordic countries to promote efforts by the UN system for the Advancement of Women. A study commissioned by the Nordic UN project, Report No. 16, 1990.

"The Polls and the 1992 Election." *The Public Perspective, A Roper Center Review of Public Opinion and Polling*, Vol. 4, No. 2, January-February 1993.

Proceedings of the European Ministerial Conference on Equality between Women and Men. Strasbourg: Council of Europe, 1986.

Proctor, Candice E. *Women, Equality, and the French Revolution*. Westport, Conn.: Greenwood Press, 1990.

Ridenour, Ron. "Vigdis Finnbogadottir." *Working Woman*, November 1981.

Roosevelt, Eleanor. *It's Up to the Women*. Frederick A. Stokes, 1933.

Rosenberg, Dorothy J. "Shock Therapy: GDR Women in Transition from a Socialist Welfare State to a Market Economy." *Signs*, Autumn 1991.

Schnitger, Elke. *Frauen und Parlamente: Verhältnisse und Verhinderungen*. Oldenburg: Bibliotheks-und Informationssystem der Universitat Oldenburg, 1990.

Sidel, Ruth. *Women and Children Last: The Plight of Poor Women in Affluent America*. New York: Viking, 1986.

Silen, Birgitta. "Women and Power." *Scandinavian Review*, Vol. 76, No. 1, Spring 1988.

Simonen, Leila. *Contradictions of the Welfare State, Women and Caring*. Research Institute for Social Sciences, University of Tampere, Finland, 1990.

_____, ed. *Finnish Debates on Women's Studies*. University of Tampere, Finland.

Sipilä, Helvi. *Woman at the Top of the World*, edited by Irma Kuntuu. Keuruu, Finland: The Otava Publishing Company, 1979.

Skard, Torild. "Women in the political life of the Nordic countries." *International Social Science Journal*.

Snyder, Paula. *The European Women's Almanac*. London: Scarlet Press, 1992.

Socialist International Women. *The Long March of Women Towards Equality*. London, May 1989.

Spirit of Finland. Special issue on women in Finland, No. 3.

The Spirit of Houston. Report of The First National Women's Conference. Washington, D.C.: U.S. Government Printing Office, 1978.

Stromberg, Erling. *The Role of Women's Organizations in Norway*. Equal Status Council. Oslo, June 1980.

Sundstrom-Feigenberg, Kajsa. "Fertility and Social Change among Women in a Stockholm Suburb." *Inside Sweden*.

Swedish Election Guide, 1988. The Riksdag (parliament), Stockholm.

Taylor, Robert. *The Economic Policies of Sweden's Political Parties*. Stockholm, Sweden: Svenska Institutet, 1991.

"Union Women on the Move." *International Confederation of Free Trade Unions*. May-June 1991.

United Nations Division for the Advancement of Women, Vienna. *WOMEN 2000,* "Women in Public Life," No. 2, 1992, "Women in Decision-Making," No. 1, 1990, "Women and Politics," No. 2, 1989.

_____ Division for the Advancement of Women. *Women in Politics and Decision-Making in the Late Twentieth Century.* A United Nations Study. Dordrecht/Boston/London: Martinus Nijhoff Publishers, 1992.

_____. *INSTRAW News.* "Women and Management," No. 17, Spring 1992.

_____. *WOMEN Challenges to the Year 2000,* 1991.

_____. *World's Women, Trends and Statistics 1970-1990.* New York, 1991

Vocation: Woman, a collection of short articles about the position of women in Finland, past and present. National Council of Women of Finland, 1988.

Weiland, Daniela. *Geschichte der Frauen Emanzipation,* ECON, Düsseldorf, 1983.

A Woman in Finland. Helsinki, Finland: The Council for Equality Between Men and Women.

Women and Men in Sweden, Facts and Figures. Equality of the Sexes, 1990. Unit for Equal Opportunity Statistics, 1990.

"Women in Denmark." *Danish Journal,* 1980.

"Women in Finland." *The Spirit of Finland.* Helsinki: Finland Promotion Board, 1991.

"Women in Power." Final Report, Athens Conference and Summit, Commission of the European Communities, Brussels, Belgium, November 1992.

Zarembka, Paul. "Poland: The Deepening Crisis." *Monthly Review.* New York, Vol. 44, 1993.

Index

United States, 179-218: affirmative action policies in, 199-200; campaign fundraising in, 181-86, 210; colonial voting rights in, 3-4; commissions on status of women, 210-13; disenfranchisement of women, 3-4; electoral gender gap, 193-99, 205-7; electoral politics, hindrances to women in, 181, 208; electoral reform proposals, 214-17; gender-balanced state appointments in, 203-5, 218 n.3; minority women candidates in, 179, 187, 214-15; 1992 elections, women candidates in, 179-82; parity strategies, 209-18; quota debate in, 199-205; term limitations in, 216-17; voting records of women legislators, 205-6; voting rights for women in, 8, 10; voting turnout in, 207; women's agenda in, 198; women's groups, support for women candidates, 181, 183-87. *See also* Democratic Party; Republican Party; *specific administration*
United States Senate, bicameral proposal for, 216
United States Women's Bureau, 213

Vanden Heuvel, Katrina, 20
Vogel-Polsky, Eliane, 29
Votaw, Carmen Delgado, 212

Voting rights. *See* Disenfranchisement; *specific country*

Walesa, Lech, 14
War: rape as tactic in, 23; and male political domination, 9-10
Waters, Maxine, 187
Wiberg, Mary, 204
Wilson, Marie, 198
Wish List, 186-87
Wistrand, Birgitta, 108
Wollstonecraft, Mary, 8
Women's Action Agenda 21, 55-56
Women's Campaign Fund, 186
Women's Environment & Development Organization (WEDO), 55
Women's peace conference of 1915, 8
Women's Rights Association of Iceland (WRAI), 150, 151
Women's status, current findings on, 17-18
Wood, Kimba, 202
Woodhull, Victoria, 4
Woods, Harriett, 180, 183, 200-201
Working women, current findings on, 17. *See also specific country*
World Women's Congress for a Healthy Planet, 55

Yeakel, Lynn, 185, 196
Yugoslavia, former: deteriorating position of women in, 20-23; rape as war tactic in, 23

Zimbabwe, 16

About the Editor

MIM KELBER, writer, editor, and feminist, has been a lifelong activist on behalf of women's rights. She served as policy adviser and speechwriter for Congress-woman Bella Abzug and as policy director for President Carter's National Advisory Committee for Women. She is a co-founder with Bella Abzug of Women USA Fund, Inc., and currently serves as editorial director of the Fund's Women's Environment and Development Organization in New York City. She coauthored *Gender Gap: Bella Abzug's Guide to Political Power for Women* (1984).

ISBN 0-275-94816-1

HARDCOVER BAR CODE

Date Due

BRODART, INC.   Cat. No. 23 233   Printed in U.S.A.